THE NATIONAL INSTITUTE OF
ECONOMIC AND SOCIAL RESEARCH

Economic and Social Studies
XXVIII

THE STRUCTURE, SIZE AND COSTS OF URBAN SETTLEMENTS

T0328319

THE STRUCTURE, SIZE
AND COSTS OF
URBAN SETTLEMENTS

P. A. STONE

CAMBRIDGE
AT THE UNIVERSITY PRESS
1973

CAMBRIDGE UNIVERSITY PRESS
Cambridge, New York, Melbourne, Madrid, Cape Town, Singapore,
São Paulo, Delhi, Dubai, Tokyo, Mexico City

Cambridge University Press
The Edinburgh Building, Cambridge CB2 8RU, UK

Published in the United States of America by Cambridge University Press, New York

www.cambridge.org
Information on this title: www.cambridge.org/9780521154482

First published 1973
First paperback printing 2010

A catalogue record for this publication is available from the British Library

Library of Congress Catalogue Card Number: 73–80480

ISBN 978-0-521-20309-8 Hardback
ISBN 978-0-521-15448-2 Paperback

CONTENTS

LIST OF TABLES

[xi]

Symbols in the tables

.. = not available

n.a. = not applicable

— = nil or negligible

LIST OF CHARTS

PREFACE

Urban form affects not only the resources required for urban development, but also those required for operating settlements and for living and working within them, and the satisfactions obtained. The forms of development interact with the spatial distribution of population and with the running of the economy. Clearly the whole field cannot be studied at once, but the effects of the form and the size of a settlement on the resources required and on the value of its amenities appeared to form a worthwhile research project. Work was planned and commenced on these lines. During the two years of the study the relationship of size and form to construction costs was examined, as was the effect of size and form on rates of return, on some operation costs and on adaptability. Unfortunately finance was not available to complete the later stages of the study, but the work which had been completed adds appreciably to available knowledge.

The purpose of this book is to review the results obtained in relation to future decisions about urban form, and to assess how far information is available for reaching decisions on the spatial distribution and form of urban Britain.

The book falls into three parts. The first is concerned with the factors affecting settlement planning and with the way the form, size and location of settlements affect their use and functioning. The second analyses the costs and returns of model settlements and provides information on population structure, and on activities, facilities, land use and unit costs. In the third, the costs of developing and operating various forms and sizes of settlements, and their financial returns, are compared with the aid of the analysis of model settlements and statistical cost data.

This work was financed partly by the then Ministry of Housing and Local Government and partly, through their good offices, by the Centre for Environmental Studies. I am most grateful to both bodies for their support.

I should like to express my gratitude to Mr G. D. N. Worswick, the Director of the Institute, and to Mrs A. K. Jackson, at that time the Executive Secretary, for their help and encouragement with this project. My thanks are also particularly due to Mr F. D. Hobbs and Mr B. D. Richardson of the Department of Transportation and Environmental Planning, Birmingham University, for their advice, and for arranging and supervising post-graduate research directed to the needs of the Institute. I would also like to thank Mr J. D. Murchland for allowing the use of his traffic programme, EGTAC. Finally I should like to acknowledge my gratitude to the many officials of central and local government, new town Development Corporations and public boards, to members of firms and to others for the information and ideas they have provided.

Mr O. E. Harris was responsible for the planning aspects of the project and for developing the models of urban form. The EGTAC programme was rewritten in Fortran by Mr Schofield of the London University Computer Science Institute. Its exploitation and further development, and the development of other computer simulation techniques, was the responsibility of Mr R. A. Arnould. Mr C. L. Day analysed population, industrial, commercial and social data, and estimated settlement population and facility needs and costs. Mr G. R. Newman analysed the facility price data. Miss V. Willmott, and later Miss S. Bliss and Miss M. Wilson, were responsible for organising the many contacts and for typing the report. The abridged version of the report, given in this book, was edited by Miss G. I. Little. The index was compiled by Miss M. Acland Hood.

My thanks are also due to my family for their forbearance while this book was being written.

P. A. STONE

NATIONAL INSTITUTE OF ECONOMIC
AND SOCIAL RESEARCH
December 1972

CHAPTER I

INTRODUCTION

URBAN FORM IN GREAT BRITAIN

Most people live in settlements. These vary in size from hamlets with populations of under a hundred to conurbations with populations of several million. In some parts of the country the settlements are evenly distributed in a hierarchy – broadly the historical pattern – in other parts they are concentrated in blocks or belts. Settlements vary in shape, in the way land uses are related, in density and in the form of their communications. There are also many ways in which settlements are related to form urban clusters.

Considerable resources are invested in the development of the built environment: currently about a twelfth of the national product, or half the total annual capital formation. When costs of maintenance and improvement are added, the resources required represent about an eighth of the national product. Over the period 1964–2004 something of the order of £200,000 million will be needed to develop, renew and maintain the built environment.[1] The consequences of urban form are, however, even wider, with this effect on the costs of industrial and social activities and, ultimately, on the quality of life. The overall scale of urban development required is determined within narrow limits by demographic factors, but the costs incurred and the satisfactions achieved vary widely with form and location.[2] The choices are not unlimited: much development already exists, or is committed, and future development must be based on what is there already. For a number of reasons, however, the freedom of choice for the future is in fact quite wide.

FUTURE URBAN DEVELOPMENT

Over the 15 years to 1967 the population of Great Britain increased by about 4·5 million. If birth rates remain at their present level there will be another 16 million people in this country by the end of the century. Population projections are very uncertain, but it is unlikely that this increase will be less than about 11 million or more than about 26

---

[1] P. A. Stone, *Urban Development in Britain: Standards, Costs and Resources, 1964–2004*, vol. 1: *Population Trends and Housing*, Cambridge University Press, 1970.

[2] P. A. Stone, *Housing, Town Development, Land and Costs*, London, Estates Gazette Ltd, 1963; R. J. Smeed and E. M. Holroyd, *Some Factors affecting Congestion in Towns*, Harmondsworth, Road Research Laboratory, 1963.

million.[1] There may also be considerable changes in the regional pattern of development; already there is considerable internal migration. Scotland is losing most if not all of its natural increase, as are the northern regions of England and Wales. In contrast the southern regions and the Midlands are gaining considerably. At the same time there is migration from the conurbations of the South and the Midlands to areas around them, and rural areas are losing population to the towns. Such movements are likely to continue, although the directions may change.

Moreover, improvements in standards will increase the rate at which urban facilities become obsolete. Because more space is required for open-air activities, for building development and for roads, the population density is reduced whenever obsolete areas are redeveloped, and some of the original inhabitants must be accommodated on new land. It is likely that, over the rest of the century, development in new areas will be required for as many as 9 million people as a result of this dispersion. When the growth in population is also taken into account, some 20 to 25 million people, nearly half the present British population, may need accommodation in new areas of development before the end of the century. Moreover, half to two thirds of the area of the present settlements will probably be redeveloped. Thus, even without reducing the size of existing settlements, the scope for changing their size and form, for developing new settlements, and for creating new locations and relationships between settlements is considerable. The face of urban Britain could be fundamentally different by the year 2000.

DECISIONS ON URBAN FORM

The extent to which a location is suitable for urban development and for particular forms of development is restricted by its physical features, by its advantages for industry and commerce, and by its attraction for people and business firms. Location and urban form also affect the costs of physical development, the costs of operating settlements and of movement between them, and the facilities and amenities which are provided. Most of the constraints are relative rather than absolute.

The best solution cannot be found either nationally or regionally without giving all the numerous factors their proper weight, and considering their effects on the need for resources and on satisfactions. It is impracticable to compare and appraise the whole range of possibilities at the level of the individual settlement, especially as they include variations in timing. The possibilities and their consequences in particular circumstances must first be analysed generally as a guide to

[1] Stone, *Urban Development in Britain*, vol. I.

the field within which the optimum solution may lie. The analysis in this book provides both a set of techniques and a bank of derived data to assist in assessing the possible alternatives in a given situation.

URBAN FORM IN A DYNAMIC SITUATION

No general study could establish a blue print for the most economic form of settlement. This depends on the life-styles, technology and availability of resources at the time the development is planned. Settlements take a long time to develop, and meanwhile conditions and requirements are all subject to change. A plan can only be optimal in relation to the conditions foreseeable at the time it is prepared, and it will need regular appraisal and revision to meet changing situations. This is not a reason for rejecting long-term planning – without it development would be *ad hoc*, taking no account of future requirements; it would then be purely a matter of chance if the development was optimal in its final form. However, it does justify examining alternative forms of development under a wide range of conditions and this is more important than being very precise in any given situation. There would be little value in determining optimal solutions in terms of current conditions only.

In principle, the development of a new town on a greenfield site is not so different from the redevelopment of an existing town. In both cases, future needs as they are foreseeable at the time, existing development and the availability of resources must be taken into account. The major difference lies in the extent of the existing development that must be considered.

THE AIMS AND CONTENTS OF THE STUDY

The major factors affecting the costs and values of settlements and settlement clusters are relations between land uses, shape, density, size and the system of internal communications; the form and extent of the clustering of settlements; the condition and potential of existing areas of development to be absorbed; and the phasing of development. The effect of these factors is studied within a range of conditions which are likely in the foreseeable future, with the object of determining under what conditions the various planning solutions would be optimal.

A purely statistical approach was not feasible because the various forms which are possible are inadequately represented by existing towns. These cover the range of sizes, but only part of the range of possible forms, and, being only the current stage of a long process of evolution involving constant adaptation to changing needs, for the most part they do not clearly reflect any specific form. The measurement of their attributes of form would therefore be a difficult and unsatisfactory exercise. Moreover, not only is there no record of their costs of construction, but there is no easily constructed schedule of the volume, age, condition and potential of their facilities. It is therefore impracticable to use existing towns for the evaluation of urban form.

At first sight the 'new towns' constructed since the war provide a more promising basis for comparing urban forms, but in practice there are still formidable difficulties. Most of these towns were built in areas where there was already substantial development, and this has been modified and expanded over a period of 15 to 20 years by a number of different agencies. The major work was done by the Development Corporations, but substantial contributions were made by urban and county councils, by the public utility boards, by government departments and by a host of private developers, ranging from large property developers and industrial concerns to church authorities and private households. Only the Development Corporations could provide a comprehensive account of their expenditures, and even they could not provide sufficient detail for our purpose.

Because development necessarily takes many years, because priorities differ and standards and price levels change, any attempt to reconstruct the physical development of an actual town and its real costs is extremely hazardous. If planners made a practice of estimating the facilities and resources required at the stage of the master plan, comparisons between master plans might be fruitful. Unfortunately the estimates are rarely detailed, accurate and comprehensive enough for this to be possible.

The data available can be used to provide two kinds of estimate: the overall scale of costs, and the provision of unit facilities and their costs. The latter can be applied to synthetic town models to give estimates of the facilities required and their costs. Thus, if models are developed to represent different forms of settlement and settlement relations, the cost consequences of form can be studied. This is the method used in this book.

Work on five aspects of the study proceeded in parallel. First, the anatomy of existing, new and proposed towns and of their relations with each other was analysed; the major parameters of size and form were selected and incorporated in models simulating the range of settlements to be studied. Secondly, population data (age, sex, marital status, economic and social groups) for settlements with various rates of growth and patterns of migration were studied and used to synthesise the population of each model settlement. Thirdly, the rates per head at which facilities are provided in new towns and their costs were used to estimate facility needs and costs in relation to the growth of the population and the form of the settlement. Fourthly, methods were devised for simulating the movement of people and vehicles around the model settlements, and for estimating road needs and travelling costs. Finally, development over time was considered and rates of return and the effects of changing forms to meet changing needs were studied. The results, brought together, provided estimates of the consequences of the various alternative forms of development.

While it was not possible, because of the constraints imposed by finance and time, to examine other factors which affect the development and functioning of settlements, this book attempts to set the results in a wider context and to compare costs with the probable scales of values.

CHAPTER 2

FACTORS AFFECTING SETTLEMENT PLANNING

REGIONAL PLANNING

In theory there must be some particular regional distribution of urban development which would provide the optimum return for all resources used. This distribution depends on the interaction of the various physical, industrial, social and economic factors.

Development could be evenly dispersed over Great Britain, or it could be concentrated in certain regions, not necessarily according to the present pattern. Since the war, policy has had a dual purpose: on the one hand, to encourage industry to move to the areas of industrial decline, mainly in the north of Britain and, on the other hand, to relieve pressure on the largest conurbations, particularly London and Glasgow. Much more weight has been given to the former than the latter, but in the less prosperous regions the two purposes are often in conflict. Up to 1963 the incentives were mainly negative – licences for industrial building were withheld in the conurbations, and in the green belts, where all development was strongly discouraged. The effectiveness of licensing is limited, since it is undesirable to stifle particular enterprises completely or to force them abroad. Complete prohibition of industrial development in an area is not feasible. After 1963, the incentive to develop in areas of industrial decline was increased by capital assistance and, since 1967, also by employment grants. However, capital costs are still about twice as heavily subsidised as labour, so that the attraction for capital intensive industry is much stronger than for the labour intensive industry that the areas need.[1]

Despite tightening control of industrial development since 1960, the effect on total employment in the largest conurbations – particularly London – was small, because employment in services, which tend to concentrate in conurbations, increased twice as fast as in manufacturing over the period 1959–66.[2] The control of development has, however, had a considerable effect in the last few years, particularly in London.

The new towns grew slowly at first, partly because of resistance to decentralisation and partly because of national financial stringency, but most of those intended for overspill from the conurbations are now

---

[1] A. J. Brown, 'Regional problems and regional policy', *National Institute Economic Review*, no. 46, November 1968.
[2] Central Statistical Office, *Annual Abstract of Statistics*, 1967, London, HMSO, 1967.

growing rapidly. They have attracted expanding industries and the consequent increase in demand for labour is likely to encourage their expansion considerably beyond the sizes planned. They have been less successful in their object of relieving pressure on the conurbations: for example, from designation to 1967 the London new towns increased their population by about 340,000, which was far less than the natural increase for London. Further, not much housing has been released, because many new town households were formed by household fission. New towns have given little relief to households in the greatest housing need, and have not prevented widespread private migration across the London green belt and an increase in commuting. These additional developments, mostly along the main lines of communication, are potential centres for further expansion.

The net effect of these movements on the pattern of existing urban development has been small. The growth of the conurbations themselves has been limited or reversed, but a ring of satellite development has grown up around the more prosperous ones, particularly London. Official policy is now to encourage larger growth points much further from the conurbations than the early new towns. Several are being established about 100 miles from London, which will double the size of existing towns to a population of about a quarter of a million. In the North the aim is to create flourishing areas of development by expanding and redeveloping the infra-structure of existing settlements. It is hoped these will attract firms which would otherwise prefer the South.

In the next decade the population of working age is likely to grow only slowly and increasing numbers of young people will stay longer in full-time education, so that the labour force will remain virtually unchanged until about 1975; over the next 15 years half its growth is expected to come from increased activity among middle-aged married women – not a situation in which mobility of employment is likely to be high. A policy of decentralisation, involving large-scale migration to new areas, may therefore be difficult to implement and, to avoid further general expansion of the conurbations, it may be necessary to promote development of finger growths from them along the main lines of communication. Against this, about 8 per cent of people move their homes each year, perhaps not far, but to this extent they are mobile.

Few, if any, of the factors affecting regional urban form result in absolute constraints. Unfavourable factors are more likely to raise costs than to prohibit any locality or form entirely. The community wishes to obtain the best value for the resources used, which implies consideration of all the factors together. The value of lost locational advantages, whether constructional, industrial or social, must be set against gains in other directions; the costs and benefits of the infra-structure can be compared with those of transport, and industrial and commercial operations.

Costs to individual agents are not usually the same as costs to the community. For example, an industrialist who moves to a new location must bear any additional costs arising from the absence of related industries or suitable labour, but he does not meet directly the cost of providing any necessary infra-structure. Similarly, neither firms nor private citizens necessarily benefit directly from migrating to, or staying in, a location with spare capacity in the infra-structure, even though savings result to the community. Thus it would be economic for the community to share the advantages of an optimum distribution of population. To some extent this already happens: firms migrating to economically stagnant localities obtain subsidies and tax advantages, whereas firms in the conurbations of the South, and particularly London, enjoy the benefits of a well-established pool of labour and services, an above-average infra-structure and subsidised communications.

It is most unlikely that the optimum distribution of population will be achieved by chance. First it is necessary to determine the whole complex of costs and the current distribution that is optimum for the community, also the way this is likely to change in the future. The second step is to ascertain the distributions which are most desirable for the various agents in the development process and for the many groups of citizens affected. The next step is to find the most suitable financial, fiscal and physical means to harmonise the interest of the developers and citizens affected with those of the community as a whole, so that the sum of individual decisions will result in the optimum distribution.

PHYSICAL FACTORS

The location and form of new settlements, and the redevelopment and expansion of existing ones are restricted by the physical structure of the site, the previous uses to which the land has been put and its location in relation to other settlements.

Other things being equal, the flatter and the more extensive the site, the easier it is to develop, the less the limitations on its use and, generally, the cheaper it is to develop and operate. Large areas of flat land are particularly important for industry. Development can also be impeded by the load-bearing characteristics of the ground, by its chemical composition and by the height of the water-table. Although hilly sites may have unstable ground and a rocky subsoil, they do not preclude urban development and may even offer some advantages. They are easier to drain; frequently, flat sites are too wet to be ideal, while rivers and streams are expensive to bridge and restrict development. Many settlements have been built on hilly sites and some of them are most successful, with particularly attractive layouts.

The micro-climate also has an important influence on development. The conditions considered favourable vary in different parts of the world: in Great Britain, long periods of sunshine and freedom from fog, frost, heavy rain and wind are regarded as desirable. People are unwilling to live where the climate is particularly unpleasant. The micro-climate also affects land use, and the form and standards of the buildings: on exposed sites buildings must be arranged to shelter the spaces between them and higher standards of cladding may be necessary.

The availability of water and other public utilities is clearly important. Services may be much more expensive to provide in some places than in others, particularly when dependent on natural resources. The availability of reserve capacity in regional and local services varies. The local supply of building materials, especially minerals, is also important.

The amount of land available for development, and the suitability of the surrounding countryside for both rural recreation and landscape, will influence the choice of site; so will its value in other uses, for example agriculture, forestry or mineral extraction. Existing and potential communications with other settlements and urban clusters are also important factors: some industries require special forms of transport, and deep coastal or river waters, or conditions suitable for the development of airports may be desirable.

INDUSTRIAL AND COMMERCIAL FACTORS

A settlement is not usually viable unless it is a suitable base for industry and commerce. In future, local services, for example, building and other trades, shops, transport, education, professions, and health and welfare, are likely to employ nearly half the total working population. Much of this employment is not created until a town reaches maturity; the larger a settlement and its hinterland, the larger the proportion of employment in service industry. Other industrial and commercial employment is created by the production of goods and services for people in other settlements at home and abroad. Such activities must be competitive in their markets and are unlikely to set up in a settlement unless it can provide the conditions they require. These conditions vary: they may include the availability of raw materials, power and suitable labour, or a suitable climate, or proximity to markets and associated industry.

Easy access to raw materials and markets chiefly benefits transport costs, but for many industries and most commercial activities these are an unimportant part of total costs. Only the basic industries, using large quantities of heavy and bulky raw materials, or those whose products are particularly perishable or expensive to transport, are severely restricted in their location by sources of supply or markets.

Climate is less important than it was before suitable conditions could easily be created artificially inside factories. More attention is now paid to the proximity of associated industry and services. There is a strong incentive to develop in the centre historically associated with the industry, which contains not only the contractors and sub-contractors but the suppliers of industrial and commercial plant, professional and scientific consultants, commercial and financial services, and frequently the central government agencies. There tends to be less saving on the direct costs of communication than on economies derived from more certain delivery and from ease of intercommunication. It is often argued that face to face contact is important in business, making it easier to settle problems and creating goodwill. These arguments may be less forceful once electronic communications can provide efficient visual as well as oral contact and convenient data transfers.

It may not be easy to attract labour to new or expanded settlements which are not established centres for an industry. Workers prefer not to be dependent on a single employer, but to have access to a number of jobs within their field to reduce the risk of unemployment; also concentration increases opportunities for education and the exchange of ideas, both of growing importance. Employers want a large pool of the types of labour they need, so that they do not have to offer large incentives to bring in additional workers, or to consider social problems when labour is redundant. These conditions are unlikely to be satisfied except in established centres of industry, and in large settlements and groups of settlements.

There are also advantages for distributive trades in large settlements rather than small ones. The greater the scale and speed of turnover, the greater are sales per unit of floor area, the proportionately smaller the stocks and the greater the savings on bulk purchases. These conditions should enable the consumer to enjoy a wider choice and lower prices.

Thus industrial and commercial interests usually favour the expansion of existing settlements, and large settlements or groups of settlements against small ones. However, the social costs of concentrating urban growth around the large economically expanding centres, as compared with dispersion and regional balance, might exceed the private benefits. Better value would then be obtained nationally by using taxes, subsidies and other financial devices to supplement the comparative private costs so that they indicated the same solution as the comparison of social costs.

SOCIAL AND PSYCHOLOGICAL FACTORS

People are influenced in deciding where to live by the available social facilities and amenities. Inevitably some services are lacking during the development of a settlement and this reduces its attraction in the early stages of construction. Many types of facility can be provided in any settlement, but their provision is less likely if costs are high. Smaller settlements will not normally be as well provided as larger ones, particularly with facilities for higher education, and cultural and recreational activities for which the minimum scale of provision is often large. However, the absence of such facilities is not absolute, since they are usually available in other settlements within the region, although distance reduces their convenience and adds to the costs of using them. As most facilities which are only viable for a substantial local population are those of minority interest, one solution is for settlements to specialise in services for ceitain types of citizen. This already occurs to some extent: for example, the smaller university towns provide facilities for music and arts, and for other higher education, on a scale often not matched by settlements several times their size. Instead of consumers travelling to facilities, the facility might travel to them; this often happens where a suitable general purpose building is available for mobile cultural enterprises.

Often more important is the range of employment opportunities; in small settlements this must inevitably be limited. Opportunities increase with the size of the settlement, but not necessarily in proportion because lengthening communications tend to inhibit travel. The effective range is therefore also a function of the form of the settlement and of its communications. Again the real range of opportunity may be improved more by specialisation than by an increase in size.

Similarly the range of social contacts increases with size, but is limited by the time and cost of communication. The effect of size and form on social contacts, especially chance contacts, is by no means fully understood. Many social contacts are important without being frequent and efficient communication with adjacent settlements may be more convenient than a larger settlement.

Both individuals and firms are influenced in their choice of location by psychological factors as well as by costs. There is often a strong preference for remaining in familiar surroundings or migrating to areas whose image is approved. Even in a country as small as Britain, regional and even local differences in climate, landscape, people and atmosphere are sufficient to inhibit movement. People and firms are often reluctant to make new social and business contacts. Differences in costs have to be substantial to overcome such psychological factors. It is often difficult to break the vicious circle created by the buoyancy of growth and optimism in the affluent areas, and by physical decay and pessimism in declining ones.

ECONOMIC FACTORS

The forms and location of a settlement affect not only the costs of constructing it, but also those of operating it, the costs to the inhabitants of living and working in it, and the imponderable advantages and disadvantages derived from it – in other words they affect the 'value for money' obtained. Different concerns will calculate 'value for money' in different ways. The solution which gives the optimum economic results to developers may not be best for all the inhabitants or for the community as a whole.

While size may bring some economies of scale, comparatively expensive types of development may be needed in consequence, adding to the costs per head of communications. Shapes and land-use relationships convenient for communications may be expensive to develop and unsatisfactory in other ways. Diseconomies, for example from the use of high-rise housing, may be more than offset by economies elsewhere. Some forms of development may be easier to phase than others and some forms easier to expand or convert to meet changing needs; but flexibility may sometimes be too expensive to be justified.

The economics of an individual settlement cannot be considered in isolation: however large, settlements are not often completely self-contained. Some advantages of size without all the disadvantages can be obtained by combining smaller settlements into related clusters. These clusters could vary considerably in size and form, up to the point where a substantial proportion of the national population lived in a single continuous area of urban development. However, the larger the urban complex the greater its impact, not only on existing settlements but also on regional and national communications, and on public utility services. Hence in studying the alternatives, a wide range of costs and benefits must be considered.

It is unlikely in a developed country that any suitable location for a new settlement will be completely without existing development. The larger the proposed development, the more likely it is that established settlements will have to be incorporated. Such existing development may have surplus capacity in its facilities which will allow substantial savings on new facilities, particularly over the period of development when they might otherwise be unavailable. However, existing settlements must often be redeveloped to relate them satisfactorily to a new development; this shortens the life of some facilities and involves costs for replacing them elsewhere. Such costs can be set against those which would have been incurred had the settlement been allowed to grow and redevelop naturally. The comparative costs of the alternatives for existing settlements – redevelopment, incorporation or expansion – hence depend both on the pattern of obsolescence and on phasing. The more demolition needs to be brought forward in time, the higher the costs of redevelopment.

The best location and form for a settlement within the national distribution of population depends on the costs of creating and operating particular forms of development, on the costs of operating within them and of the values they create. Far too little is known of the effects of the size and form of a settlement either on construction and operating costs or on the consequences of development for living and working. The costs of physical development vary not only with size and form, and with the interaction with existing development, but also with phasing and locality. Prices of construction vary from one region to another with differences in labour rates, productivity, material prices and competitive conditions. When a development project causes a large increase in local activity, there is likely to be a large increase also in prices of construction work.

Little is known either about the way people and firms operate in different types of settlement, or the way they evaluate the amenities the settlements provide. Information is needed on the frequency of different types of shopping, of visits to places of amenity and of attendances at places of education. Not enough is known of people's reactions to the provision of better housing, to changing jobs, to standards of public transport or to the staggering of hours or work, or of their relative preferences for such qualities as accessibility, freedom from noise, privacy and urbanity.

CHAPTER 3

THE STRUCTURE OF SETTLEMENTS

RESIDENTIAL AREAS

The most basic function of a settlement is to provide shelter. Very small settlements consist mainly of housing, with some shops, a church and other local communal services, which are usually those essential in any residential area, whether free-standing such as a village or part of a larger settlement. The proportion of land needed for housing (the net residential area) naturally varies with the density of development and the functions of the settlement. Generally in this country, the net residential area takes rather over half the total land. The proportion is usually highest in very small settlements, or in those which function as a dormitory, the inhabitants working either in the countryside around or in another settlement.

The extent to which housing areas are provided with local services varies considerably. Most villages contain shops for daily purchases, a school for the younger children, essential service industry (which may be no more than a garage and repair workshops), churches, minimum communal, social and health services, and some public open space. For historical reasons towns have, in this respect, often developed as a collection of villages; the planning concept of a neighbourhood is largely based on the village. Neighbourhoods, as generally understood in the context of the planned town of the early postwar years, provide all the basic daily services for about 10,000 people. The concept drew attention to the lack of local services in many housing estates built between the wars.

A residential neighbourhood is made up of a small group of housing areas – around a neighbourhood centre providing shopping and other services – and some local recreational areas. It is small enough for the housewife to do her daily shopping on foot, and the primary school, medical and other communal services, and some open space are all within walking distance. The inhabitants have to leave the neighbourhood for most employment, for higher education and for more specialised commercial, cultural and recreational purposes.

It is desirable to exclude heavy and fast traffic from the housing areas. This is not difficult provided that the housing areas are not too large; if they house only a few thousand persons each they can be contained within the secondary distributor roads. Through traffic can be dis-

[14]

couraged or prevented by the layout of the access roads, or by speed limits.

The size and the cost of housing areas depends not only on the standard of the dwellings but also on the density of development. Very low densities tend to be expensive both in land and in other resources. As density rises costs per head fall until high-rise development becomes unavoidable. Beyond this point, while land requirements continue to fall, the cost in other resources rises substantially.

COMMERCIAL AND SOCIAL CENTRES

The neighbourhood centre provides for daily needs only – broadly, shopping for convenience goods, a local library, a general practitioner and other such services. Most durable goods and more specialised convenience goods, other services and entertainment are found elsewhere. In most towns there is a major shopping and service area placed centrally and, especially in large towns, there may also be intermediate shopping centres. The larger the centre the greater the variety of services it can provide, but the further it will be from some of the housing areas it serves. The best distribution of shopping and service areas therefore depends on balancing the convenience, efficiency and possibly lower prices of large centres against the inconvenience and costs of travelling to them.

Recently the conditions for which a neighbourhood was devised have changed in a number of ways. First, the ownership of cars has increased and probably most households will possess one eventually. A housewife who has a car available is more likely to shop outside the neighbourhood, particularly if she works herself. Supermarkets, if they are more efficient and cheaper, attract shoppers from a wide area to larger shopping centres. Evening and weekend shopping arrangements may even extend this to housewives without a car, but many who have young families or are elderly will continue to prefer local shops. Public transport to the shops is not an adequate substitute for a private car, even where pick-up points are convenient and the service frequent, because of the weight and bulk of goods to be carried, and the difficulty and cost of taking children.

For other types of journey public transport is more satisfactory, so that medical, cultural and recreational facilities can be centralised more conveniently, although additional inconvenience and cost might discourage their use, particularly by young people. The neighbourhood centre cannot therefore be dismissed as a planning concept, but the alternatives are worth considering.

Shops for convenience goods and some services – the local newsagent is an example – need an intensive localised market. For these, neighbourhood centres are not essential, since comparatively few shops of this kind are needed and they can be corner-shops within the housing areas. In large settlements, a single major commercial centre would not be convenient for all shopping that could not be done in the corner-shops, and if no neighbourhood centre was provided, district centres catering for intermediate requirements would be necessary. Such district centres might also take over some functions of the central commercial area and provide a location for nationally and regionally orientated service industries.

INDUSTRIAL AREAS

Villages usually contain some industry, although this is often only service workshops or food processing plants related to local agriculture. However, in larger settlements where there is no close relationship between home and workplace, accessibility is not as strong a reason for siting industry and other workplaces in residential neighbourhoods. Noise and pollution are no longer always associated with industry and some commercial and industrial buildings can be sited in the residential areas without spoiling them. Nevertheless many factories are still out of scale in relation to other development and generate considerable heavy traffic; they often need large areas of open storage which, even if kept tidy, detract from the amenities of residential areas, as do the necessary terminal facilities for public utility services – electricity, gas and other fuels, water, sewage and refuse disposal. Areas set aside for industrial use therefore seem likely to continue to be needed on a considerable scale, even though the proportion of the working population employed in manufacturing is likely to decline.

There is little firm evidence on the best size for industrial concentrations. Clearly there are advantages in sub-contracting plants being near the main consumer of their services, but it is usually considered important that a settlement should contain a wide variety of industries and firms. If this principle is followed, it is not possible also to create complexes of linked firms except in very large settlements, and this makes it difficult to attract to newly developed settlements, however large they expect to become, the kind of firm and industry for which linkages are important.

There is now usually little advantage in industry concentrating about public utility terminals, or special transport terminals such as rail yards and docks, which are usually important only in large cities and transport centres. Dispersal, on the other hand, is likely to simplify communications generally. By decreasing the average journey to work the spread of traffic is improved and the efficient use of both roads and public transport is promoted, leading to lower costs. Goods traffic also is spread more evenly over the road system if industry is not too concentrated. However, the benefits are not unlimited: the more industry is widespread the less will be the relative gains from traffic dispersion. Road costs increase abruptly once potential demand exceeds the capacity of a single lane, and the smaller industrial areas are, the more difficult and expensive it is to insulate residential and other areas from them.

EDUCATIONAL AND OTHER FACILITIES

A primary school should be within walking distance of all its pupils. For secondary schools this is not necessary and the catchment area has to be larger to provide for a variety of needs at this level. Colleges of art and technology, for which the demand is limited, are usually in the central area and then only in fairly large settlements. Newly created residential areas are often populated within a short period of time. Typical migrants have predominantly young families, so that their children are concentrated in a narrow age band. This creates a large demand for school places, which moves in a wave through the schools. If enough school places are provided to meet the maximum demand, there will be a surplus once the wave has moved on. This difficulty can be met in various ways: for example, development can be phased over several residential areas, each of which grows slowly, or schools can be built to serve residential areas at different stages of development. Flexible buildings with alternative functions, or demountable buildings which can be moved, are also possible solutions.

A settlement also needs facilities for outdoor recreation, various types of institution and communications. Recreational land is required for organised games and athletics, for gardens and parks, for allotments and for open space available to the public. Space is also taken up by landscaped strips between the main types of area, and beside major roads and other transport links to mask unsightly development and noise. Land is also needed for a hospital and other residential institutions, for the main road network, for car parks, and possibly for railways and other forms of transport.

CHAPTER 4

LAND USE AND DENSITIES

THE ARRANGEMENT OF LAND USES

Each type of facility needs land. The form of a settlement depends on the way these different land uses are related, as well as on shape and size, on the way communications are arranged and on density. All the factors of urban form interact and their effects on the operation of the settlement cannot be completely separated. Nevertheless, it is convenient to discuss each factor in turn.

The different land uses are not always separated physically; in unplanned settlements they are often very mixed. There is little agreement on how far separation is desirable. In planned settlements, and when existing settlements are replanned, a distinct area is usually allocated to each use.

Historically, shops and other services tended to be at the communication centre of a settlement, the point where the main roads met, but there was little clear cut separation of other land uses. Entrepreneurs often set up in business in their homes and expanded on to adjacent land and property. Business centres grew as houses around were converted to business use, or as sites were redeveloped. The business demand for central land inflated prices above the levels acceptable for housing, and displaced residents, migrants and natural increase were housed at the periphery, where land was cheaper and easier to obtain. In earlier periods housing was often built beside the business which employed the occupants, but the nose, dirt and squalor of nineteenth century industry encouraged separate zoning. While these factors are now much less important, traffic problems have to some extent taken their place. Open space was distributed more or less haphazardly, originating partly as common land, partly as gifts from public benefactors and partly as any suitable land which happened to be available when the local authority could finance its acquisition.

Planned land uses can be specialised or mixed, and centralised or dispersed. Some specialisation is generally attempted, its degree depending on the minimum size of unit. The smaller this is, the greater the possible dispersion and the wider the selection of functions in each district.

Journeys usually originate and terminate at home. Since housing occupies about twice as much land as all other facilities apart from outdoor recreation, travelling distances are shorter if housing is grouped round the other facilities than if the arrangement is reversed. When a journey to any other facility is equally likely, total travelling is minimised if all non-housing is in the centre of the settlement. Since the area required for commerce and industry will normally be small compared with the residential area surrounding it, as long as the settlement is not too large any point in the central area will be easily accessible from the home. Any member of the household could therefore change his place of work or patronise different facilities without excessive travelling.

As the size of a settlement increases, the facilities needed daily, whether shopping and other services, or recreation, are duplicated. The real choice is not much improved by continued duplication and, up to a point, not much reduced by grouping such facilities in various parts of the settlement. As the settlement centre becomes less accessible with increasing size, the advantages of grouping with the housing the facilities for daily needs tend to outweigh the loss of choice; hence the value of neighbourhood centres and local recreational space and, at a lower level, the corner-shop and the doctor's surgery in the housing area itself. Similarly, at a higher level, district centres are needed in larger settlements, and centres serving yet more people in the largest settlements. A trade-off between accessibility and choice determines the best sizes for the centres in each settlement.

In settlements of any size some facilities are indivisible because only one is needed – for example, the department store, the high-class specialist furnisher or tailor, the concert hall, the municipal offices and the hospital. However, each will only be visited infrequently, and not all are required on the same occasion, so they do not need to be together but can be distributed among various district or other high-level centres. If they were in associated groups in convenient local centres, total travelling might be less than if they were all in a single centre, since people could choose to live near the centres catering for their particular interests. The grouping is clearly important: one centre might specialise in advanced education and cultural activities, another in sport and another in popular entertainments.

Similar considerations apply to places of employment. Employment in tertiary industry obviously follows the pattern of the facilities themselves, but nationally and regionally orientated industry can be centralised or dispersed; each area can provide a variety of employment or it can specialise. Whereas people patronise many shops and other service facilities, they usually have only one place of work at any given time, although this may continue for only a few months or for a lifetime. Hence, in the short term, travelling is minimised by dispersing employment so that people can live near their workplace. However, dispersal also decreases flexibility, so that people may be unable to change their jobs or their homes independently without a substantially longer journey to work. This effect on total travelling can be reduced if each area specialises in industry which creates a limited range of jobs, so that every worker has the maximum opportunities for his type of employment within one area. For example, firms employing wood-workers, or metalworkers, or workers in textiles could be grouped together, as could insurance, banking and other financial firms. Such an arrangement would probably suit management as well as the employees, but difficulties arise where there is more than one worker in a household. Working wives usually have less specialised skills than their husbands, but they need work close to home for domestic reasons. Thus some female employment should be provided in each industrial area. Younger members of the household may be just as specialised as their fathers, but they will probably form their own households soon after starting work, so that local employment opportunities for them are not a long-term problem.

The relationship between employment areas and shopping and service areas depends largely on convenience and the effect on traffic generation. There are advantages in coupling functions which generate traffic at different times. For example, shopping journeys tend to be made between the peak times of the journey to work, so that the same roads can be used, although separate parking facilities are necessary, and the lunch time trade of employees in a shopping and service area generates no extra traffic or parking. These advantages would be even greater if opening times for shops and other services coincided less with the working hours for commerce and industry. Cultural and entertain-ment areas also can be coupled with shopping and service areas or with employment areas; here the one set of parking facilities as well as of roads can be used for both.

Residents of housing areas prefer their recreational space to be as close as possible. However, in this position rather than at the edge of the settlement, it may duplicate an amenity and cause the development to spread and need longer communications. In small settlements or narrow ribbons of development, recreational space can be at the periphery while still adjacent to the housing area it serves.

SETTLEMENT SHAPE

Unless there are external influences, the unplanned settlement grows fairly evenly around its centre. Frequently, of course, a narrow valley, or a barrier formed by a river or the sea forces the settlement into a linear shape. The effect of shape must be considered in relation to other factors such as land-use relationships, size and density.

A centralised settlement with facilities evenly spread provides the greatest overall accessibility if it is circular. With fingers projecting from the circle to create a star shape, distances from points in the settlement to the centre increase but, since the length of periphery is increased, average distances to the surrounding agricultural land and recreation space outside are reduced. Changing a circular settlement to an elliptical, rectangular or linear one has a similar effect. Longer internal distances increase the road area required and also the public utility links. It is more difficult to generalise about the effect of shape on decentralised and partly centralised settlements, since the relative value of accessibility for each land use has to be considered. As the centre becomes less important and districts more self-contained, the advantages of a circle decline and the value of proximity to the country-side rises relative to other values.

A star or linear shape instead of a circle increases distances to the centre, but does not add to the traffic generated. A linear central area reduces distances to the centre as a whole and spreads the traffic, but increases distances to particular parts of the centre (reducing the density of the central area has similar consequences); overall it improves accessibility only if parts of it are duplicated, and these might be better detached as district centres. The efficiency of a system of public trans-port, particularly tracked transport, is affected by town form differently from private cars, because the load necessary for a viable route is so much greater in the former case than in the latter. Usually public transport must attract all the traffic within range and maintain an even flow of traffic in both directions all along the route and throughout the working day. These conditions are most likely in narrow bands of development. For private cars the road system should also be as evenly loaded as possible in both directions, but only up to full capacity of the roads – the more lanes required the more complex the system and the greater the costs per lane.

Other things being equal, distances increase if the central area functions are outside the settlement and in a new settlement this arrangement would be unlikely to simplify the traffic system. A free-standing 'out of town' shopping and service area has the merit of adaptability, but in operation has advantages only if it either serves several new settlements or relieves congestion in existing ones. In both cases areas with other functions might just as well be added to make it into a balanced settlement.

Shape of settlement also has an important influence on expansion and again the effect has to be related to the pattern of land use. The more nearly circular a settlement is, the more growth all round reduces accessibility both internally and to the surrounding countryside. The

more centralised a settlement is, the more difficult is expansion of the
central area to meet the needs created by peripheral growth. Generally
shape is less important if dispersion is greater so that more needs are
satisfied locally.

SIZE OF SETTLEMENTS

Settlements vary considerably in size; the smallest do not provide even
for all daily needs. The larger the settlement the greater the range of
facilities but the less accessible they are, so that traffic increases more
than proportionately with size. Reducing densities has similar effects on
accessibility and traffic to those of increasing the settlement size.

Facilities can conveniently be divided into those required universally,
such as most convenience goods, many shoppers goods and a large
proportion of services, and those required by only part of the community, for example, other goods and services, and employment opportunities. A full range of the facilities needed can generally be provided
if the settlement is large enough to support them, or is one of a related
cluster of settlements of adequate total size. For the specialised facility,
it matters more what proportion of the inhabitants require it; as this
increases, the minimum size of settlement for which the facility is viable
falls and access becomes easier. Thus specialisation by type of employment and by cultural, leisure and other services enables a much smaller
settlement to provide all the facilities needed by a correspondingly
specialised population. A settlement with specialised facilities attracts
people requiring the services it provides, but the matching of facilities
and population is never complete. People change their employment and
their interests, and young people grow up with different interests from
their parents. Some movement to other settlements for facilities and
employment is therefore inevitable, but the cost to the community as a
whole is small, even if the facilities are at a considerable distance, if
they are used only by a minority.

Larger settlements not only have more facilities, but may enjoy
economies of scale in some functions. Moreover, the range of firms and
trades increases with size, providing greater stability and adaptability
to meet economic fluctuations. The tendency of the traffic to increase
more than proportionately can perhaps be damped by dispersion into a
cluster of smaller specialist settlements, even though, without specialisation, dispersion has the opposite effect. A cluster in place of a single
settlement spreads the area of development and reduces the distinction
between town and country, but specialised settlement clusters may make
urban concentration more acceptable.

Size has no meaning unless the extent of a settlement is defined.
Continuity of development is not essential and parts of a settlement may

be detached, but they cannot be considered part of the settlement if they are so far from the main development that it is inconvenient for their inhabitants to go there for daily and weekly shopping. Thus villages some distance from a town may not be part of the same settlement. Nevertheless, settlements can be clustered, so that while each is self-sufficient for daily and weekly needs, together they comprise a single continuous settlement in terms of facilities. Such clusters are best considered as sub-regional developments. Compared with single settlements they have both advantages and disadvantages: individually they are more compact and more convenient for local services and the open country, but services provided centrally in one settlement are less accessible. The organisation and operation of such clusters will be considered later.

COMMUNICATIONS SYSTEMS

Settlement planning is largely dominated by the great mobility of current western society. The difficulties arise as much from the nature of personal transport as from the distances travelled. In existing settlements the problems which arise from the density of development and its scale, as well as the form of transport, can only be resolved by extensive redevelopment – not always convenient or economic. In very high density developments, such as Hong Kong, bicycles, handcarts, or even perambulators would cause congestion if everybody used them. Had horse-drawn vehicles been widely owned, the planning problems they posed would probably have been greater than those posed in existing towns by private motor cars.

A private car is not only a useful form of transport, but also a possession currently almost universally desired for prestige reasons. Even if public transport were comprehensive, convenient and cheap, not much reduction is likely either in the ownership of private cars, or in their use for internal journeys, or for journeys out of the settlement except to other major settlements. The extent to which public transport might replace private cars for journeys within settlements depends on the level of charges. Once people possess personal transport they compare its marginal costs with the fares on public transport. The marginal costs of private transport normally include parking charges, but not necessarily any allowance for depreciation, tax, insurance and repairs, or for travelling time. In fact driving may be regarded as a satisfaction and be set against the inconvenience of walking to public transport, waiting and changing. In contrast the charges for public transport are based on average costs and are inflated by the 'peakiness' of demand. As more people buy private cars, public transport becomes less competitive, but its complete elimination is unacceptable on both social and planning grounds.

Clearly the transport for a settlement needs to be considered as a whole. The optimum system, that which gives the best value for money, can only be found by examining all the consequences. These are complex and include not only the capital and operating costs of roads, tracks and vehicles (including the costs of replacing property lost during redevelopment), but the costs of special buildings. The forms of settlement convenient for systems of mass transport, for example narrow, linear or necklace high-density developments, might have very high capital and operating costs, so that the savings from cheaper kinds of transport could be more than offset by the diseconomies of the urban form. Again, while special types of personal transport for use in the central areas of settlements, or even in settlements generally, might reduce the costs of roads and parking facilities, they might also add to overall costs if, as seems likely, private cars were still required for journeys out of the settlement. Savings on general development resulting from the use of public transport could be used to subsidise it. However, subsidies may lead to a waste of resources, and it might be better to levy direct charges on the use of roads and car parks, so that each journey incurred its true costs.

Many short journeys are made on foot, especially to local shops and services, and to school. Children, old people and parents with young children are more likely to walk, and are more dependent on public transport than others. It is, therefore, important that pedestrians and vehicles should be adequately separated, particularly on fast distributor roads, and this is usually achieved by independent networks of footpaths and roads. Within the residential areas, where usually only access roads are provided, the systems can be interleaved so that footpaths do not cross roads too frequently. This concentrates through traffic on the distributor roads, which need underpasses or bridges wherever a pedestrian way crosses. Cycle tracks, if required, could be provided parallel to the footpath system.

Buses can operate entirely on the distributor roads, but in some forms of settlement this is unsatisfactory because the hinterland within walking distance on either side of the road does not always provide sufficient passengers. In such cases the buses can be routed either along special bus-only roads, or along estate (access) roads. The additional costs of the latter, even with special links to prevent other through traffic in residential areas, are likely to be small compared with the former, but inevitably some amenity is lost. Tracked transport is probably not viable in small settlements, but it might be in large settlements or settlement clusters, and could either follow the line of the primary road network or take some route better suited to its own economies.

Networks for public utilities are usually less difficult to provide than transport systems, since pipes and conduits can run anywhere, although preferably not under buildings or main roads. There is less interaction with the form of development and the level of services required is probably more important than settlement form, although costs may fall as centralisation and density increase. Clearly the effects of settlement form on public utilities need to be investigated.

DENSITY OF DEVELOPMENT

The density of a settlement depends on many factors: internal and external space standards, the standards of internal environment, the way the buildings are laid out and the nature of the site. In Great Britain, internal space standards are among the highest in the world: residential space is perhaps five times that accepted in less developed parts of the world so that, other things being equal, densities can only be about a fifth as great.[1] Again, British external space standards are relatively high and expected to increase with affluence.[2] In a conventional new town only about an eighth of the land is covered by buildings.[3] With an average storey height, except for industry, of just under three storeys, relatively little land can be saved by building higher. The space required for private access, storage and parking is actually greater than that covered by buildings. About a sixth of the land is needed for roads and three fifths for private gardens and public open space, of which nearly half is private.[3] Saving land to obtain a more compact town is therefore difficult without losing amenities.

In Britain, a satisfactory internal environment requires daylight, sunlight, privacy and freedom from noise and pollution. Their provision depends on the arrangement and spacing of buildings. Daylight can penetrate over roofs and between buildings, and is reflected from one building to another, but sunlight depends on turning buildings so that windows face the right direction. All these factors affect the possible density. The rise in density from building higher is far less than proportionate because the buildings must be further apart.[4] Mixed development and the natural features of the site can often be used to increase density without sacrificing amenities, but some land is unsuitable for development because of its shape, slope, bearing capacity or amenity,

[1] Department of Scientific and Industrial Research, *Densities of Housing Areas*, by P. H. H. Stevens, London, HMSO, 1960.
[2] International Federation for Housing and Planning, *Growing Space Needs in the Urbanized Regions*, Stockholm, 1965.
[3] P. A. Stone, 'The impact of urban development on the use of land and other resources', *Journal of the Town Planning Institute*, vol. 47, no. 5, May 1961.
[4] Stone, *Housing, Town Development, Land and Costs*.

so that densities achieved are usually much lower than those theoretically possible.

About a third of the land in a typical new town is used for housing – more than any other land use.[1] An artificial environment is becoming acceptable for circulation space and bathrooms, but it is unlikely ever to be widely accepted for living rooms and bedrooms. This restricts the arrangement and spacing of dwellings, so that, although in theory densities of 200 or more habitable rooms per acre are feasible with blocks of ten to fifteen storeys, in practice they are rare.[2] In calculating net residential densities, land within the curtilage and space for access roads are included. Densities can therefore be increased by using the space above other land uses to admit daylight and sunlight, and to provide a barrier against noise and pollution from surrounding land uses. If dwellings are built around open spaces, on the banks of rivers or lakes, or on the edge of a hill or the sea, on that side they can abut the boundary of the site. Daylight and sunlight can also be obtained across main roads, car parks, industrial storage or railway lines, but not freedom from noise and pollution. Building at one-room depth against the walls of buildings not requiring windows is another device to increase density. In favourable circumstances three-storey buildings can give densities as great as high-rise blocks. However, high densities can only be attained over limited areas of a settlement.

As densities increase the space about buildings per room and hence per person falls, and it becomes difficult to fit in all the facilities required in a housing area. Private gardens are only practicable for houses and bungalows; privacy in a small garden is rare even so, and clearly non-existent for flatted blocks. With a smaller area of private gardens more communal space is required for play and other amenity areas, and each inhabitant still needs space for car-parking, access and other purposes. In fact, densities higher than those normally obtained with two-storey housing are difficult to achieve without some loss of amenity. The space about buildings per habitable room falls with increasing density whatever the number of storeys (table 4.1). On average about 200 square feet per habitable room is required for access of all kinds and parking,[3] so that, even if high flatted blocks are used, play spaces, areas of planting and other amenities can only be provided at densities of 150 habitable rooms per acre or less. Densities much greater, however high the blocks, are impossible without a serious sacrifice of amenities, since the gain in space about buildings from building higher is soon exhausted. Residential areas without private gardens give an impression of

[1] R. H. Best, *Land for New Towns*, London, Town and Country Planning Association, 1964.
[2] See Stone, *Urban Development in Britain*, vol. I, fig. 7.1, p. 105.
[3] Stone, *Urban Development in Britain*, vol. I.

Table 4.1. *Space about buildings per habitable room*

Square feet

Habitable rooms per acre	Average number of storeys							Decrease in space
	1	2	3	4	5	6	7	
50	621	746	787	808	821	829	835	436
100	185	310	351	372	385	393	399	
150	40	165	206	227	240	248	254	145
200	—	93	134	155	168	176	182	72

source: NIESR estimates.

spaciousness because there are no divisions; a similar effect can be obtained by building around the edge of the site. However, no such device increases the space about buildings per room and, although on a large site playing fields or a park could be created, the land thus used is lost to the residents for normal activities around their home. Perhaps only a minority would want larger gardens, but with increasing numbers of private cars, boats and caravans, and more leisure generally, the demand for space about homes is likely to grow.

Housing densities per acre can be measured in dwellings, habitable rooms, bedspaces or persons. The relationship between these measures depends on size of households and on the way dwellings are divided into rooms and occupied. Smaller households mean that more bathrooms, kitchens and space for access, circulation and garaging are required per person, so that maximum density is low. However, the way households are fitted to dwellings is the major factor. The average for Great Britain in 1961 was about 0·68 persons per habitable room, or 0·69 after allowing for statutory overcrowding and unwanted rooms.[1] New settlements have populations younger than average, with more children and hence a high occupation rate per room – sometimes over unity where all the bedspaces are occupied. Such occupation rates are possible in new housing, although not often achieved in private housing, but they cannot be maintained without considerable overcrowding of some households, unless families are rapidly moved to larger or smaller dwellings every time their size and composition changes. Neither the overcrowding nor such mobility would normally be acceptable.

Dwellings usually have about one bedspace per habitable room and can easily be built to provide 37 rooms an acre. If these bedspaces were all fully occupied, which is unlikely even in subsidised public housing, this would be equivalent to the new town average density of (say) 270 acres for 10,000 people. If the occupation rate was similar to that found

[1] Stone, *Urban Development in Britain*, vol. 1.

nationally in 1961, about 54 habitable rooms per acre (or slightly less under new town conditions) would be needed to house the same number of people. Houses built by public authorities provide about 50 rooms per acre,[1] so about 10 per cent of such dwellings would need to be flatted, or more if some were built privately at lower densities. (Since current government policy is for equal proportions of public and private dwellings, about 20 per cent of the former would need to be flatted to maintain the average density.) By 1989, the maturity date taken for the model settlements, the effect of migration on the proportion of young families will not be exhausted, so that some households will be at their maximum size and the occupation rate might still be above the national average, although well below that frequently assumed for new public authority housing estates. Of course, a low occupation rate is associated with improved amenities per head.

Net housing densities vary widely: the town maps for England and Wales provided an average of 283 acres for 10,000 people:[2] ranging between 234 acres in county boroughs and 461 acres in small towns. These figures reflect the historic situation and what was considered possible in that light. In 1964, the average for planned new towns was 269 acres,[3] but it ranged from 117 to 393, with Cumbernauld lowest because of its high proportion of local authority dwellings, many of them flats, and its policy of high-density development.

Internal space with an artificial environment is already accepted for some commercial uses such as large shops, warehouses, restaurants and public entertainment buildings and, to some extent, for offices. The core of large deep buildings could provide such space, and space for circulation and subsidiary functions, with uses requiring a natural environment on the periphery. Even without such radical changes, densities could be increased, at least in theory, by siting buildings close together and using artificial light to compensate for inadequate daylight at the back of the rooms. However, an artificial environment is not necessarily the most economic solution.

The amount of land about buildings required in commercial areas for circulation, storage and parking is about four times that covered by buildings. A considerable area is also needed for access roads and public car parks. Increasing the number of storeys alone would save little land. Storage, circulation and parking space can be provided on decks above the access roads, but this entails heavy construction, vertical (and probably mechanical) circulation systems, lighting and ventilation, and sophisticated fire precautions. Moreover, the floor

---

[1] Stone, *Urban Development in Britain*, vol. i.
[2] *Report of the Ministry of Housing and Local Government, 1958*, Cmnd 737, London, HMSO, 1959.
[3] Best, *Land for New Towns*.

space used for circulation and by mechanical plant increases with the number of storeys.

Inevitably increased density leads to higher costs of construction, maintenance and operation, but optimum densities are not necessarily those that minimise direct costs – indirect costs and amenities need to be considered. Neighbourhood centres are usually on one level, but with larger centres it becomes more difficult to provide convenient access to all facilities and to separate traffic from pedestrians without multi-level development. Either a decked centre, usually with access roads at ground level and parking between them and the pedestrian decks, or a ground-level pedestrian precinct surrounded by multi-storey car parks, are the principal solutions for district and town centres. Operational efficiency alone is not the criterion for how much multi-level development is economic in each case. Development on the ground is most adaptable – not unimportant when future needs are so difficult to anticipate. Ground-level parking, for example, can easily be decked over should the need arise.

The area loosely described as commercial includes all the cultural and social functions not specifically allocated to other areas. Although it is analytically convenient to group these facilities, they are not confined to a central area, whether in a neighbourhood, district or settlement, but spread into the residential areas, some being completely detached. There are also some flats over shops and service premises, which increases slightly the area of the centres and reduces the residential areas, but the effect on residential density is small.

Commercial land in existing and new towns is planned at between 35 and 50 acres for 10,000 persons.[1] These figures underestimate requirements, partly because they exclude some uses included as commercial in this study and partly because requirements will increase with rising standards – for example, more roads, parking space and commercial garages will be needed for the increase in private cars. An analysis of land uses in new towns suggests 45 acres per 10,000 persons, about half for roads and parking, which would be divided between the different types of centre according to their facilities. Larger settlements with more facilities would generally be developed at higher densities, so the commercial area would not increase proportionately with size.

More land is needed by manufacturing industry in the new towns, which are designed for health and convenience, than is used for the congested and inconvenient sites in the old industrial towns, for example in the Midlands.[2] After the war standards were often set unrealistically

---

[1] *Report of the Ministry of Housing and Local Government, 1958.*
[2] Department of Scientific and Industrial Research, *The Economics of Factory Buildings*, by P. A. Stone, London, HMSO, 1962.

high;[1] moreover incoming industrialists tend to allow for expansion, so that the area per worker falls as establishments expand towards their planned size. Land classified as industrial is, of course, used also for public utility services and for service industry.

Usually single-storey production areas, which need be no more than light-weight sheds, are more economic than multi-storey buildings, which need a heavy construction to carry the usual industrial loads. On one floor the whole building can be lit naturally through the roof, which usually minimises the costs-in-use,[2] and the absence of vertical circulation saves space. Except where gravity flow is important, a production flow on one level is most efficient, and a single factory floor is easier to supervise and more adaptable to production changes. At present the land per worker needed for production and for his car park is not very different. In future, automation will tend to increase the production area per worker, but more shift working might decrease it. Workers' car parks may have to be substantially larger in future in relation to the production area, so that nearly as much land might be saved by multi-storey car parks as by multi-storey production areas, and they are also likely to be more economic.

In existing towns, land for industry is planned at about 52 acres per 10,000 persons – rather more in the smaller towns.[1] The corresponding figure for London new towns in 1964 was 53 acres, which was also the average for all new towns in Great Britain.[3] Land needed for this purpose is likely to increase a little, especially as more cars are used for the journey to work.

In existing towns, planned open space averages about 126 acres per 10,000 persons.[1] A decade ago the new towns were planning for even more, being largely influenced by the standards suggested by the National Playing Fields Association.[4] These figures are now considered too high, but there are no authoritative alternatives. In 1964, the London new towns were planning for 99 acres per 10,000 persons; the average for the other new towns was a little over 100 acres.[3] An analysis of the space requirements per participant for organised games and play weighted by currently projected peak activity rates suggests about 40 acres per 10,000 persons. The area is expected to increase with peak activities to 46 acres by the 1990s. A similar approach indicated a figure of about 20 acres per 10,000 persons for parks and gardens. For landscaped areas and other amenity space, 20 acres per 10,000 persons

---

[1] *Report of the Ministry of Housing and Local Government, 1958.*
[2] DSIR, *The Economics of Factory Buildings.*
[3] Best, *Land for New Towns.*
[4] Ministry of Housing and Local Government, *Open Space*, Technical Memorandum no. 6, London, HMSO, 1956.

appeared reasonable, and a recent estimate for allotments gave a figure of 14 acres per 10,000 persons, which is unlikely to fall in future with leisure time increasing and gardens becoming fewer and smaller. Thus 100 acres per 10,000 persons might be appropriate overall for open space.

Playing fields take up 90 per cent of the land needed for education, so that the height of buildings has no appreciable effect on density. Standards are largely determined by those set for public authority schools by the Department of Education and Science,[1] which indicated that in nursery and primary schools about 0·015 acres were required per pupil, and in secondary schools about 0·030 acres for children under 15 and 0·025 acres for older children. Total needs for land depend, of course, also on numbers of pupils, which are determined by the age and sex structure of the population and by educational activity rates. New settlements have more schoolchildren than average.

Most settlements also contain institutions such as hospitals, residential homes for children and old people, and places of detention, but generally these institutions do not use much land. There is, however, a substantial land requirement for the distributor road network. Space for estate (access) roads is included in the land allocated for residential and other purposes. Distributor roads are wide, and large areas are needed for interchanges and for screening the roads on either side, although open space can be used for the latter. The total land required for main roads is inevitably uncertain, depending on future changes in vehicle owner-ship and use. Adaptation to changing needs requires reserves of land, perhaps best in the form of transport corridors along the line of the main network, which can be landscaped as open space until needed. About 37 acres per 10,000 persons might be sufficient for settlements catering for full motorisation, that is for road systems adequate for all journeys to work to be made by private car. Some settlements will also need space for railways, ports and other transport.

The overall density of a settlement is largely determined by residential densities, housing being the largest user of land. Plans for county boroughs use about 534 acres per 10,000 persons for all urban purposes, while large towns use 811 acres.[2] The figure currently planned for British new towns is 550 acres.[3]

[1] Department of Education and Science, *Playing Fields and Hard Surface Areas*, London, HMSO, 1966.
[2] *Report of the Ministry of Housing and Local Government, 1958.*
[3] Best, *Land for New Towns.*

CHAPTER 5

SETTLEMENT MODELS

THE BASIS OF THE ESTIMATES

Neither existing towns nor the new towns of the last two decades can provide adequate data to show the effect of the size and form of settlements on their costs of development and operation. No new town is, of course, ever complete and many are in comparatively early stages of development, so that information on their final form is particularly incomplete, but they provide some data – on parts of towns and the provision of some facilities – which can be used to estimate facility requirements and their costs in theoretical model settlements.

Such models have to cover the whole range for each factor on which information is required. To determine this range, the shapes and sizes of conventional towns – generally the result of location and past economic forces – and of new towns, both existing and planned, were examined.

Most free-standing towns are roughly circular with major facilities concentrated in the centre, although there are some mixed land uses, indicating a continuing expansion of the centre to match peripheral growth of residential areas. The centre itself is often surrounded by an area of decaying residential and other properties, made obsolete partly by physical and functional change, a product of their age, and partly by an incomplete process of change to new uses of the area. Where the town has engulfed other smaller settlements, there are usually sub-centres providing district or local services. The continuity and density of land use and the shape of the town are affected if some land is unsuitable for development, or if there are private estates within the settlement. Where a great deal of land cannot be developed for any reason, the development that exists is often very dense, particularly in settlements which have grown rapidly. Constraints on available land are the main reasons for non-circular development: river and coastal settlements are frequently fan-shaped; valley settlements are often linear. Small settlements may be linear because of ribbon development which avoids the need for new roads.

Transport within settlements is usually by road; railways only exist in the largest developments with substantial suburbs. Generally the road systems are radial, meeting in the central area. The form of the road system is determined by the form of the settlement; independent road patterns such as grids have not been used on any scale in this country except within residential estates.

PARAMETERS OF THE MODELS

The object of this study was to examine settlements large enough to be mainly self-sufficient, and so villages and small towns were omitted and three model sizes were taken – to house 50,000, 100,000 and 250,000 persons. Some indication of the costs of larger or smaller settlements

Chart 5.1. *Shapes of settlements and settlement clusters*

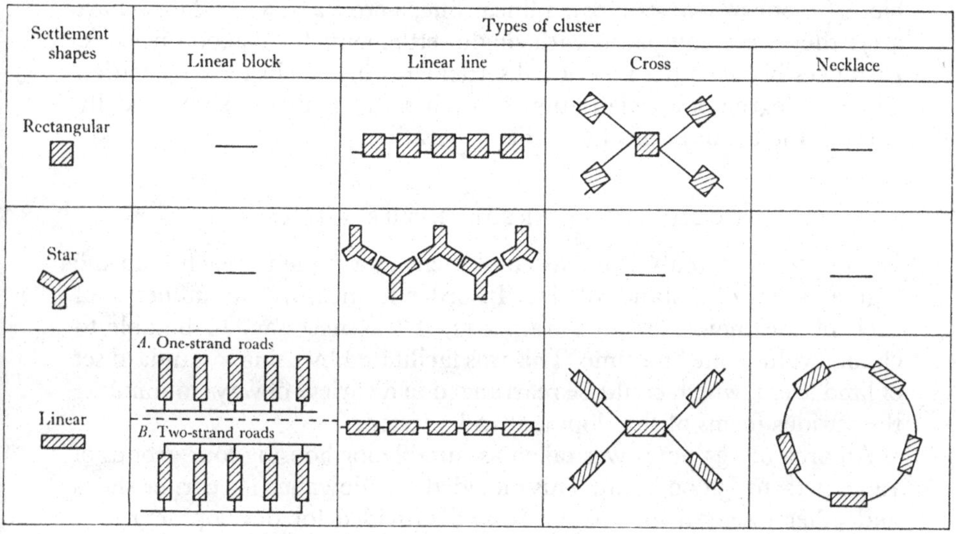

Settlement shapes	Types of cluster			
	Linear block	Linear line	Cross	Necklace
Rectangular	—			—
Star	—		—	—
Linear	A. One-strand roads B. Two-strand roads			

can be obtained by extrapolating the results. Studies of various effects of settlement size on the scale of development and costs indicate that some costs increase with size, but probably other costs first fall as size increases.[1] It was therefore necessary to study a range of sizes to determine the optimum for various conditions.

The form of settlement was defined by the arrangement of the central functions. Centralised settlements, in which most shops, offices and service establishments are in one central area, would be impracticable in very large settlements, so models based on this form were examined

---

[1] Smeed and Holroyd, *Some Factors affecting Congestion in Towns*; K. S. Lomax, 'The relationship between expenditure per head and size of population of county boroughs in England and Wales', *Journal of the Royal Statistical Society*, vol. 106, part 1, 1943.

only for 50,000 and 100,000 persons. Decentralised settlements were those where a neighbourhood centre provides those central facilities needed daily or weekly by about 10,000 persons, with the remainder in the central area. Between the two extremes, partly centralised settlements were based on districts for about 25,000 persons, each with a district centre providing all services except those that could only be met on a settlement basis in the town centre.

For purposes of evaluating shape, model forms were created to simulate the range from circular to linear. Three main shapes of settlement were studied: rectangular, star and linear. Large settlements were also designed as a cluster of five small settlements each for 50,000 persons. Five types of settlement cluster were considered – a linear block (in one or two strands), a linear line, a cross and a necklace (chart 5.1); they were compared with single settlements for 250,000 persons. Distances between the individual settlements in the cluster were varied and the degree of specialisation of each settlement was simulated by varying the assumptions for traffic generation.

COMPONENT AREAS IN THE MODELS

For purposes of analysis it was convenient to assume for each land use regular areas of a standard size. In order to measure the influence of each of the major design parameters, it was necessary to be able to change values one at a time. This was facilitated by using a standard set of land areas, which could be rearranged in a variety of ways to simulate the various forms of development to be tested.

An area of 135 acres was taken as suitable for housing four groups of 1,250 persons, 5,000 in all. This included an allowance for corner-shops and other essential local services, and provided for development at a density of about 37 persons per acre or 270 acres per 10,000 persons (table 5.1).[1] The average figure planned for British new towns in 1964 was 269 acres per 10,000 persons.[2] Open space (23·5 acres) and a primary school site suitable for a population of 5,000 (6·5 acres) were added to each residential area.

---

[1] The densities to be tested in the models were set at 30, 37 and 50 persons per acre. The effect of varying the density could be measured by making various changes in the models. In the majority of linear and star-shaped settlements the depth of the housing areas could be increased or reduced without changes other than adding to or subtracting from the lengths of secondary road. This was also possible in the outer housing areas of the other models. Changing the scale of the model, another possibility, would, of course, change the density of all the areas in the same proportion. A third method was to vary the population in some housing areas; while this affected the traffic loads on the distributor roads and the layout of the residential area, it did not affect the form of the settlement. The effects of relatively higher densities in some areas and of reducing the number of residential areas were tested by these methods.　　　　[2] Best, *Land for New Towns*.

Table 5.1. *The use of land in the model settlements*

Acres per 10,000 persons

	Residential areas	Central areas	Industrial areas	Other areas	Total land
Housing					
Dwellings[a]	236·0	—	—	—	236·0
Access roads	34·0	—	—	—	34·0
Commercial					
Buildings	—	17·1	—	—	17·1
Central parking[b]	—	6·6	—	—	6·6
Central roads[b]	—	4·5	—	—	4·5
Social etc.					
Buildings	—	7·6[c]	—	—	7·6
Access roads[b]	—	5·5[c]	—	—	5·5
Industrial					
Buildings	—	—	28·0	—	28·0
Estate roads	—	—	8·0	—	8·0
Schools and colleges	13·0	—	—	28·0[d]	41·0[d]
Hospitals	—	—	—	7·0	7·0
Main roads	—	—	—	37·0	37·0
Public utilities	—	1·0[c]	21·0	—	22·0
Parks and gardens	—	5·0[c]	—	7·0	12·0
Playing fields	37·0	—	18·0	13·0[e]	68·0
Other open space[f]	10·0	2·7[c]	10·0	—	22·7
Total	330·0	50·0	85·0	92·0	557·0

SOURCE: NIESR estimates.

[a] Based on 37 persons per acre, includes curtilages.
[b] Average figures: see table 9.12 for details with different degrees of centralisation.
[c] Central area facilities which could be supplied in residential areas.
[d] Excludes a college of further education, which would be provided only in larger settlements (see p. 54).
[e] Includes a golf course and sports stadium.
[f] Includes landscaped areas.

A basic neighbourhood for 10,000 persons, comprising two residential areas and a centre of 40 acres, would therefore cover 370 acres in all (chart 5.2). It was convenient to assume a rectangular neighbourhood, but the shape could be varied to suit the needs of some settlement models. Conceptually, for purposes of the model, facilities other than housing will be described as if they formed a compact centre, but in practice this would not necessarily be so – some of them could be integrated into the residential areas.

Two other types of commercial area were also considered – district centres and town centres. The district centres were conceived as serving 25,000 people in five housing areas. They would replace neighbourhood centres and the services provided there, but not the incidental shops and

Chart 5.2. *Component areas of settlement models*

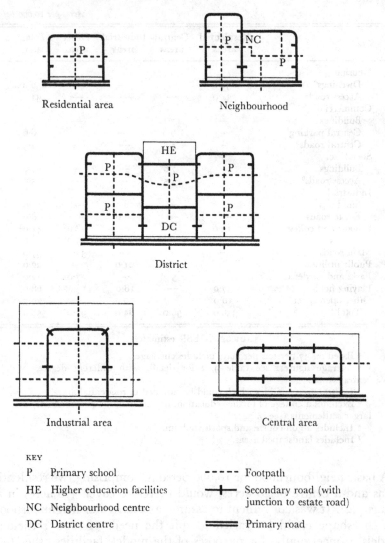

Residential area   Neighbourhood

District

Industrial area   Central area

KEY

P	Primary school	----- Footpath
HE	Higher education facilities	—+— Secondary road (with
NC	Neighbourhood centre	junction to estate road)
DC	District centre	=== Primary road

surgeries in the housing area itself, nor the other non-centralised neighbourhood functions. Town centres would also be needed to provide all a settlement's central functions and the balance of other functions not provided in the district or neighbourhood centres. Again the areas were conceived for simplicity as simple rectangles, which could be drawn out to suit different settlement forms (chart 5.2).

An analysis of the use of land in new towns for central area functions gave a figure of 45 acres per 10,000 persons. This figure compared satis-factorily with the average figures for existing towns[1] and was used in the model settlements (table 5.1). It excluded parks and gardens, but included the land required for all commercial, cultural and social buildings, including residential institutions, for parking and roads, and for incidental open space, whether the central area functions were provided in a single town centre or were partially or wholly decentralised.

Rectangles were also used to simulate industrial areas (chart 5.2). These could be combined to simulate areas for larger settlements or those with greater industrial concentration. Settlements for 50,000 or 100,000 persons would have two industrial areas, larger settlements four. The total of land for industrial areas required in the model settle-ments was estimated on the basis of the projected number of workers (see chapter 6 below) and the site area per worker in London new towns in 1968. This gave figures per 10,000 population of 28 acres for factories, offices and warehouses, 8 acres for roads and 21 acres for public utility services and reserved sites for industrial and other purposes (table 5.1). This total of 57 acres per 10,000 persons compares with an average of 52 acres planned for towns in England and Wales[2] and 53 acres for both the London new towns and those in Great Britain.[3] The higher figure adopted in this study allows for increasing use of cars for the journey to work.

In addition to land within residential areas provided for primary schools, sites for higher education facilities were provided for each 25,000 people (chart 5.2). Total land for schools in the model settle-ments was estimated from the projected number of pupils in schools and from officially recommended site areas per pupil. The figure, 41 acres per 10,000 population, agrees closely with the average (39 acres) planned for towns in England and Wales.[2]

The models also provided land for various other uses. Hospitals and other large institutions were allocated 7 acres per 10,000 persons, the figure indicated by new town plans.

Open space in the model settlements was taken as just over 100 acres per 10,000 persons (table 5.1), the average planned for new towns in Great Britain.[2] Rather more than half would be for playing fields, a fifth for landscaped and natural areas, and just over a tenth for formal gardens and parks. Some playing fields and other open spaces were assumed to be within each residential area, and some in the central areas; the balance would be in separate areas related to each 25,000 people. Most of the open space being at the edge of the model settlements, only large

---

[1] Stone, *Housing, Town Development, Land and Costs.*
[2] *Report of the Ministry of Housing and Local Government, 1958.*
[3] Best, *Land for New Towns.*

changes in the areas allocated would make any significant difference to roads or to costs generally.

The allocation of land for communications created special difficulties, since the size of roads and the space they would occupy could not be estimated until all land uses had been decided, but, on the other hand, distances could not be estimated until the plans were complete. Advantage was therefore taken of the need for landscaping roads, and for providing some barrier between them and the adjacent areas, to allocate corridors large enough to accommodate primary and secondary roads and to provide for landscaping. In the model settlements the allowance for primary and secondary roads was 37 acres per 10,000 persons, based on information from new town plans (table 5.1). Access roads were included in functional areas.

The total basic areas of the model settlements of 557 acres per 10,000 persons compares with 534 acres planned for county boroughs[1] and 550 acres planned for British new towns.[2] Other existing towns have much larger acreages per 10,000 mainly because of much lower housing densities.

THE ARRANGEMENT OF COMPONENT AREAS

Clearly it was not possible to simulate the whole range of possible arrangements in the models. A selection was therefore made to provide a broad cross-section (chart 5.3).

In centralised settlements, all shopping and services not provided in the housing areas, and about half the nationally and locally orientated service industry were concentrated in a single centre. This was adjacent to, or surrounded by, a single industrial area containing also the balance of nationally and locally orientated service industry. Open space and land for higher education facilities, a hospital and other institutions, all requiring large sites but not generating much vehicular traffic, were located at the periphery of the settlement.

In partly centralised settlements, districts consisted of five housing areas around a district centre, which provided shopping and other services exclusively required for 25,000 persons. The balance of shopping and services and the service industry remained in the town centre. The number of industrial areas was doubled for the smaller settlements (up to 100,000 persons) and doubled again for the larger settlements. Again the large space users were located at the periphery of the settlement.

In decentralised settlements, neighbourhoods consisted of two housing areas around a neighbourhood centre, which provided shopping and

---

[1] *Report of the Ministry of Housing and Local Government, 1958.*
[2] Best, *Land for New Towns.*

Chart 5.3. *Forms of settlement by degree of centralisation*

Centralised

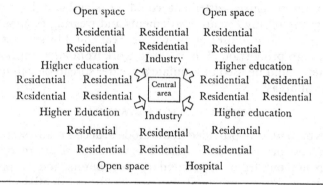

Open space		Open space
Residential	Residential	Residential
Residential	Residential	Residential
Higher education	Industry	Higher education
Residential	Residential	Residential Residential
Residential	Residential	Residential Residential
Higher Education	Industry	Higher education
Residential	Residential	Residential
Residential	Residential	Residential
Open space	Hospital	

Partly centralised

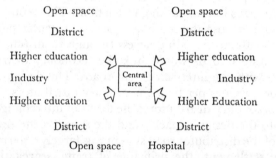

Open space	Open space
District	District
Higher education	Higher education
Industry	Industry
Higher education	Higher Education
District	District
Open space	Hospital

Decentralised

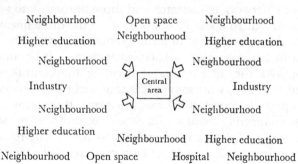

Neighbourhood	Open space	Neighbourhood
Higher education	Neighbourhood	Higher education
Neighbourhood		Neighbourhood
Industry		Industry
Neighbourhood		Neighbourhood
Higher education	Neighbourhood	Higher education
Neighbourhood	Open space	Hospital Neighbourhood

other services exclusively required for 10,000 persons. Again, the balance of shopping and services and other service industry remained in the town centre. Other areas were dispersed as in the partly centralised settlement.

Other relations between land uses could be simulated by combining the component parts in other ways, by grouping small settlements or by allowing for different types of movement in estimating traffic. For example, a multi-centre settlement could be simulated by putting together a group of single centre settlements and treating them as one; the development of specialised employment areas could be simulated by assuming a high proportion of journeys to work from adjacent housing areas; clusters could be used to simulate a greater spread of commercial and industrial areas.

COMMUNICATIONS SYSTEMS

Three types of road were provided in the models: access roads, secondary distributors and primary distributors. The access or estate roads were assumed to fan out from the secondary distributors and to provide access to the buildings and land uses within the residential or other areas, but not to provide routes across the areas. There would be speed limits on these roads but no parking restrictions. The secondary distributor roads would enclose the residential areas and enter industrial and central areas, without providing access through them (chart 5.2). The primary distributor roads would link the secondary distributors and connect them with the inter-settlement roads. The design speeds were assumed to be 40 miles per hour for primary distributors and 30 miles per hour for secondary distributors; the forms of interchanges would be appropriate to the design capacity and the speed of the traffic.

The form of the distributor road system was largely determined by the shape of the settlement, the principle of traffic segregation and the volume of traffic. The obvious road system for a linear settlement was a central primary network of collector and through roads into which the secondary roads fed. In a star (Y-shaped) town the three linear strands would join at the central point to form a radial system. As the depth of development in a linear or star settlement increased, it became worthwhile to consider the alternatives of dividing the central strand of primary road into two, with some areas sandwiched in between, or of joining and up-grading peripheral roads to form a three-strand primary system. Cross-connecting roads would have to be provided to form a box or a hierarchical grid as in a rectangular settlement. The relationships between the settlement forms and primary road networks are illustrated for settlements for 100,000 persons in chart 5.4.[1]

Footpaths were provided to link the various parts of each area and to

---

[1] There were two sub-forms of rectangular settlements; both were based on the same physical areas, but (A) adhered strictly to the component shapes and road alignments, while in (B) shapes were varied to fit the overall shape of the settlement and secondary roads were allowed to pass through the component areas. As a result primary roads were longer and secondary roads shorter in (B) than in (A).

Chart 5.4. *Road systems in various settlements*

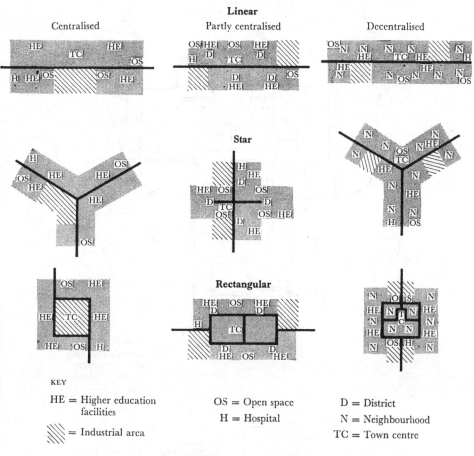

KEY

HE = Higher education facilities

\\\\ = Industrial area

OS = Open space

H = Hospital

D = District

N = Neighbourhood

TC = Town centre

Notes: (i) All settlements shown are for 100,000 persons.

(ii) In rectangular settlements the sub-forms illustrated are (A) for centralised and partly centralised, (B) for decentralised (see footnote on p. 40).

separate pedestrians from vehicular traffic; they were assumed to be connected right across the settlement to provide an unbroken footpath system.

A detailed picture of the form of the model settlements can be obtained by drawing the separate areas with their secondary distributor roads and footpath systems on the broad model plans. Part of the model for a 250,000 person rectangular settlement with district centres for which this has been done is illustrated in chart 5.5, on which bus routes

Chart 5.5. *Alternative bus routes*

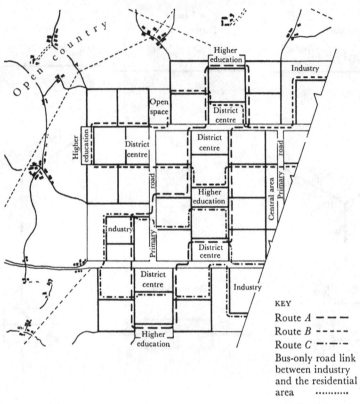

KEY

Route *A* — — —

Route *B* - - - - -

Route *C* —·—·—

Bus-only road link
between industry
and the residential
area   ··········

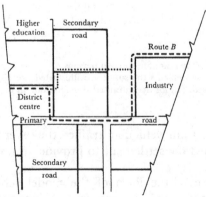

in a model settlement are also considered. Since only the primary and secondary distributors are through roads, bus routes would tend to follow these, which would have the advantage of keeping buses out of housing areas. The principal disadvantages of this system would be the distance passengers would have to walk to and from a bus stop, and the indirectness of the bus routes. The first difficulty could be overcome by running buses through housing areas and creating links for buses only between the major cul-de-sacs in those areas. A complete road system for buses only might shorten their routes, but would not necessarily reduce walking distance to the bus stops.

In the largest size of settlement some land uses could be rearranged to provide for a railway as an alternative passenger transport system (chart 11.2).[1]

[1] See p. 145 below.

CHAPTER 6

POPULATION AND FACILITIES

POPULATION OF A MATURE SETTLEMENT

The population of a mature settlement depends partly on the structure of the base population in the vicinity at the beginning of planned development and its rates of natural increase, and partly on the demographic characteristics of the migrants and their rates of natural increase. It is possible that the structure of the base population could interact with the economics of the settlement form, but as shown in appendix A[1] this is not the case, and an analysis of rates of natural increase indicated no significant departure from normal in any class of town. Thus, there seemed no strong reasons against projecting the population for the model settlements from a base with the national demographic structure and growth at national rates. (In fact, since the growth of the migrant population usually dwarfs the natural increase of the base population, even extreme distortions in the latter would have little effect on the final population.) The demographic structure of migrants, which affects their rate of natural increase and its timing, can be shown by a study of the population in new towns to be similar throughout the country, and there is no reason to foresee any substantial change. One such structure was therefore sufficient for use in the models and, as the best available data were for the 1964 population of Crawley – then a settlement in the middle of its growth period, with a more balanced selection of migrants than one in the early years of growth – these were the figures used.

Most comparisons in this study are made at the maturity of a planned settlement, that is when planned migration is at an end. The period of migration could be anything from 10 to 30 years depending on the initial population, the final size proposed and the annual rate of net immigration. The characteristics of the population at maturity were examined for 18 combinations of different levels of these factors, but the proportions of population in the age and sex groups significant for the provision of urban facilities varied very little, and least in the groups of major importance. The study of town size and form was therefore based on one average set of planning factors, which gave the demographic structure shown in table A.9.[2]

[1] See p. 257. [2] See p. 268.

THE NEED FOR FACILITIES

To estimate facility needs from the demographic and economic structure of the population, the numbers in each population category were related to their requirements. The method naturally varied with the facility: with schools for example, the relevant population category could be estimated closely and figures were available of floor area required per pupil place; in other cases the statistics were not sufficiently precise for such treatment, and it was necessary to relate a certain size and standard of facility to a population category of given size. Road needs were estimated as described in chapter 7 below.

Allowance was made, as far as possible, for conditions in 1989, taken as the maturity date of the settlement. Thus it was necessary to assume education policy, shopping organisation, employment distribution, car ownership and so on at that time, but since this study is comparative, errors in these assumptions are not important provided there is no interaction with the settlement forms under discussion, which in general appears unlikely.

HOUSING

The projection of population described in appendix A was extended to produce an analysis of households by type and size (tables 6.1 and 6.2).[1] Naturally, the continuous intake of predominantly young people into a developing settlement results in households younger and larger than the national average. The average household at maturity of the settlement will be 3·42 persons as against 2·92 in the population as a whole. Had the headship rates expected nationally[2] been applied to the settlement population structure, the average household would have been about 4·2 persons, but, of course, the rates of household formation will be higher in new settlements than in the country generally.

The next stage was to fit the households to dwellings of the appropriate size. There were two approaches, neither of them completely satisfactory: the first was arbitrarily to relate rooms to household sizes and the second to use observed fitting standards. The adequacy of a fitting standard varies with the composition of a household and with its own space standards: some households, particularly large ones,

---

[1] An extension of the EMCON programme took any one quinquennial output of the main programme and broke the population down into a likely distribution of households. The basic data (from the General Register Office, *Census 1961. England and Wales, Household Composition Tables*, London, HMSO, 1966) provided a distribution among 32 types of household differentiated by size and composition. The household distributions for the national and migrant populations for each quinquennium were used as building blocks, like the population structures (see p. 263), to obtain the household structures resulting from the different population histories.

[2] Stone, *Urban Development in Britain*, vol. 1.

Table 6.1. *Projections of household distribution*

	Percentage distribution of households							Total no. of households[a]
	1 person	2 persons	3 persons	4 persons	5 persons	6 persons	7+ persons	
	Migrants							
1966	4·8	27·1	25·3	24·4	11·2	4·4	2·8	*3,267*
1971	5·3	19·3	22·9	25·3	15·0	7·3	4·9	*3,376*
1976	5·8	16·6	21·8	24·6	16·3	8·7	6·2	*3,515*
1981	6·8	14·9	23·5	26·0	15·5	7·7	5·6	*3,814*
1986	8·0	17·2	27·0	25·5	13·2	5·6	3·5	*4,429*
1991	8·2	23·7	26·7	23·3	10·9	4·3	2·9	*5,147*
	National average							
1986	14·0	22·6	23·7	20·9	11·1	4·6	3·1	*37,668*
1991	14·2	22·3	23·6	21·0	11·1	4·7	3·1	*39,113*

SOURCE: NIESR estimates.

[a] Formed by the projected populations shown in table A.5.

may be adequately housed with one bedroom for each two members; others may require a separate bedroom for each member and possibly spare rooms for visitors. Again, some households may find one living room acceptable, whereas others will require several. It is useful to examine the relationship between fitting standards and occupancy ratios. Fitting standard (A) (table 6.3) implies eating and sitting in the same living room, which would be a very low standard unless a second bedroom was shared to provide another living room. Moderate fitting standards (B) and (C) produce occupancy ratios of between 0·7 and 0·8 for a population with household structures as projected for the new settlements.

Table 6.2. *Households in a mature settlement*[a]

Persons per household	Households per 10,000 persons	Percentage distribution
1	270	*9*
2	560	*19*
3	710	*24*
4	700	*24*
5	390	*14*
6	180	*6*
7+	120	*4*
Total	2930	*100*

SOURCE: NIESR estimates.

[a] Taken as 1989.

Table 6.3. *Fitting standards and occupancy ratios*

Persons per habitable room

	1 bedroom per married couple plus 1 bedroom for each other member of household	1 bedroom per married couple plus 1 bedroom for each other member plus 1 bedroom extra for expanding households
Fitting standard:		
(A) 1 extra room per household	0·91	0·86
(B) 1 extra room for 1- and 2-bedroom households and 2 extra rooms for others	0·81	0·76
(C) 2 extra rooms per household	0·72	0·69

Note: A kitchen with dining area would count as a habitable room.

However well a dwelling fits a household when it is first allocated, the fit inevitably becomes less satisfactory with time. As a household grows in size and wealth it will generally move to a larger dwelling, but the reverse is not so usual, partly because smaller dwellings are not appreciably cheaper, especially if newer, and partly because spare rooms are often required for visiting children. Thus the occupancy ratio decreases with time; in 1961, in Great Britain as a whole, it was 0·69 persons per habitable room after eliminating statutory overcrowding and involuntary under-occupation. Although the fit at the maturity of a planned

Table 6.4. *Distribution of dwellings in a mature settlement*

Dwelling size (habitable rooms)	Dwellings per 10,000 persons		Occupancy ratios	
	Numbers	Percentage distribution	Persons per room	Persons per dwelling
1	13	0·4	1·00	1·00
2	116	4·0	0·82	1·64
3	332	11·3	0·75	2·26
4	838	28·6	0·70	2·78
5	1061	36·3	0·70	3·50
6	374	12·8	0·64	3·85
7	132	4·5	0·64	4·45
8+	60	2·1	0·54	4·99
All dwellings	2926	100·0	0·73	3·42

SOURCE: NIESR estimates.

settlement would be tighter than the national average, space standards are expected to rise with increasing affluence; it was, therefore, decided to fit households to dwellings at the 1961 national occupation rates adjusted for overcrowding and under-occupation.[1] However, since the households in the settlement at maturity would be larger than the national average in 1961, the average occupancy ratio would be greater – 0·73 persons per habitable room (see table 6.4) – and the average dwelling would have 4·6 habitable rooms instead of 4·4.

SHOPPING AND SERVICE TRADES

The calculations of shopping space required commenced with estimates of turnover per head of settlement population, divided between convenience and durable goods, which were projected forward to the maturity date. Factors for turnover per square foot were related to the figures for turnover per head to give the area required per head.

Table 6.5. *Turnover per head of population
in towns of different sizes, 1961*

£s, 1967 prices

Sample		Turnover per head		
No. of towns	Population	Average	Median	Quartile range
99	40,000– 59,999	185	182	134–230
52	80,000–119,999	200	199	105–232
10	200,000–299,999	224	230	188–238

SOURCE: Board of Trade, *Report on the Census of Distribution and Other Services, 1961*, part 1: *Establishment Tables*, London, HMSO, 1963.

Turnover per head of the population of a town is not the same as expenditure per head by the population, because some retail sales are made to visitors and, conversely, some of the residents' purchases are made in other towns. Whether these effects result in a net inflow or outflow of purchasing power depends upon the relative attraction of the town in its locality, which is determined partly by the town's size and geographical situation, and partly by historical factors. The effect of town size on turnover needs to be isolated.

Regional variations in turnover per head of population are very small: in 1961, only Greater London and Wales varied by more than

[1] Stone, *Urban Development in Britain*, vol. I, table 5.8.

7 per cent from the national average of £174.[1] Both extremes are irrelevant to this study: the figure for Greater London is obviously related to its special status, and a new settlement in Wales is unlikely to have a turnover typical of Wales as a whole – it would probably be populated by Birmingham overspill with unchanged behaviour patterns and income levels. No regional adjustments in sales per head therefore seemed necessary.

If the figures for turnover per head of population are analysed in relation to town size, the differences again are small, and seem unlikely to be significant as the quartile ranges overlap considerably (table 6.5).

The regional marketing status of a town has more effect on sales per head than either region or size. Clearly status cannot be defined in terms of turnover per head in this context, so samples of subordinate and predominant towns were selected from the map. The criteria can best be defined by the lists of towns, but approximately they were:

Subordinate – urban districts clearly overshadowed by a large neighbouring centre.

Predominant – municipal and county boroughs well away from other centres.

The towns selected were:

Subordinate

Fareham (Hampshire)
Hove (Sussex)
Bedworth (Warwickshire)
Oadby (Leicestershire)
Sutton-in-Ashfield
    (Nottinghamshire)
Hoylake,
    Wirral (Cheshire)

Cheadle and Gatley (Cheshire)
Bentley-with-Arksey (Yorkshire)
Thornton Cleveleys (Lancashire)
Brandon and Byshottles (Durham)
Longbenton (Northumberland)
Musselburgh (Midlothian)
Paisley (Renfrewshire)
Prestwick (Ayrshire)

Predominant

Derby (Derbyshire)
Salisbury (Wiltshire)
Colchester (Essex)
Reading (Berkshire)
Plymouth (Devon)
Scarborough (Yorkshire)
Darlington (Durham)
Worcester (Worcestershire)
York (Yorkshire)
Dundee (Angus)

Great Yarmouth (Norfolk)
Norwich (Norfolk)
Ipswich (Suffolk)
Cambridge (Cambridgeshire)
Preston (Lancashire)
Swindon (Wiltshire)
Hereford (Herefordshire)
Chester (Cheshire)
Ayr (Ayrshire)
Inverness (Inverness-shire)

[1] Stone, *Urban Development in Britain*, vol. II: *Non-residential development* (forthcoming).

Table 6.6. *Turnover per head of population by town status, 1961*

	Status of town	
	Subordinate	Predominant
Number in sample	14	20
Annual turnover per head	(£s, 1967 prices)	
Average	133	270
Median	137	271
Quartile range	92–149	249–88
Proportion of turnover in	(percentages)	
Convenience goods*a*	*73·1*	*49·9*
Durable goods*b*	*26·9*	*50·1*

SOURCE: as table 6.5.

a From grocers and provision dealers, other food retailers, confectioners, tobacconists, newsagents and 45% of other non-food retailers.

b From clothing and footwear stores, household goods merchants, general stores and 55% of other non-food retailers.

Average turnover for predominant towns was about twice as high as for subordinate towns and the quartile ranges were completely separate (table 6.6). Of the smallest towns in table 6.5, 35 per cent had a turnover per head within the quartile range of subordinate towns and only 4 per cent within the range of predominant towns. The corresponding figures for the middle group were 20 per cent and 6 per cent, and for the largest group 0 and 10 per cent.

It would appear from a comparison of tables 6.5 and 6.6 that differences in turnover per head result from status rather than size, so that the average value for all settlements – £203 per annum in 1961 – could be used in the models.

On the other hand, the variation in turnover per head with shopping status was important; moreover the durable goods share of turnover rose with increasing status (table 6.6). This is compatible with the common pattern of frequent short trips for food and small articles, and fewer longer journeys for furniture and clothes.

The figures needed for turnover per square foot were the national averages at a given date, not the best achieved at that date. It was assumed that in 1989 the minimum value would be the 1961 best; implying that, by then, all shops having a lower turnover per square foot than the best that could be achieved in 1961 would have been eliminated. A distribution with this cut-off but nonetheless skewed, like the national average, toward the lower levels, seemed plausible for a new town started in the mid-1960s and completed by 1989. Most shops

Table 6.7. *Space requirements for retailing by town status*

	Subordinate	Average	Predominant
Annual turnover per head[a]	(£)	(£)	(£)
1961 Convenience goods	98·0	110·8	134·2
Durables	36·0	92·2	134·8
1989 Convenience goods	104·6	118·3	143·2
Durables	70·8	181·3	265·1
Floor area per head	(sq. ft.)	(sq. ft.)	(sq. ft.)
1989 Convenience goods	2·3	2·6	3·1
Durables	2·2	5·7	8·3
Total	4·5	8·3	11·4

SOURCE: NIESR estimates.

[a] At constant, 1967 prices.

in the settlement would have been built well before the maturity date and would be similar to the national pattern. Improvements in turnover per square foot would therefore be limited – any major reorganisation requiring rebuilding or at least refitting. The level of efficiency would probably not be far from the national average, but the factors used for turnover per square foot and expenditure per head were scaled down to discount improvements in the quality of the goods sold, which only obscure improvements over time in the efficiency of distribution. The results for sales per square foot in 1989 were £46 per annum for convenience goods and £32 per annum for durable goods.

The estimate of floor space for shopping was very sensitive to variations in turnover per square foot – much more than to variations in expenditure per head. The accuracy of the former was therefore more important and, as the values in 1961 varied widely, the possible error in the estimates was large. The differential in shopping space requirements for towns of different status was also difficult to determine. Sales to visitors in predominant towns increased turnover per square foot as well as per head. The only indication of the different rates was provided by rack rents per square foot. Hence, the estimates of retail area required were based on 1989 turnover per person and per square foot, modified by a measure of differential sales per square foot associated with the status of the town (table 6.7).

For service trades, the rise in turnover per square foot by 1989 (table 6.8) seemed unlikely to be very large, in view of the limited possibilities for improvement and the small units general in new settlements. The rate of improvement per annum was assumed to be the

Table 6.8. *Space requirements for service trades*

	Turnover per head[a]		Turnover per sq. ft.[a]		Floor area per 10,000 pop. 1989
	1961	1989	1961	1989	
	(£)	(£)	(£)	(£)	(sq. ft. 000s)
Showrooms					
Electricity	1·07	2·10	} 25	} 33	0·6
Gas	0·96	1·89			0·6
Catering[b]	6·35	12·49			3·8
Launderettes	0·11	0·22			0·1
Dry cleaners	0·77	1·51			0·5
Motor trades					
Motor sales	32·24	103·43	30	40	25·9
Service	11·16	35·80	12	16	22·4
Petrol sales	10·18	34·68	20	27	12·8
Miscellaneous sales	2·11	6·77	30[c]	40	1·7
Hairdressers	1·90	3·74	} 25	} 33	1·1
Boot and shoe repairs	0·50	0·98			0·3
Total	67·35	203·61			69·8

SOURCES: Board of Trade, *Census of Distribution, 1961*; Central Statistical Office, *Annual Abstract of Statistics*, 1961; *Board of Trade Journal*, 17 March 1961; NIESR estimates.
  [a] At constant, 1967 prices.
  [b] Includes cafes, restaurants, fish and chip shops, etc.
  [c] Assumed the same as motor sales.

same as in retailing durable goods. Similarly, turnover per head in the service trades (apart from motor trades) was assumed to rise at the same annual rate as turnover per head in retailing durable goods. This was better founded, since both depend mainly on the level of personal incomes remaining after the purchase of basic necessities, so that both are likely to rise in proportion to this residual, although in the early stages durable goods may take more than their share and later services might predominate. For motor trades, turnover per head was assumed to follow the projected rise in car ownership, which was estimated as 0·389 cars per head in 1989 compared with 0·12 in 1961.[1] The total floor area per 10,000 persons for service trades in 1989 was estimated at 69,800 square feet.

EDUCATION

The Department of Education and Science published projections of the school population for maintained schools (primary and secondary) and for all schools. The difference included children at public authority special schools as well as at private schools. We made an arbitrary division between these two groups because no data were available and, since in a new settlement fewer children than the national average are

[1] Stone, *Urban Development in Britain*, vol. II.

Table 6.9. *Projected school population[a] in a mature settlement*

Percentages

Age group	National projections		Estimates for new settlements	
	Maintained primary and secondary schools	All schools	All maintained schools	Other schools
2–4	10·06	11·63	10·5	1·1
5–10	96·21	99·38	97·0	2·4
11–15	92·83	98·99	94·0	5·0
16	58·10	63·83	59·0	4·8
17	23·49	27·40	23·5	3·9
18	8·15	9·50	8·2	1·4
19	0·69	0·78	0·7	0·1

SOURCES: Department of Education and Science, *Statistics of Education, 1965*, part 2, London, HMSO, 1966; NIESR estimates.

[a] Expressed as a proportion of each age group.

likely to be privately educated, the figures for maintained schools were rounded upwards and the possibility of boarders ignored (table 6.9).

Numbers of children of nursery, primary and secondary school age were taken from the population projections (table A.9), and combined

Table 6.10. *School requirements[a] in a mature settlement*

	Children per 10,000 population	Pupil places per 10,000 population		Standard per pupil	Built area		Land area	
		Public	Private		Public	Private	Public	Private
Nursery schools					(square feet)		(acres)	
Age 2–4	588	59	12	42	2,478	504	1·0	0·2
Primary schools								
Age 5–10	1,145	1,111	29	42	46,662	1,218	11·5	0·3
Secondary schools								
Age 11–15	979	920	54					
16	192	113	10					
17	187	44	5	72	78,696	5,184	26·2	1·8
18	184	15	2					
19	179	1	1					

SOURCE: NIESR estimates.

[a] Per 10,000 population.

with the rates of attendance to give estimates of the number of pupil places required (table 6.10). Space standards for schools were obtained from an analysis of information provided by the education authorities.[1] In a new settlement most private schools would be specially built, to probably much the same standards as those built by the public authorities. Total floor areas and land areas for schools for the children of 10,000 persons are also given in table 6.10.

No facilities for higher education would be provided in towns for 50,000 persons but there would be a college of further education in each of the larger towns. Estimating the demand for places for this type of education was very difficult, partly at least because many colleges draw students from far outside the towns in which they are sited. It was thought that about 1,750 full-time equivalent places would be required in an ordinary 100,000 person town. This figure was increased *pro rata* for a town of 250,000 persons. The floor area per full-time place was 130 square feet (based on an analysis of such colleges), so a building of 227,500 square feet would be required in the 100,000 person town and one of 568,750 square feet in the 250,000 person town. A site area of 7 acres without playing fields was suggested for the smaller college and therefore one of 17·5 acres was allocated to the larger. Playing fields were assumed to be separate from the college and included in the total provision for the town.

INDUSTRY AND COMMERCE

Employment

Employment requirements could be calculated by estimating the numbers in the economically active population and distributing them between industries. The total employable population was found by applying activity rates to the population in each age group.

Projected activity rates for the period 1966–81 published by the Ministry of Labour[2] were extrapolated to 1989. Only trends in the rates for married women aged 35–59 were expected to show a noticeable change. The article stated: 'For married women aged 35 and over, continuing marked increases in activity rates were assumed. The rates of increases were reduced slightly in the latter parts of the forecast period because it cannot be expected that steady rates of increase will continue indefinitely.' A slight further downturn was therefore assumed in the growth of these particular activity rates (table 6.11).

Men and unmarried women aged 15–24 presented certain problems;

---

[1] Stone, *Urban Development in Britain*, vol. II.

[2] 'Forecasts of the working population 1966–81', *Ministry of Labour Gazette*, November 1966.

Table 6.11. *Projected activity rates by age and sex*

Percentages

	15–19	20–4	25–9	30–4	35–9	40–4	45–9	50–4	55–9	60–4	65–9	70+
Men												
1966	..	..	97½	98	98	98	98	98	96	90	38	14
1971	..	..									35½	12½
1976	..	..									33	11
1981	..	..									30½	10
1989[a]	53	93									26½	8½
Single women[b]												
1966	..	..	95	87½	87½	82½	78	71	62	29	5	5
1971	..	..					80	73			5	5
1976	..	..					81	74			4½	4½
1981	..	..					82	75			4½	4½
1989[a]	56	89					83½	77			4	4
Married women												
1966	40	39	30	33	43	48	49	47	39	21	8	8
1971		35			45½	52	53	51	44	23	8½	8½
1976		35			48	55	56	55	48	25	9	9
1981		35			50½	58	59	58	52	26	9½	9½
1989[a]		35			52½	61	62½	61½	56	27½	10½	10½

SOURCE: 'Forecasts of the working population 1966–81', *Ministry of Labour Gazette*, November 1966.

[a] Derived as described in the text.
[b] Including widowed and divorced.

Table 6.12. *Working population per 10,000, by age,*
sex and marital status in a mature settlement

	Males	Females			Total working population
		Single	Married	Total	
15–19	255	238	12	250	505
20–4	385	156	77	233	618
25–9	324	55	83	138	462
30–4	296	28	97	125	421
35–9	323	22	173	195	518
40–4	344	21	206	227	571
45–9	325	21	187	208	533
50–4	269	20	140	160	429
55–9	200	19	90	109	309
60–4	147	12	34	46	193
65–9	36	2	20	22	58
70+	17	8	11	19	36
All ages	2,921	602	1,130	1,732	4,653

SOURCE: NIESR estimates.

the numbers expected to be still at school in 1989 were available (table 6.9), but not those attending places of higher education. Approximate figures were deduced primarily by comparing the Ministry of Labour's figures for the working population in 1981 with the Government Actuary's projection of total population, but also by reference to another projection of all 15–24 year olds undergoing further and higher full-time education.[1] An allowance was made for those in education in each quinquennial age group who were also working in part-time and holiday jobs. The projected activity rates were applied to the projected population in 1989 (table A.9) to give the estimated working population (table 6.12).

All areas have both nationally and locally orientated industry, the presence of the former being dependent on the attractions of the developing settlement and of the latter arising from the settlement's need for services. This division does not conveniently follow the categories in the Standard Industrial Classification and can only be an approximation. All manufacturing and extractive industry (SIC I–XVI), together with wholesale distribution (part of SIC XX), was placed in the nationally orientated group, and construction and all other services in the locally orientated group.

Employment opportunities develop in a small number of discrete units, each probably unique, so that employment varies radically from one town to another, especially in nationally orientated industry. It is

[1] Stone, *Urban Development in Britain*, vol. II.

Table 6.13. *Structure of nationally orientated employment*

		1961 percentage distribution	Projected growth factor 1961–89	1989 percentage distribution
III	Food, drink, tobacco	5·82	*0·97*	4·9
IV	Chemicals etc.	5·84	*1·03*	5·3
V	Metal manufactures	3·46	*0·95*	2·9
VI	Engineering, electrical goods	40·70	*1·30*	46·5
VII	Shipbuilding, etc.	0·06	*0·91*	—
VIII	Vehicles	18·36 }	*1·03*	{ 16·6
IX	Metal goods n.e.s.	4·11 }		{ 3·7
X	Textiles	0·85 }		{ 0·5
XI	Leather and fur	0·11 }	*0·73*	{ 0·1
XII	Clothing and footwear	3·70 }		{ 2·4
XIII	Bricks, pottery, glass	3·73 }		{ 3·7
XIV	Timber, furniture, etc.	2·90 }		{ 2·9
XV	Paper, printing, publishing	3·83 }	*1·12*	{ 3·8
XVI	Other manufacturing	4·03 }		{ 4·0
XX (part)	Wholesale distribution	2·50	*1·22*	2·7
	Total	100·00		100·0

SOURCE: NIESR estimates.

not yet clear whether there are types of firms particularly attracted to developing settlements, or whether they are simply mobile firms which are unable to obtain planning consent in established settlements; some firms are undoubtedly attracted by a particular location. Generally the firms in growth industries are the most mobile, and the same industries are expected to continue growing in the foreseeable future. The most plausible assumption was that, despite some differences between conditions in new settlements and in existing new towns, averaging the employment structure of existing new towns to minimise the importance of their individual features should provide a typical structure. The best available data were provided by the 1961 Census.[1] From the figures for 15 new towns,[2] a weighted average distribution was calculated. The results for nationally orientated industry are shown in the first column of table 6.13, excluding extractive industry (SIC I and II), which was insignificant in the new towns and declining nationally.

The structure of employment in manufacturing and wholesale distribution changes with the growth of the component industries, so that by 1989 employment will be distributed between industries in a

[1] The distribution of employment between SIC categories, derived from a 10 per cent sample, is given in General Register Office, *Census 1961. England and Wales, Occupation, Industry and Socio-Economic Groups* (county volumes), London, HMSO, 1966.

[2] Aycliffe, Basildon, Bracknell, Corby, Crawley, Cumbernauld, Cwmbran, East Kilbride, Glenrothes, Harlow, Hatfield, Hemel Hempstead, Peterlee, Stevenage and Welwyn Garden City.

Table 6.14. *Structure of locally orientated employment*
(excluding shopping)

		1961 employment per 10,000 population			Projected growth factor 1961–89	1989 employment per 10,000 population[a]
		Towns under 50,000	Towns 50,000 to 100,000	Towns over 100,000	All urban areas[a]		
XVII	Construction	300	340	340	320	*1·03*	330
XVIII	Gas, electricity, water	80	90	100	90	*0·89*	80
XIX	Transport	260	350	420	330	*0·79*	260
XXI	Insurance, banking, finance	70	90	110	90	*1·11*	100
XXII	Professional services	420	450	440	430	*1·63*	700
XXIII	Miscellaneous services	420	460	460	440	*1·23*	540
XXIV	Public administration	260	310	280	270	*1·04*	280
	Total	1810	2090	2150	1970		2290

SOURCES: General Register Office, *Census 1961. Industry Tables*, part 1, table 8 and *Age, Marital Condition and General Tables*, table 7, London, HMSO, 1966 and 1964.
[a] All urban areas excluding conurbations.

very different pattern from that prevailing today. This change will be reflected in the new settlements in two ways. First, since the fast growing industries tend to be the most mobile, the pattern of incoming employment will change. Secondly, since the growth of a firm is related to the growth of the industry in which it operates, firms in fast growing industries are likely to grow faster than other firms in the settlement. The 1961 employment structure was, therefore, modified by projected rates of growth from 1961 to 1989, which were obtained by projecting forward the growth rates for the period 1960–75 given by Beckerman.[1]

Most of the new towns were too young in 1961 to provide useful evidence on employment in locally orientated industry. As would be expected, national figures indicated that service employment per head tends to increase with size of town, but if distribution was excluded, towns of over 100,000 population showed only a small increase over those of population between 50,000 and 100,000 (table 6.14). Substantial differences over the size range under discussion were therefore

[1] W. Beckerman, *The British Economy in 1975*, Cambridge University Press, 1965.

Table 6.15. *Numbers employed[a] by industry group
in a mature settlement*

	Industry group	No. of jobs
III	Food, drink, tobacco	90
IV	Chemicals, etc.	100
V	Metal manufactures	50
VI	Engineering, electrical goods	860
VII	Shipbuilding, etc.	—
VIII	Vehicles	310
IX	Metal goods n.e.s.	70
X	Textiles	10
XI	Leather and fur	10
XII	Clothing and footwear	50
XIII	Bricks, pottery, glass	70
XIV	Timber, furniture, etc.	50
XV	Paper, printing, publishing	70
XVI	Other manufacturing	70
XVII	Construction	330
XVIII	Gas, electricity, water	80
XIX	Transport and communication	260
XX	Distribution	
	Retail	500
	Wholesale	50
XXI	Insurance, banking, finance	100
XXII	Professional and scientific services	700
XXIII	Miscellaneous services	540
XXIV	Public administration and defence	280
	Total	4650

SOURCE: NIESR estimates.

[a] Per 10,000 population.

unlikely. It could be that differences in service employment are related to status, but it is improbable that towns would be subordinate or predominant equally in all services. Apart from shopping, few services are particularly orientated to consumers, and nationally orientated service firms would not be drawn to particular towns any more than industrial firms. The national employment rates were, therefore, used. Again it was necessary to adjust for changes over the period 1961–89, and this was done in the same way as for nationally orientated industry (table 6.14).

Employment in shopping was calculated from the figures previously derived for shopping turnover. Labour productivity is not closely related to turnover, nor to settlement size. In 1961 average turnover per employee (full-time equivalent) in Great Britain (excluding Greater London) was £3,960 per annum; the corresponding figure for towns having a turnover of £10 million a year or more was £4,129.[1] A figure

[1] R. D. George, *Productivity in Distribution*, Cambridge University Press, 1966.

Table 6.16. *Space requirements for manufacturing industry in a mature settlement*

Industry group	Floor areas per employee				Per 10,000 population	
	Trading estates[a]	Middle-sex[b]	New towns[c]	Midland region[d]	Jobs projected[e]	Floor area
	(square feet)				(nos.)	(sq. ft. 000s)
III Food, drink, tobacco	116–310	385	183–306	286	90	25·7
IV Chemicals, etc.	264–366	263	417	410	100	41·0
V Metal manufactures	280–435	303	371	339	50	16·9
VI Engineering, electrical goods	142–329	161–85	150–235	252	860	216·7
VIII Vehicles	174–300	263	313	251	310	77·8
IX Metal goods n.e.s.	218–627	227	241	258	70	18·1
X Textiles	203–573	286	..	336	10	3·4
XI Leather and fur	59–234	..	..	87	10	0·9
XII Clothing and footwear	22–276	..	173	164	50	8·2
XIII Bricks, pottery, glass	237–672	312	316	445	70	31·2
XIV Timber and furniture	109–90	435	360	272	50	13·6
XV Paper, printing, publishing	76–378	250–357	320	265	70	18·5
XVI Other manufacturing	204–614	..	253	204	70	14·3
Total					1810	486·3

SOURCES: [a] E. H. Doubleday, *The Future of Industry in Central Hertfordshire*, Hertford, Hertfordshire County Council Planning Department, 1956.
[b] Middlesex County Council, *First Review of the Development Plan: report of a survey*, London, 1962.
[c] From analysis of returns.
[d] DSIR, *The Economics of Factory Buildings*.
[e] Table 6.15.

of £4,045 was taken for the settlements considered in this study. Between 1951 and 1957 British output per head in retail trade rose between 1·5 per cent and 2·0 per cent a year. The rate of increase was 2·9 per cent a year over the period 1957–61, but the exceptional growth of self-service stores probably contributed to this,[1] so that this rate of innovation was unlikely to continue. An increase in productivity of 2 per cent a year, probably all that could be expected, gave an average turnover per employee (full-time equivalent) in 1989 of £7,038 per annum. For a 100,000 person settlement with a total turnover of £2,996,000 (table 6.7), the staff requirement in full-time equivalents would be 4,257. Because of its considerable complexity and minor effect

[1] They increased more than seven-fold over this period; see W. G. McClelland, *Studies in Retailing*, Oxford, Basil Blackwell, 1963.

Table 6.17. *Areas of buildings for service industry in a mature settlement*

	Floor area per employee	Per 10,000 population	
		Jobs projected	Total area
Construction	(sq. ft.)	(nos.)	(sq. ft. 000s)
In offices	150	16	2·5
In workshops and stores	269	16	4·4
Site workers and drivers	—	297	—
Gas, electricity and water[a]	—	80	—
Transport and communication			
In offices	150	24	3·6
On maintenance, in stores, etc.	400	19	7·6
Mobile and Post Office workers	—	217	—
Retail distribution[b]	n.a.	500	83·0
Wholesale distribution	400	50	20·0
Insurance, banking and finance[c]	150	100	15·0
Professional and scientific services			
In offices	150	470	70·5
Medical, educational, etc.	—	230	—
Miscellaneous services[d]	n.a.	540	69·8
Public administration			
In offices	150	140	21·0
In workshops and stores	269	40	10·8
In other facilities	—	100	—
Total		2839	308·2

SOURCE: NIESR estimates.

[a] See discussion of public utilities.
[b] See discussion of 'shopping'.
[c] All assumed to be employed in offices.
[d] See discussion of service trades: 35 per cent assumed to be employed in other facilities and therefore needing no extra working space.

on this study, no attempt was made to project the proportion of part-time workers; the value of 31 per cent given by George for 1965 was used.[1] This gave a full-time staff of 3,476, and a part-time one equivalent to 1,562; the total of 5,038 was rounded to 5,000, or 500 per 10,000 population.

The complete distribution of employment between industrial categories in 1989 could then be compiled (table 6.15). Employment in locally orientated industries having been derived absolutely as 2,290 per 10,000 population plus a further 500 in shopping, this left 1,860 jobs in nationally orientated industry, of which 50 were counted as in wholesaling and the balance in manufacturing. These were distributed according to the proportions previously derived (table 6.13).

[1] George, *Productivity in Distribution.*

The distribution of the working population between the sexes was checked against the total assumed to be employed in each industry, divided into males and females according to the national ratios calculated from 1961 Census data; there was no marked discrepancy. As well as checking that the employment structure was compatible with the population, it would be useful in planning an actual town to check that it produced a balanced social structure.

Space requirements

In manufacturing industry both the nature of the product and the form of organisation affect the space required per employee: greater automation is likely to increase it, while more shift working and a growing proportion of administrative, technical and clerical workers is likely to decrease it. Space per person employed in factories is determined by the relation between current conditions (organisation and output) and those which existed when the space was originally provided. Survey figures could, therefore, only be a rough guide, and the only complete survey available covered the Midland region in the late 1950s.[1] However, other less complete data confirmed that those results were of the right order, so they were used as a basis for calculating floor area for industry (table 6.16). It will be noted that two thirds of the labour was employed in two industries and that much the same estimate of floor space was obtained whichever set of figures was used.

It was difficult to obtain systematic information on space requirements for service industry other than shopping. The figures used were from many sources and were thought broadly to reflect current tendencies. No allowance was, of course, made for people who either did not work in buildings, for example, building operatives and drivers of vehicles, or who worked in buildings already counted elsewhere, for example, teachers and hospital staff (table 6.17).

HOSPITALS AND OTHER BUILDINGS

The need for hospitals depends on the age structure of the population and on the rates at which relevant groups need bedspaces. These were calculated elsewhere,[2] and are shown in the first column of table 6.18.

The projected numbers, at maturity of the settlement, of those aged 65 and over and under 1 year was 779 and 194 respectively in each 10,000 persons (table A.9). The projected number of births after adjusting for infant mortality was 199. Average floor space per bed was estimated for a general hospital at 900 square feet and for a psychiatric

---

[1] DSIR, *The Economics of Factory Buildings.*
[2] Stone, *Urban Development in Britain*, vol. II.

Table 6.18. *Hospitals in a mature settlement*

	Bedspaces per 10,000 relevant persons[a]	Per 10,000 population		
Type of bed		Relevant persons[a]	Number of beds	Floor space (sq. ft. 000s)
General	33·3	10,000	33·3	} 42·93
Geriatric	100·0	779	7·8	
Maternity	329·0	199	6·6	
Psychiatric	32·6	10,000	32·6	11·74

SOURCE: NIESR estimates.

[a] Taken as total population for general and psychiatric hospitals, population aged 65 and over for geriatric hospitals, and births for maternity hospitals.

hospital at 360 square feet.[1] These figures could be combined as shown in table 6.18 to give space requirements. A hospital as small as that required for a 50,000 person settlement would not usually be built; provision would be made in larger settlements. No hospital was, therefore, included in the smallest settlement model.

Table 6.19. *Built areas of minor building facilities in a mature settlement*

Square feet, thousands

	Town centre	Sub- centre	Open space
Court house	3·5	—	—
Libraries	1·2	4·0	—
Police, fire, ambulance stations	5·0	—	—
Post Office	3·6	—	—
Museum/Art gallery	2·0	—	—
Concert hall/Theatre/Cinemas	2·0	—	—
Dance hall/Amusement centre	5·5	—	—
Churches	0·5	20·0	—
Hotels	3·5	—	—
Bus station	5·0	—	—
Market	0·5	—	—
Public conveniences	0·1	0·6	—
Public houses	—	8·0	—
Residential institutions	—	10·5	—
Community centres/Clubs	—	9·0	—
Health centres/Surgeries	—	5·0	—
Miscellaneous buildings	—	—	15·0
Total	32·4	57·1	15·0

SOURCE: NIESR estimates.

[1] Stone, *Urban Development in Britain*, vol. II.

There remained a number of minor facilities of great variety but relatively not of great importance. Systematic data were not available, and information might be either in terms of units or of floor area. The exact composition of the group was less important than its overall balance (table 6.19).

CAR PARKS

Car-parking is a public problem only in central areas; elsewhere cars can be parked on private premises or for short periods on access roads. Central areas generate a large demand for car parks in relation to their size, and generally private space is not available, being completely filled with buildings, and storage and circulation areas. It would be both wasteful of space and inconvenient to provide separate parking for each building.

Table 6.20. *Parking in central areas per 10,000 population*

	Fully centralised town centre	Partly centralised		Decentralised	
		Town centre	District centre	Town centre	Neighbour-hood centre
Shopping					
Number of workers	584	81	503	342	242
Car spaces (31% of workers)	181	25	156	106	75
Other businesses					
Number of workers	1035	260	775	762	273
Car spaces (62% of workers)	642	161	481	472	169
Total workers' car spaces	823	186	637	578	244
Area of shopping and quasi-shopping (sq. ft. 000s)	*102*	*14*	*88*	*60*	*42*
Car spaces for shoppers					
Saturday peak[a]	680	93	440	400	168
Weekday peak[b]	374	51	242	220	92
Total car spaces					
Saturday peak[c]	861	118	596	506	243
Weekday peak[d]	1197	237	879	798	336
Land for car parks (acres)					
Ground level (250 sq. ft. per car)	*6·87*	*1·36*	*5·05*	*4·58*	*1·93*
or Multi-storey (50 sq. ft. per car)	*1·37*	*0·27*	*1·01*	*0·92*	*0·39*

SOURCE: NIESR estimates.

[a] Estimated at one space per 150 sq. ft. of town centre shopping, per 200 sq. ft. of district centre shopping and per 250 sq. ft. of neighbourhood centre shopping.
[b] 55% of figures for Saturday peak.
[c] For workers in shops only, plus shoppers.
[d] For all workers plus shoppers.

Car parks are needed in the central areas for both workers and shoppers, the latter including people visiting offices and other service establishments during the working day. Workers only require their parking space during working hours, so that in non-working hours it is available for those attending places of culture and entertainment, and parking for office workers is available for the Saturday peak of shoppers.

In all settlements some people would travel by public transport, walk or cycle, so that it was thought unlikely that the proportion of workers travelling by car would exceed 80 per cent. Assuming 1·3 persons per car, this implied about 62 cars per 100 workers. The ratio might be only half this for people employed in shops, of whom a large proportion, being women, would be less likely to drive their own car to work, and some, being van drivers, might either use the vans as personal transport or park their cars in the van park when out on deliveries.

The number of car spaces required for shoppers would depend upon how many people the centre attracted, the distances they travelled and the availability of cars for their use – these would not, of course, be independent variables. The number of people attracted would be reflected in turnover, although the relationship would not be directly proportional because of variations in income levels and in the shares of different types of goods. These shares affect car park requirements through both turnover and the average size of transaction; also because the husband, and hence the car, is much more likely to come on a shopping expedition to buy durables than on an ordinary weekly shopping trip. The distances people travel for their shopping depend upon the geographical area and regional status of the settlement. Within a settlement, the size of catchment areas varies with the arrangement of central area functions, and a lower proportion of shoppers would use cars from a smaller catchment area.

Availability of cars and drivers is an important factor in generating retail trade. The present pattern of demand for car parks may change radically with social habits, but there has been no exhaustive analysis even of current parking requirements for shopping. An estimate of future requirements could only be made by averaging the current figures and adjusting for expected changes in car ownership. On this basis it was assumed that one car space would be needed for each 150 square feet of town centre shopping, each 200 square feet of district centre shopping and each 250 square feet of neighbourhood centre shopping. These figures applied to the Saturday peak hours; the Monday to Friday values were taken at about 55 per cent of those for Saturday (table 6.20).

CHAPTER 7

TRAFFIC IN THE SETTLEMENTS

TYPES OF MOVEMENT

The greatest volume of movement generally occurs during the journeys to and from work. In the morning, journeys to school often coincide with the journey to work, as do some journeys for shopping and, on the roads, some movement of industrial vehicles, for deliveries both in and out of the settlement. Of personal journeys (other than pedestrian journeys of under a mile), 39 per cent were to and from work, 9 per cent to and from school or college, 19 per cent for shopping or personal business, and the balance journeys to social functions or journeys for recreation.[1] A few workers might also go home at lunch time; the smaller the settlement the larger this movement would be, but on average probably not more than 10 per cent of the movement to and from work.

Other types of journey seldom cause traffic too heavy for the facilities provided for the journey to work. Special provisions are often made to deter shoppers and other travellers from using cars during peak periods of the journey to work: for example, car parks may be reserved for shoppers and business travellers and opened only between peak periods. Usually there are one or two peak shopping periods each week when shopping traffic might be comparable with that for the journey to work, but shopping journeys are generally well spread over time, and most movement for neighbourhood and district shopping is short distance and confined to the secondary roads. Journeys to entertainments, or to cultural or sports facilities do not normally coincide with the journey to work, and additional capacity is only needed at the destination. Social journeys also occur largely outside peak periods and do not generate heavy traffic. Most of the areas of Great Britain suitable for development have a large network of rural roads, to which settlement roads could be connected to facilitate filtering traffic on recreational journeys. Generally, through traffic is segregated on a separate route, by-passing the settlement.

Except in the largest settlements, railways play only a small part, except, perhaps, for people commuting to and from other settlements. It is convenient in the first place to consider settlements without a railway.

[1] Ministry of Transport, *National Travel Survey, 1964: preliminary report*, London, 1967.

[66]

THE GENERATION OF MOVEMENT

The volume of movement depends on the relationship between homes and other facilities, and on people's propensity to spend time in travelling. Clearly less travelling is necessary if more facilities are provided close to the home and, except perhaps for recreation, people do not travel unnecessarily, so that, other things being equal, they patronise the nearest facility. However, facilities might not be evenly spread over the settlement and sometimes people might be willing to travel some distance to obtain slightly better goods, services, or jobs. Moreover, if it is necessary to travel further to reach special facilities, other journeys may be included in the same trip; it might be more convenient to do all the weekly shopping in the town centre, even though much of it could be done in the neighbourhood centre.

Various models have been suggested to describe the distribution of jobs in relation to homes. One of the best known is the Gravity Model, which relates the probability of a trip from a given area (origin) to a particular location (destination) directly to the proportion of jobs in that area and inversely to a function of the distance between origin and destination.[1] The formula can be written:

$$f_{ij} = a_i \, b_j \exp\left(-\lambda t_{ij} - n \log t_{ij}\right)$$

where f_{ij} is the number of journeys from origin i to destination j, t_{ij} is half the round trip from i to j, a_i and b_j are constants reflecting the size of the areas, and λ and n are constants with values which provide maximum agreement with the observed values for an appropriate settlement.

Tanner and others have estimated values of λ and n for parts of London and for a few other towns. The values varied not only with the size of the town but with the arrangement of the housing and places of work; journeys to work would be longer, even in settlements of the same size, where the main employment opportunities were further from the housing than where homes and jobs were close together. Again, journeys would probably be longer in towns with cheap and efficient communications than in those without such facilities. Moreover, some types of workers are prepared to travel further than others; generally professional and clerical workers will travel further than manual workers, and men further than women.

The Tanner constants could, of course, be calculated only for existing settlements and reflected their characteristics. For model settlements the best compromise was to use values estimated for actual towns of the same size. Strictly comparable towns were difficult to find and, clearly,

---

[1] Department of Scientific and Industrial Research, *Factors affecting the amount of Travel*, by J. C. Tanner, London, HMSO, 1961.

Table 7.1. *Tanner constants for non-specialised settlements*

	Tanner constants	
	λ	n
Probability of journey unaffected by distance	0·0	0·0
Cathedral and industrial town, population 75,000	0·014	0·5
Riverside industrial town, population 150,000	0·1	1·0

SOURCE: DSIR, *Factors affecting the amount of Travel.*

the results needed to be studied with care. Since the constants were available only for non-specialised settlements, they could not be used for models of specialised settlements, and for these it was impossible to do more than make broad assumptions about the traffic between jobs and homes.

For purposes of the model studies, the constants in the gravity formula were set at various values which simulated movement in actual towns of the same order of size. They were also set at zero to simulate the situation when journeys are made irrespective of distance, so that the probability of travel from each origin to any given destination was dependent only on employment opportunities (table 7.1).

THE INFLUENCE OF THE TANNER CONSTANTS

Since the values of the Tanner constants reflected the arrangement of homes and jobs in the towns for which they were calculated, the effect in the model settlements of different degrees of deterrence of the length of the journey to work could only be measured comparatively. Capital costs of main roads and travelling costs were, therefore, estimated for a range of Tanner values, including zero to provide a basis of comparison.

As would be expected, the larger the area of the settlement the greater in general, was the effect of the Tanner constants (table 7.2). Not much importance could be attached to individual results since inevitably these reflected the spare capacity in the system. It appeared that, broadly, compared with the situation of zero deterrence (both constants nil), the capital costs of the road system would be reduced by between 3 and 6 per cent and the length of the journey to work by between 5 and 10 per cent with $\lambda = 0·014$ and $n = 0·5$. The effects in the cluster settlements, where distances could be substantially greater, were more

Table 7.2. *The effects of Tanner constants on capital costs of roads and the length of the journey to work*

Percentages of results with $\lambda = o$, $n = o$

	Capital costs		Length of journey	
	$\lambda = 0.014$ $n = 0.5$	$\lambda = 0.1$ $n = 1.0$	$\lambda = 0.014$ $n = 0.5$	$\lambda = 0.1$ $n = 1.0$
Individual settlements				
50,000 persons				
rectangular	92	92	92	77
100,000 persons				
rectangular	97, 95	94	91, 96	87
linear	95, 98		94, 98	
star	99		94	
250,000 persons				
rectangular	94, 97	90	93, 93	80
linear	94		89	
star	95		92	
Cluster settlements				
250,000 persons	90	63, 73, 75	78	38, 45, 47

SOURCE: NIESR estimates.

Chart 7.1. *Distribution of journeys by travelling time in a settlement[a] for 50,000 persons*

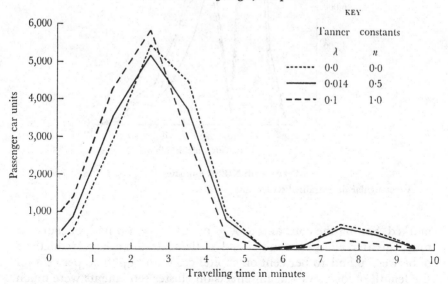

SOURCE: NIESR estimates.

[a] A rectangular decentralised settlement.

Chart 7.2. *Distribution of journeys by travelling time*
in a settlement[a] for 250,000 persons

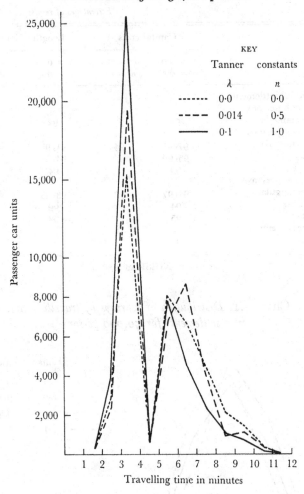

SOURCE: NIESR estimates.

[a] A rectangular decentralised settlement.

marked. Setting the constants at $\lambda = 0.1$ and $n = 1.0$ had, of course, a
much greater effect – in individual settlements there were reductions
of between 6 and 10 per cent on capital costs, and up to 20 per cent on
the length of journeys – again effects on cluster settlements were much
greater. The reductions for the smallest rectangular settlement were
surprisingly large and these might not be representative. However, the

geographical relationship between homes and jobs clearly interacted in a significant way with the deterrent effect.

The results obtained for an actual town with 150,000 inhabitants were comparable: the value of λ had little effect on the length of journeys, which was determined largely by the value of n. The larger the value of n, the less effect changes in the value of λ appeared to have. With $n = 0.5$, the journey time fell about 8 per cent, with $n = 1.0$ the fall varied from 15 to 25 per cent; while for $n = 2.0$, the fall was 40 per cent.

The distribution of journeys by length was influenced by the location of homes and jobs, and hence departed from normality. For example, in a rectangular settlement with 50,000 population the distribution was bimodal (chart 7.1): as λ and n increased, the number of very short journeys rose substantially and the number of medium and long journeys fell. These tendencies were even more marked in a rectangular settlement with 250,000 population (chart 7.2). In terms of the geography of the settlements, more workers travelled to the nearer employment areas as n increased, and the second mode represented the effect on journeys to more distant employment.

TANNER CONSTANTS AND MOVEMENT BETWEEN SETTLEMENTS

The effect of the deterrence as simulated by the Tanner constants on the pattern of journeys to work in cluster settlements was interesting. If workers were not deterred by the length of the journey, in a cluster of five equal settlements they would be equally likely to work in any settlement, and so nearly 80 per cent would work in settlements where they did not live (chart 7.3). With moderate values for the Tanner constants ($\lambda = 0.014$; $n = 0.5$), the proportion of workers working outside the settlement where they lived would fall to between 50 and 60 per cent, and with high values ($\lambda = 0.1$; $n = 1.0$) to between 15 and 25 per cent.

Clearly the distance between the settlements affected the results. The above figures related to adjacent settlements in a linear cluster. The percentage of workers leaving their settlement for work also fell as the settlements became further apart (chart 7.3). When the distance between one settlement and the next was increased from one mile to two, the proportion who worked outside the settlement where they lived fell by about an eighth, and by another fifth when the distance was increased to three miles. With a high deterrence ($\lambda = 0.1$; $n = 1.0$) and settlements 4 miles apart, only about 10 per cent of workers did not work and live in the same settlement. A high degree of job specialisation in each settlement would have had similar effects.

Chart 7.3. *Traffic flow between five 50,000 person settlements*[a]

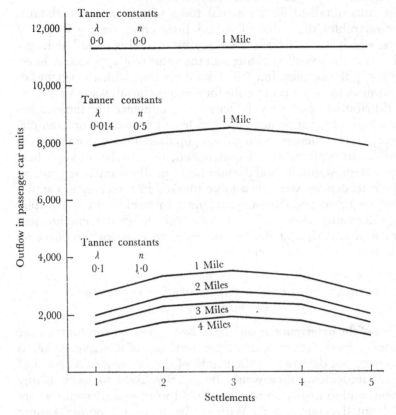

SOURCE: NIESR estimates.

[a] Variations with Tanner constants and with distance between the settlements.

In a linear cluster, workers living in peripheral settlements have fewer jobs within a given distance of their homes than those in central settlements, and a smaller proportion of them travel to work in other settlements. Thus, other things being equal, there was less movement outside the settlement of residence in linear clusters than in star or ring clusters, and less movement the larger and more widespread the cluster. The amount of movement was also a measure of the accessibility of jobs.

TRAVELLING PERIODS

In a settlement, the intensity of movement depends on its timing and on the extent to which different types of movement overlap. The critical movement in determining the size of roads is the journey to work. The longer the period over which journeys to work (and similarly the return journeys) are spread, and the less these overlap with other journeys, the lower the volume of traffic to be carried at any one time. For example, road capacity could be less in a settlement working three or even two shifts than in one working a single shift; it might be less in a settlement with a mixture of social–economic classes than in one of mainly the same class. The staggering of working hours, the arrangement of school hours (particularly for secondary and higher schools), and the discouragement of shopping at the times of the journeys to and from work, including the lunch period, would all help to spread the load of traffic and to reduce the size of roads and junctions needed. Roads are very 'lumpy' investments because they can only be built in units of a lane.

To a large extent the capacity of a road system limits the actual demand, since overloading discourages journeys. In contrast, generous capacity encourages the increase of traffic to fill it. These behaviour patterns do not, of course, justify limiting initial capacity to the minimum acceptable at that time without provision for expansion. Clearly a limited capacity involves forgoing amenity, and if taken to extremes would be unacceptable politically and affect the viability of a new settlement. As a result it might be necessary to expand subsequently beyond the provision made, which could be very expensive.

Table 7.3. *Peaking factors*

Percentages

	Level (1)		Level (2)	
Work trips in peak period	66·7	50·0	50·0	40·0
Additional peaking[a]	—	15·0	5·0	12·0
Gross peaking factor	66·7	65·0	55·0	52·0
Allowance for other trips[b]	6·7	8·1	6·9	10·4
Peaking factor	73		62	

SOURCE: NIESR estimates.

[a] Estimated at 0, 30, 10 and 30 per cent respectively of the percentages of work trips in the peak period.

[b] Estimated at 10, 12·5, 12·5 and 20 per cent respectively of the gross peaking factors.

The intensity of traffic was measured in the models by peaking factors applied to the critical movement, usually the journey to work. The traffic was assumed to be spread evenly over the peak hour, or to rise within it by a given percentage. In the latter case a gross peaking factor was calculated by multiplying the factor for the whole peak period by the percentage of peaking within the peak. Other types of movement within the peak period were estimated as a percentage of the gross peaking factor and added in. The range of peaking factors used is given in table 7.3.

THE MODAL SPLIT

The main forms of movement in a settlement are walking, cycling, private cars, buses and possibly tracked transport (trams, rail-buses, trains or monorails). Moving pavements, and automatic or remote controlled vehicles do not yet appear practical or economic except for limited application.

Most people are not prepared to walk more than short distances, perhaps about a mile, and this only in fine weather. In bad weather those who normally walk might use public transport or their own cars, thus increasing traffic at such times. Sheltered pedestrian ways are likely both to increase the amount of walking and to stabilise it, reducing extra traffic in bad weather.

Cycling is now more a leisure activity, particularly for children and young people, than an important form of general transport. Again it is likely to depend on the weather; people who cycle to work on fine days might add to private or public vehicular traffic when the weather was bad.

Both walking and cycling also vary with conditions in the settlement, being less popular in one built on a hilly or exposed site. It was thought unlikely that over 10 to 15 per cent of journeys to work would be made on foot or bicycle. By 1989, cycling to work might be most unusual, so it was, perhaps, unnecessary to make provision for cycle ways in the models, although they could be constructed adjoining pedestrian ways and the two combined in the future. The amount of cycle traffic on main roads would probably be very small and, since a bicycle takes up only a third of the road space for a private car, the effect on the road system would be minimal.

Private cars would be by far the most numerous vehicles used during the journey to work. The number varies with the social–economic structure of the labour force: generally, the higher the social–economic class the more cars owned and the more likely they are to be used for going to work. Similarly, men are more likely to own cars and use them to go to work than women, and professional and semi-professional

Table 7.4. *Modal splits*

	Occupancy rate	Road space	Persons per PCU	Modal split		
				(1)	(2)	(3)
	(persons)	(PCUs)		(percentages)		
Walkers	—	—	—	7	5	15
Cycles	1·00	0·33	3·00	—	5	10
Cars	1·30	1·00	1·30	93	80	25
Buses	69·00	3·00	23·00	—	10	50
				(PCU index)^a		
All forms				1·4	1·6	4·0

SOURCE: NIESR estimates.

^{a} Harmonic mean of rate for each form weighted by the percentage modal split, e.g. in (3), $100/(10/3\cdot0+25/1\cdot3+50/23\cdot0) = 4\cdot0$.

workers have a particularly high propensity to do so, since they often need their cars for business. With increasing affluence car ownership is likely to be spread more evenly; in the short run, however, the road capacity required for the journey to work depends both on the social–economic structure of the housing area and on the social–economic and sex structure of the employment area.

The proportion of workers using public transport depends on the social–economic and sex structure of the population and on the comparison between the charges for public transport and the marginal costs of the private car. Since, by 1989, most working heads of households and many other workers are likely to own a car, for most people the marginal costs of going to work by car would amount to little more than the cost of petrol and oil (assuming that they parked on the premises where they worked, or in a free public park). Unless an extra car had to be kept especially for the journey to work, or there was a change in the pattern of taxes and subsidies, workers would be likely to find their private cars cheaper to use than public transport.[1] Convenience would also be important; public transport should be reasonably frequent and within easy distance of homes and the destinations of journeys. Half a mile might be the limit for the distance of the pick-up

[1] Costs of private and public transport could be equalised either by charging track costs (or perhaps parking costs) to the private motorist, or by subsidising public transport. Costs of roads and car parks increase because cars are used, and it would be logical to charge the users direct if this could be done fairly without unreasonable collection costs. Subsidies for public transport can be justified by the needs of young and old for a convenient service and their difficulties in meeting its costs unless the general public uses it too. To avoid directly encouraging wasteful use it might be better to subsidise the optional users, and thus increase the load factors; the young and old could then be subsidised indirectly through social benefits.

point from origin or destination, and the minimum frequency every 5 minutes during the main travelling periods.

In estimating traffic, different modal splits were measured by indices for persons carried per passenger car unit of road capacity. A road lane can accommodate three times as many cycles as cars, but only a third as many buses. Usually cars on the journey to work carry an average of 1·3 persons, cycles carry 1 person and buses in peak periods about 69 persons. Combining these figures gave persons per passenger car unit (PCU) for each form of transport, and any modal split could be characterised by an average for persons per PCU, calculated by weighting the rates for each form by the percentage modal split.[1] The result was very sensitive to the proportion travelling by car; the lower this was the higher the average, the smaller the traffic load, and the cheaper the roads and interchanges. On the other hand, public transport would cost more if more people travelled by bus; the overall economics of transport depend on the combined costs of public transport, private transport and the road network.

The majority of the road estimates were based on a modal split index of 1·6 and a peaking factor of 62 per cent. A limited investigation was made of the effects of using modal splits of 1·4 and 4·0 and a peaking factor of 73 per cent. Table 7.4 shows some of the assumptions which could give these modal splits. As with the peaking factors in table 7.3, they could be derived from other combinations of circumstances. Combined with each other and with the Tanner constants the modal splits and peaking factors determined the load of traffic to be accommodated on the roads and their costs.

FUTURE TRAFFIC CONDITIONS

Before the effects of different modal splits and peaking factors could be assessed, it was necessary to consider how traffic conditions might change by 1989. The traffic load during peak periods is dependent on the proportion of workers travelling by each method, the occupancy rate in persons per vehicle, the proportion of workers travelling during the peak period, the number of journeys to work each week and the scale of other vehicular movements during the peak period.

The main determinant of the mode of travel is probably car ownership, which might never be as universal as is often anticipated. The rates forecast by Tanner[2] combined with the demographic structure of the

---

[1] In practice those walking and, to a lesser extent, those cycling would make shorter journeys. These forms of travelling were therefore overweighted in the average indices, the bias increasing with the size of settlement.

[2] J. C. Tanner, 'Forecasts of vehicle ownership in Great Britain', *Roads and Road Construction*, November/December 1965.

population of a mature settlement implied that about 70 per cent of workers would have their own car by 1989. Thus, even with an occupancy rate for cars of 1·3 persons, 9 per cent of workers would have to walk, cycle or use public transport. Probably only about one married woman in seven would have a car of her own, so that the family car might sometimes have to be left at home for other trips. Thus, only in a high-income dormitory town was 93 per cent thought a possible level for journeys to work by car, and then very much an upper limit. Even 80 per cent seemed high, although at 1·3 persons per car quite feasible, leaving about one wife in three with a car to use during the day. On the other hand, the economics of travelling by public transport would have to become very favourable for the proportion travelling by car to be reduced to 25 per cent.

However, if car ownership increases, the occupancy rate might decrease because more people travelled in their own cars, even though this raised costs compared with public transport. With no sharing in cars, a modal split index of 1·4 could represent 70 per cent going to work by car, 20 per cent by bus and 10 per cent walking; an index of 1·6 would imply about 30 per cent travelling by bus. The direct effect on the modal split of the occupancy rate for buses is much smaller because a bus can carry so many more passengers in relation to the road space used. Generally, occupancy rates affect road requirements and costs much less than the modal split itself. If both the modal split and the occupancy rates varied, a situation in which about 65 per cent of journeys to work were made by car at about 1·1 persons per car, 25 per cent by bus at not quite capacity occupation, a small proportion by cycle and the balance walking, would be simulated by a modal split of 1·6, which was thought a reasonable measure of future conditions.

The proportion of workers travelling during the peak period would increase if hours of work in offices, factories and other places of employment became standardised, but then other journeys in peak hours might decrease since those hours would be shorter. On the other hand, more shift working or more staggering of working hours would reduce the proportion of workers travelling in the peak period.

It was considered unlikely that the number of journeys to work each week would rise. If the working week was reduced to four or even three days and working days were staggered, the numbers travelling during the peak period would be reduced by 20 to 40 per cent. The usual volume of journeys to work is probably little affected by longer annual holidays, as they are taken seasonally, mainly during the summer.

Not all traffic during the peak period is going to work; some journeys are for other personal reasons and some for commercial purposes. During the morning peak most other personal journeys are school journeys, but even with a high level of car ownership, few of these would be in separate vehicles, so that their effect on the flow of traffic is small. In the evening peak, shopping, social and business journeys are more important. There was little comprehensive information on traffic flows applicable to the model settlements. Data for the West Midlands[1] suggested that in the evening peak period other traffic was about 20 per cent of the traffic from work, although the figure for Stevenage was only 10 per cent.[2] In London, non-work journeys were expected to increase much faster than work journeys.[3] Commercial traffic during the evening peak was nationally just over 30 per cent of the car traffic, although in the suburbs of Birmingham this figure was 20 to 25 per cent and in the centre of Birmingham about 15 per cent.[4] (Of course, some commercial vehicles are used for the journey to work.) Buchanan's estimates for 2,010 of all other traffic (commercial vehicles, buses and cars) in the peak period were 10–25 per cent of cars going home from work in Newbury (population under 40,000), 33 per cent in Norwich (population 200,000) and 41 per cent in Leeds (population 524,000).[5] A figure of 30 to 40 per cent seemed reasonable for the model settlements.

Probably not more than about 45 per cent of journeys to work would be made during the peak period, so that if other traffic amounted to between 30 and 40 per cent of this, all traffic in the peak period would be between 59 and 63 per cent of the total. A change in working hours might cause traffic on the journey to work to coincide more with other traffic peaks, for example the journey to school, but even a 60 per cent allowance for other traffic would only raise the peaking factor to 72 per cent. There would always be some absenteeism, though with a less than proportionate effect on traffic loads, so that a peaking factor of 62 per cent seemed reasonable for conditions in a mature settlement.

The effects of changes in the modal split and in peaking factors on the costs of the road system depended on the spare capacity available, and on the extent to which the size of roads and form of interchanges had to be modified. Generally, the larger the settlement the more a given change in the traffic load affected costs. A change of modal split from 1·6 to 4·0 reduced the road capacity required by 60 per cent and the

[1] Freeman, Fox, Wilbur Smith and Associates, *West Midlands Transport Study, Summary Report*, London, 1967.
[2] Birmingham University (Department of Transportation and Land Use Planning), *Travel and Land Use Survey*, Birmingham, 1966.
[3] Greater London Council, *London Traffic Survey*, vol. 2, London, 1966.
[4] Ministry of Transport, *Research on Road Traffic*, London, HMSO, 1965.
[5] Ministry of Transport, *Traffic in Towns*, London, HMSO, 1963.

costs of the main roads in model settlements with populations of 50,000, 100,000 and 250,000 by 18, 20 and 34 per cent respectively. The combined effect of changing the modal split from 1·6 to 1·4 and the peaking factor from 62 to 73 per cent was to increase the road capacity required by 35 per cent, and the costs of the main road system in the same models by 13, 17 and 22 per cent respectively. A similar change in the peaking factor alone had far less consistent results – it gave increases in costs of 12, 8 and 9 per cent respectively.

THE TRAFFIC MODEL

A traffic model was needed to determine the size of roads to be constructed, and to cost them and the journeys on them. At the time few suitable models were available and it was decided to use EGTAC, a model already developed by J. Murchland of the London School of Economics.[1]

The EGTAC programme could only handle a limited number of vertices on the road network of each settlement model, so they were confined to junctions between access roads and secondary distributors, and between secondary and primary roads. All journeys were therefore assumed to start and finish on the distributor road network, each section of road being specified by its initial and terminal vertices, and by its length and average speed.

The number of vehicles (in PCUs) originating and terminating at each vertex was calculated from the number of persons living or employed in the area served by that vertex. This was divided by the modal split index (table 7.4) and multiplied by the peaking factor (table 7.3). The numbers originating a journey at any vertex and terminating it at another were assumed to be related as in the Gravity Model, that is the probability of a journey was proportional directly to the numbers at each destination and inversely to a function of travelling time, with constants λ and n as in table 7.1. Average speeds along the arcs between the vertices were assumed, and the traffic was allocated to each road on the assumption that the quickest route was followed. Other traffic, for example through traffic or commercial traffic, could be simulated by adding PCUs. The number of PCUs along each arc

[1] B. A. Farbey and J. D. Murchland, 'Towards an evaluation of road system designs', *Regional Studies*, vol. I, no. I, February 1967.

Essentially EGTAC is a research tool, not a design tool. Its great virtue is that it is comparatively cheap to use, so that many alternatives could be investigated to build up an understanding of the effects of a range of parameters. A number of possible improvements might save work on preparing runs but, generally, greater sophistication was likely to add considerably to operational costs and to result in a model as expensive to operate as some highway design models; this would be unsatisfactory for research work.

was converted to the number of lanes required by using appropriate lane capacities. Each arc was costed using a unit cost per mile of lane and a unit cost for its initial and terminal interchanges (vertices). Travelling time was also calculated and costed per unit of journey time.

EGTAC AND ROAD DESIGN

The EGTAC traffic programme produced a specification for a workable road system, but not necessarily the optimum specification. This was due partly to the basic assumptions and partly to the way the assumptions were applied. Generally the road system tended to be overdesigned.

In choosing routes, traffic was allocated to the first route in the programme with a minimum travel time. Thus, where there was more than one such route, traffic was concentrated on the first on the list. The amount of traffic on a route was unlimited, so that the favoured routes might have been over-specified, with unnecessarily complicated interchanges, while capacity remained spare on other routes. This feature was not very important in the road systems of the model settlements studied, because they provided few alternative routes; it did, however, limit the range of road systems considered.

Road sizes were estimated by dividing total flow by the design capacity of a lane. Flows in each direction were handled separately, so that sufficient lanes were provided in both directions to handle the morning and the evening flows. The total capacity might, therefore, have considerably exceeded the actual flows. The assumption of dual carriageways also resulted in extra capacity, since their width could only be increased by whole lanes and not by small increments. However, single carriageways were clearly less safe and convenient, besides providing less capacity.

Finally, the form of the interchanges had to be specified before the traffic flows or the number of lanes were known, so that over- or under-specification was possible.

For all these reasons, before the results of the EGTAC programme were accepted, it was necessary to study them in detail and compare them with manual results obtained by plotting peak traffic loads on plans of the main road networks. It was not feasible to make a detailed appraisal of every road network, so a cross-section of five settlement models was selected, covering three different settlement forms for 50,000 persons, and linear forms of 100,000 and 250,000 person settlements.

In the manual calculations, many of the rigidities imposed by the EGTAC programme were relaxed. For primary distributors, and other cases where capacities were high enough to warrant urban motorway standards,[1] dual carriageways were retained, but elsewhere 'all-purpose' road standards were used, with graded interchanges and correspondingly reduced capacities. Where a large number of lanes was required, for example near the central area in the settlement for 250,000 persons, the route was divided into inner carriageways at motorway standards and outer carriageways at 'all-purpose' standards.[1] For secondary distributors a lower standard of 'all-purpose' road was used, in a two-way form where a dual carriageway appeared unnecessary – and further, road widths were not restricted to units of a lane (12 feet). For secondary distributors in the industrial areas, tidal flows of traffic were envisaged. Each interchange was considered separately and a roundabout, signals, or a priority junction was specified according to the traffic load.

The effect on costs of modifying the network varied from one settlement model to another. In two cases the spare capacity in the EGTAC specification was so small that the savings from relaxing the lane requirements were more than offset by the wider roads needed to make up for lost capacity resulting from other changes. In the other three cases costs fell as a result of the changes, but the resulting network would not, of course, have been as safe as one based on lanes, nor would traffic necessarily flow as smoothly.

Manually specified interchanges showed savings over those in the EGTAC programme of about two thirds in the three smallest settlement models, about a third in the 100,000 person settlement and about a sixth in the largest settlement. Since savings on primary interchanges of two thirds of the costs would be equivalent to about 10 per cent of the total main road costs, these were taken into account for the smallest settlement. Otherwise, since none of the differences appeared to be systematic or likely to distort the comparisons seriously, the alternative standards were not accepted, and the EGTAC results were used despite their shortcomings. Possibly the main road network of the medium-sized settlement might have been costed about 2 per cent too high and of the larger settlement perhaps as much as 4 per cent too high. For cluster settlements the error probably fell somewhere between these values.

RESULTS FOR THE ROAD SYSTEM ASSESSED

The settlement models were designed with a set of standard components to provide comparability, but this did not of course ensure that each model represented the most efficient way of laying out that form. For example, the road system might have been more efficient if the component parts of the settlement were resited, or varied in size and density,

[1] Ministry of Transport, *Roads in Urban Areas*, London, HMSO, 1966.

so that each part of the road system was loaded to capacity. Hence too much weight could not be placed on individual results from the programme, but the consistency of the pattern of main road costs for different settlements was very striking (see chart 8.1, page 88).

Since the movement of workers from origin to destination was inversely proportional to a function of travelling time, any change in the road network changed the distribution of journeys over the whole settlement. A change in settlement form which reduced travelling time between homes and jobs would raise the proportion of people working outside their locality and the distances travelled, and might result in increased road costs. Moreover, the deterrent effect of distance was doubtful in the settlements under consideration, with road networks on which crossing the settlement took only a few minutes.[1] Many of the comparisons of road construction and travel costs were therefore made on the basis of the situation represented mathematically in the traffic programme by the Tanner constants $\lambda = 0\cdot0$, $n = 0\cdot0$, which gave a measure of the maximum road requirements and maximum travel costs.

The accuracy of the traffic programme was severely limited by the restricted number of vertices at which vehicles could be recorded as entering, leaving and changing routes. The assumption that traffic entered the network in the model at the interchange points between access and distributor roads meant that access roads were excluded from the programme, and hence from the estimates of construction and journey costs; also that journeys on the access roads were not taken into account in determining the deterrent effect of the length of the journey to work. These difficulties could be overcome to some extent: the construction of access roads was costed with estate development; an allowance for journeys on access roads and for parking and unparking was included in journey costs; the Tanner constants used were estimated excluding traffic on access roads.

Even so the number of vertices available on the first version of EGTAC programme, 75, though adequate for the smallest settlements, was about 10 per cent short for the medium-sized ones and 50 per cent short for the largest ones. Various approximations based on pairing interchanges were tested, but though the length of roads was unaffected, the positions on the secondary roads at which traffic entered the main road system were altered and hence lane mileage. The total length of journeys tended to increase, so that both construction and

[1] Journeys between the most distant parts of the main road networks of 50,000 person rectangular settlements would take less than 10 minutes, and for 250,000 person settlements less than 12 minutes. Thus, even allowing for extra travelling on estate roads, for changing from estate to main roads and for parking, the maximum journey was unlikely to take longer than 20 minutes.

journey costs were biased upwards, although the former were affected much less than the latter. The bias in the main road costs of medium-sized settlements appeared within the acceptable margin of error, but that for 250,000 person settlements and settlement clusters was inevitably larger and more serious.

Various other techniques for overcoming the shortage of vertices proved unsatisfactory; instead the EGTAC programme was rewritten to provide 149 vertices.[1] Some calculations on the largest settlements had been made before the expanded programme was available and the costs for the rectangular models were obtained by the approximations described above. The effect of doubling the number of vertices in two types of linear, 250,000 person settlements was to reduce main road costs by 1 per cent and 5 per cent (table 8.2) and journey costs by about 13 per cent (table 10.1).

EGTAC AND ACTUAL TRAFFIC FLOWS

Suitable traffic data from existing towns were sought to test the accuracy of the EGTAC estimates of traffic flow. Since the model assigned traffic to routes without any limit on volume, agreement between actual and estimated flows could only be expected in towns where road capacity did not limit the volume of traffic which ideally would like to use the route. Only in new towns was this condition met even approximately, and only Stevenage was able at the time to provide the data required. Stevenage was designed on a neighbourhood principle similar to that used in certain of the model towns, but it differed from them in two important ways: first, Stevenage has only one industrial area, in the extreme west, whereas the models have two to four; secondly, Stevenage is a net importer of labour.[2] A further difference, although less important, was that, whereas the model assumed that all routes, and hence all interchanges, were equally efficient, in Stevenage the northern routes are slower than the southern ones due to the design. Agreement between the theoretical and actual traffic flows could not therefore be expected to be very close.

The total of the observed and theoretical flows over a period differed by just under 1·5 per cent. The relative differences between the flows at different times were found to be inversely correlated with the rate of flow: as the rate increased from 0 to 2,000 PCUs per hour the range of error declined from ± 100 to ± 5 per cent. Thus the errors in predicting

[1] It seemed feasible to increase the number to about 200, which would be essential for sub-regional and regional studies. Unfortunately increasing the number of vertices sharply increased the costs of a run.

[2] About 20 per cent of labour commutes into the town each day, although there is also a substantial daily outflow of labour.

journey times were relatively small, and errors in predicting the flows, even if large, would have no effect on the sizes of roads where the flows themselves were relatively small, since a minimum of one lane in each direction must be provided. Thus errors in sizes were small and so were errors in costing construction. Hence the estimates of road and journey costs were all probably reasonably accurate, especially as positive and negative errors would tend to cancel each other out.

CHAPTER 8

MAIN ROADS AND THEIR CAPITAL COSTS

COSTING MAIN ROADS

In the model settlements the main roads were defined as distributor roads, and excluded the estate and service roads which provided access to the properties and communication within the environmental areas. The separation of distributor and access functions has been widely accepted only in the last few years and cost data on this basis were limited. Both actual and estimated road costs for new towns and expansion schemes were analysed and compared with various figures supplied by the Ministry of Transport. Costs for roads of the same class vary considerably; in particular they depend on the specification and scale of interchanges, on how much existing development is involved and on the terrain.

The EGTAC model required unit costs per lane and per terminal vertex.[1] Lanes were standard so that only one figure was needed for lane costs, but the type of interchange depended on the speed of the traffic, the number of roads joining and the number of lanes involved, and so a range of costs was required for terminal vertices. Only the new town data provided separate lane and interchange costs. Typical road costs, covering both lanes and interchanges, were therefore calculated by applying these data to the roads in the models to give average costs for primary and for secondary distributors. These were then adjusted to agree with the Ministry of Transport figures for comparable roads, although these unfortunately did not differentiate between roads in virgin areas and other roads. The adjusted averages might therefore have been too high for settlements constructed largely on virgin sites, but, on the other hand, the exclusion of costs of bridging and of altering levels by more than 10 feet would tend to make them too low. The results (table 8.1) were therefore probably of the right order. They implied that a primary road of four lanes with one major and one minor intersection would cost about £350,000 a mile to construct, while a secondary road with two lanes and two light-controlled junctions would cost about £150,000. This assumed that the ground was reasonably level and that little in the way of tunnels, cuttings or embankments was required.[2] Both primary and secondary distributors would be all-

---

[1] Each lane generates one terminal vertex on each interchange.

[2] Elevated motorways are seven times as expensive as those on the ground, roads in retained cuttings ten times as expensive, cut-and-cover twelve times as expensive and bored

Table 8.1. *Main roads: unit costs of construction*

£s, 1967 prices

Road lanes (per mile)	59,630
Interchanges	
Priority junction	1,250
Traffic signals[a]	3,130
Separate grade intersection[b]	12,500
'At grade' roundabout[c]	
Primary distributor	50,000
Secondary distributor	37,500

SOURCE: NIESR estimates.

[a] Per road end.
[b] Per lane end.
[c] Dual carriageways assumed.

purpose roads, not motorways. The design standards followed those recommended by the Ministry of Transport.[1]

Costs per head for main roads in all the models of individual settlements lay between £60 and £130 (table 8.2). These figures covered lanes and interchanges, also pedestrian underpasses, but not inter-settlement roads outside the developed area. They were based on typical site and contour conditions and did not allow for the need to change road alignments because of contours or to avoid obstructions. Analysis suggested, however, that such requirements were unlikely to add more than about 1·5 per cent to lane costs and they did not affect interchange costs. As lane costs were some 70 per cent of the total, road costs could not be increased by more than about 1 per cent on this account. Inter-settlement roads were likely to cost about £2 per mile per head, so that even an allowance for a mile of such road on either side of the settlement, as well as for contour and other effects, would not add more than another £5 per head to the main road costs.

The value taken for the Tanner constant n reflected the proportion of workers who are deterred by distance from making long journeys to work; hence the lower n was assumed to be the more people travelling on the network and the greater its costs. Reducing the value of n from 1·0 to 0·0 had the effect of increasing the costs of the road network by about 5 to 10 per cent (table 8.2). The actual increase in each case depended on the amount of unused capacity in the road network; since the smallest unit of road is a lane, some capacity would usually be spare. Similarly, the PCU index for the modal split was a measure of the number of vehicles needed to transport a given number of passen-

tunnels over fifty times as expensive (see A. Goldstein, *Motorway Route Location Studies*, Keele, Town and Country Planning Summer School, 1966).
[1] Ministry of Transport, *Research on Road Traffic* and *Roads in Urban Areas*.

Table 8.2. *Capital costs of main roads in individual settlements*

Settlement	Tanner n	Modal split[b]	Peaking factor	50,000 persons	100,000 persons	250,000 persons 75 vertices	149 vertices
			(%)	($£$s per head, 1967 prices)			
Rectangular[c]							
Decentralised[d]	0·0	1·6	62	66[e]	80	99	..
	0·0	1·4	73	72	96	122	..
	0·5	1·4	62	60	86	105	..
	0·5	1·4	73	70	93	114	..
	1·0	1·4	73	70	90	110	..
Partly centralised[e]	0·0	1·6	62	..	91	114	..
	0·5	1·6	62	..	86	111	..
Centralised[f]	0·0	1·6	62	90	98	..	..
Star[g]							
Decentralised	0·0	1·6	62	88	107	..	123
Partly centralised	0·0	1·6	62	..	99	..	119
	0·5	1·6	62	..	99	..	113
Centralised	0·0	1·6	62	104	114	..	..
Linear[h]							
Decentralised	0·0	1·6	62	80	101	126	121
	0·5	1·6	62	..	..	115	114
Partly centralised	0·0	1·6	62	80	105	..	117
	0·5	1·6	62	..	100	..	113
Centralised	0·0	1·6	62	98	111	..	..
	0·5	1·6	62	..	109	..	..

SOURCE: NIESR estimates.

[a] Excluding costs of estate roads.
[b] PCU index.
[c] Rectangular settlements have grid road systems (see chart 5.4).
[d] For sub-form (B) of a rectangular settlement (see chart 5.4).
[e] The corresponding cost using sub-form (A) would be $£$76.
[f] For sub-form (A) of a rectangular settlement (see chart 5.4).
[g] Star settlements have radial road systems (see chart 5.4).
[h] For 1-strand roads only: costs for 2 and 3 strands in table 8.8.

gers, and the lower it was the higher the road costs. On the other hand, the peaking factor, which measured the proportion of vehicles travelling in the peak period, varied directly with road capacity required. Over the values tested for these factors, differences of up to 10 per cent were found in the costs of the network (table 8.2).

SETTLEMENT SIZE AND ROAD COSTS

The results of the model studies of main road networks appeared on the whole remarkably consistent (chart 8.1). Costs rose but at a declining rate as the size of settlement increased. Increases with size in the rectangular settlements were biased upwards by the inadequate number of vertices for large settlements on the EGTAC programme. In settlements for 250,000, costs per head were higher by about £35 to £40 (or 50 per cent) than in settlements for 50,000 (table 8.2). Thus the main road network of the largest settlement would cost £9 to £10 million

Chart 8.1. *Main road costs and settlement factors*

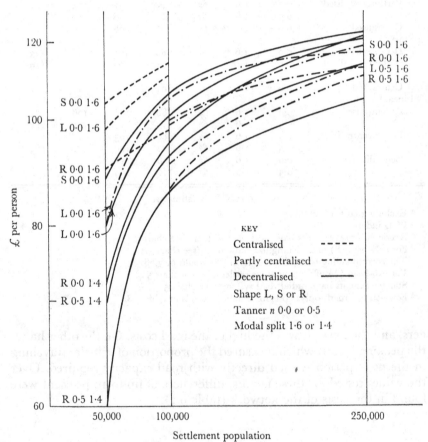

SOURCE: table 8.2.

Note: Costs at 1967 prices; shapes—L=linear, S=star, R=rectangular.

more than the network for five of the smallest settlements, even though both catered for the same number of people.

Table 8.3. *Settlement size and capital costs of main roads*

Settlement	Traffic Tanner *n*	Modal split	Peaking factor	50,000 persons	100,000 persons	250,000 persons 75 vertices	149 vertices
			(%)		(percentages)		
Rectangular							
Decentralised	0·0	1·6	62	82	100	124	..
	0·0	1·4	73	75	100	127	..
	0·5	1·4	62	70	100	122	..
	0·5	1·4	73	75	100	123	..
	1·0	1·4	73	78	100	122	..
Partly centralised	0·0	1·6	62	..	100	125	..
	0·5	1·6	62	..	100	129	..
Centralised	0·0	1·6	62	92	100	..	..
Star							
Decentralised	0·0	1·6	62	82	100	..	115
Partly centralised	0·0	1·6	62	..	100	..	120
	0·5	1·6	62	..	100	..	114
Centralised	0·0	1·6	62	91	100	..	..
Linear							
Decentralised	0·0	1·6	62	79	100	125	120
Partly centralised	0·0	1·6	62	76	100	..	111
	0·5	1·6	62	..	100	..	113
Centralised	0·0	1·6	62	88	100	..	..
Averages							
Decentralised settlements				77	100	122	
Partly centralised settlements				76	100	119	
Centralised settlements				90	100	..	
Rectangular settlements				79	100	125	
Star settlements				86	100	116	
Linear settlements				81	100	115	
Overall				81	100	121	

SOURCE: table 8.2.

Note: In this table and the two following (also tables 10.2–10.4) costs per head under various conditions are expressed as percentages of the costs for one value of the parameter being considered. An arithmetic mean of these percentages is an approximate average which is not influenced, as would be the mean of the actual figures, by lacunae in the data, e.g. the absence of any partly centralised results in the averages for rectangular and star settlements for 50,000 persons. Because of the limitations of the traffic model (see chapter 7) little significance can be attached to any particular result, so that the exact method of calculating the averages is immaterial. What is important is that the trends are shown to be consistent by both tables and charts, with no sign of interaction between traffic factors and settlement factors.

The rise in costs with size varied with the shape and the degree of centralisation: centralised settlements, which were only studied in the two smaller sizes, showed the least change (table 8.3). Possibly the result of the concentration of all job opportunities in the centre was that small changes in size had little effect on the road network. There was also a variation with shape – rectangular settlements showing the largest increase,[1] but, of course, the figure for the largest rectangular settlements was likely to be biased upwards.

No firm conclusions on the relationship between road costs and form in settlements with over 250,000 population could be drawn without models for the relevant sizes; but speculation from the results for the three settlement sizes examined indicated that costs would probably continue to rise with increases in size but at a falling rate (chart 8.1). Costs per person might average about £130 in a settlement for half a million (about 30 per cent more than in one for 100,000 persons). At that size the advantages of the rectangular shape might have been lost, so that a linear settlement might have the cheapest roads.

Work by Smeed and Holroyd lent some support to these figures.[2] They examined the road space required in the centre of a town where people lived outside the central area but worked within it. Road space per person was found to vary with the type of routing, with road width, with the duration of the peak travelling period and with the form of transport. On average, however, a ten-fold increase in population increased central road space by a factor of about three. Since costs would increase less than in proportion to road space and road space in the central area more than in proportion to total road space, these relationships appeared compatible with those obtained above. At the very least they helped to confirm the direction and proportions of the cost variations.

SETTLEMENT SHAPE AND ROAD COSTS

Over the range examined, main roads were least expensive in rectangular settlements; costs were about 17 per cent higher in star settlements and about 14 per cent higher in linear ones (table 8.4). Since the costs for the rectangular settlements were likely to be overestimated, they might compare even more favourably than the figures indicated. Broadly, a 1 per cent difference was equivalent to about £1 of capital costs per head of the population.

[1] The differences between the two rectangular sub-forms (see chart 5.4) were not large enough to change the trends described. The capital costs of (A) were £10 per head more than those for (B), but running costs were slightly lower in (A).

[2] Smeed and Holroyd, *Some Factors affecting Congestion in Towns*.

Table 8.4. *Settlement shape and capital costs of main roads*

Settlement	Tanner n^a	Variation of costs		
		Rectangular	Star	Linear
50,000 persons		(percentages)		
Decentralised	0·0	100	133	121
Centralised	0·0	100	116	109
100,000 persons				
Decentralised	0·0	100	134	126
Partly centralised	0·0	100	109	115
	0·5	100	115	116
Centralised	0·0	100	116	113
250,000 persons				
Decentralised	0·0	100	124	124[b]
Partly centralised	0·0	100	104	103
	0·5	100	102	102
Averages				
Settlements for				
50,000 persons		100	125	115
100,000 persons		100	118	118
250,000 persons		100	110	110
Decentralised settlements		100	130	124
Partly centralised settlements		100	107	109
Centralised settlements		100	116	111
Overall		100	117	114

SOURCE: table 8.2.

[a] Only results for standard modal split (1.6) and peaking factor (62%) included in this table.
[b] Average of results with 75 and 149 vertices in the EGTAC programme.

While rectangular settlements were always substantially cheaper than the other shapes, the relative positions of star and linear were rather confused. The disadvantage of star as compared with rectangular declined steadily with size, but in the linear results that for 100,000 persons did not follow this pattern. The linear shape was cheaper than the star by about the same amount in centralised and decentralised settlements, but more expensive in partly centralised ones, due no doubt to the compactness of the star 100,000 person settlement in this form.

The results were logical: in small settlements compactness minimised the costs of the main road system, but this advantage was lost as size increased because the traffic built up faster in compact than in dispersed settlements and expensive interchanges were needed. Costs were lowest in a circular settlement but increased with the ratio of length to breadth. Star settlements needed special consideration since they can take many

forms: as arms are pushed out from the circle the advantages of compactness are lost, but whether costs were higher than in a linear settlement depended on the actual characteristics of the settlements compared.
Most star settlements considered here were more expensive than the
corresponding linear settlements because the sum of the lengths of their
arms was greater than the length of the linear settlements; the 100,000
person, partly centralised, star settlement (chart 5.4) of cruciform shape
was the exception. Perhaps it would be better to regard star settlements
as circles with finger-shaped developments.

Some theoretical work by Reynolds confirmed the above results.[1] He
concluded that, unless there were special geographical or cost features,
a circular or square town was optimum for both centralised and dispersed patterns of travel; shape was not critical as long as extreme
linear shapes were avoided.

DEGREE OF CENTRALISATION AND ROAD COSTS

In general, decentralised settlements had the lowest main road costs
per person and centralised the highest (table 8.5). Costs for the centralised settlements were systematically greater for every size and shape
and, on average, about 19 per cent above those for decentralised
settlements. The disadvantages of centralisation were, as would be
expected, greater in rectangular settlements than in the other shapes;
they also greater in smaller than in larger settlements, but this
probably reflected a particular combination of circumstances rather
than a trend. The difference in costs between decentralised and partly
centralised settlements was small, only about 3 per cent. Partly centralised settlements showed themselves at a disadvantage mainly when they
were rectangular, which might have reflected the comparative advantages of sub-form (B) as compared with sub-form (A) (chart 5.4), the
former being used for the decentralised estimates and the latter for the
partly centralised ones. The comparisons again reflected clearly the
advantages of the cruciform (star) shape for the 100,000 person, partly
centralised settlement.

The main road system would be most economic when the traffic
generators were distributed uniformly over the settlement. Dwellings
were distributed fairly evenly in all the models, so that it was the distribution of jobs which distinguished the centralised model settlements
from the others, and to a lesser extent the decentralised from partly
centralised settlements (table 8.6). There were the same number of
jobs in the industrial areas in all the settlements: the variation was in

---

[1] D. J. Reynolds, *Urban Layout and Transport Systems: a theoretical/practical study*, Ottawa,
Roads and Transportation Association of Canada, 1971.

Table 8.5. *Degree of centralisation and capital costs of main roads*

Percentages

Settlement[a]	Decentralised	Partly centralised	Centralised
50,000 persons			
Rectangular	100	..	136
Star	100	..	118
Linear	100	100	122
100,000 persons			
Rectangular	100	114	122
Star	100	93	107
Linear	100	104	110
250,000 persons			
Rectangular	100	115	..
Star	100	97	..
Linear	100[b]	97	..
Averages			
Settlements for			
50,000 persons	100	100	125
100,000 persons	100	104	113
250,000 persons	100	103	..
Rectangular settlements	100	114	129
Star settlements	100	95	112
Linear settlements	100	100	116
Overall	100	103	119

SOURCE: table 8.2.

[a] Only results for standard traffic conditions (n = 0·0, modal split = 1·6, peaking factor = 62%) included in this table.
[b] With 149 vertices on the EGTAC programme.

central areas. In decentralised settlements for 100,000 persons there were about 700 jobs in each neighbourhood centre and 11,000 in the town centre; the proportions remained about the same for other sizes. In partly centralised settlements, there were about an equal number of jobs in the town centre and in each district centre in the 100,000 person town, but the proportions varied with size. Generally, the advantages lay with the widest possible dispersion. The decentralised settlements might have shown up even better if jobs had been distributed more evenly between neighbourhood and town centres. A better distribution could also be obtained by having more industrial areas; there seemed no adequate reason for industry to be in large local aggregations.[1] Dispersion of central areas, in so far as it implies dispersion of shops and

[1] There might be a gain if some of the factories generated a great deal of noise, since other areas could then be protected by siting such factories in the centre of large industrial areas.

Table 8.6. *Distribution of jobs by form of settlement*

Degree of centralisation	Settlement size (persons)	Number of jobs in:			
		Town centre	Sub-centres	Industrial areas	Other areas
Decentralised	50,000	5,520	5× 695	2× 6,603	2×150
	100,000	11,040	10× 695	2×12,930	{4×150, 1×550}
	250,000	27,600	25× 695	4×16,231	{10×150, 2×550}
Partly centralised	50,000	1,900	2×3,547	2× 6,603	2×150
	100,000	3,800	4×3,547	2×12,930	{4×150, 1×550}
	250,000	9,500	10×3,547	4×16,231	{10×150, 2×550}
Centralised	50,000	8,995	—	2× 6,603	2×150
	100,000	17,990	—	2×12,930	{4×150, 1×550}

SOURCE: NIESR estimates.

other retail services, probably has more effect on the roads needed for shopping journeys, than for journeys to work.

No data were available to show the results of varying the sizes of local units, but since standard neighbourhoods accommodated 10,000 persons and districts 25,000, rough estimates for localities of those sizes could be made from costs already calculated for decentralised and partly centralised settlements. Similarly, costs with localities for 50,000 and 100,000 persons were estimated from costs for centralised settlements of those sizes. The latter estimates illustrate, of course, the complete centralisation of jobs, but those for the two smaller localities were based on only partial local centralisation of employment, most jobs in industry being elsewhere. If the jobs in the industrial areas and the town centre were transferred to the local centres, local self-sufficiency would be maximised and the settlement would have a uniform distribution of employment.[1] Thus, if people felt some reluctance to make long journeys to work, the costs of main roads in decentralised and partly centralised settlements would be lower than those in the models, while in centralised settlements costs would remain unchanged. The indications from the figures available (chart 8.2) were that settlements with localities of 10,000, 25,000, 50,000 and 100,000 persons had road costs in the ratio of about 73:78:94:105.

[1] The greater the reluctance to travel long distances to work, the greater the effect on costs of dispersing jobs evenly in relation to homes. Unfortunately, it was not possible to test this without sacrificing more important tests.

Chart 8.2. *Main road costs[a] and size of locality*

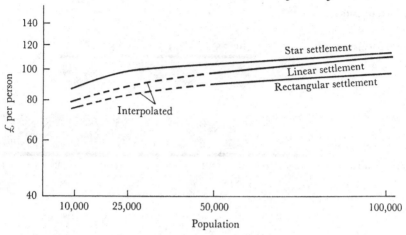

SOURCE: NIESR estimates.
[a] At 1967 prices.

DENSITY AND ROAD COSTS

The effect of changing densities was tested in two limited exercises. Since, at basic densities, nearly half the area of a settlement was used for residential purposes and there was much less choice for other densities, only alternative residential densities were considered.

First, residential densities were changed uniformly without any other alteration in layout. This resulted in different road lengths but did not affect the intersections. In linear, partly centralised settlements a decrease in residential density from 37 to 30 persons per acre increased

Table 8.7. *Effect on road costs of eliminating neighbourhoods[a]*

Size of settlement	Neighbourhoods		Adjusted density[b]	Road costs[c]	
	Standard	Adjusted		Standard	Adjusted
(persons)			(ppa)	($£$s per head)	
100,000	10	8	46·25	101	93
250,000	25	{ 21	44·00	121[d]	113[d]
		{ 17	54·41	121[d]	124[d]

SOURCE: NIESR estimates.
[a] In linear decentralised settlements.
[b] Standard density is 37 persons per acre.
[c] At 1967 prices.
[d] With 149 vertices.

Chart 8.3. *Variations on road systems*

Adjusted densities

100,000 population
8 neighbourhoods

250,000 population
21 neighbourhoods

250,000 population
17 neighbourhoods

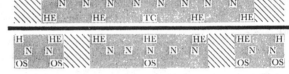

Number of strands

2 strands

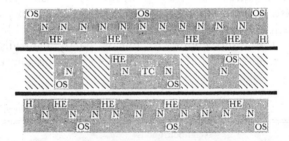

3 strands

Note: For key see chart 5.4.

road lengths by about 4 per cent and costs by just over £2 per head; an increase in density to 50 persons per acre reduced them by about the same amounts. The changes were similar for all sizes of settlement, and it seemed unlikely that very different results would have been obtained for other forms. The effect on housing costs of the changes in densities would be greater than these differences in road costs (see chapter 9 below).

A more radical exercise was the elimination of some localities, all densities being raised to absorb their residents and facilities (chart 8.3). Tests were made on two sizes of linear decentralised settlements (table 8.7). Savings on road costs were again substantially lower than the increased housing costs which would have resulted from using higher densities. When eight neighbourhoods were eliminated, road costs increased because the average journey lengthened, which indicated the importance of locating the main centres of employment relatively close to homes.

THE ROAD NETWORK AND ITS COSTS

Given the shape of a settlement and the assumption of rectangular environmental areas, the form of road network was largely determined. To begin with it was assumed that the protection of environmental areas would be given high priority, and that speed limits (40 miles per hour on primary roads, 30 miles per hour on others) would be imposed, to force as much traffic as possible on to the primary roads from which the environmental areas could be insulated. Even so the traffic on some secondary roads would be heavy and open space would not always provide adequate protection against noise.

Only one set of road network alternatives could be tested, and since the number of strands of primary road in a linear settlement was much under discussion, this aspect was examined. Costs in a 250,000 person, linear decentralised settlement were compared for one strand, two strands and three variations of three strands, of which the first consisted only of intermediate link roads (table 8.8). The three-strand systems implied the same land uses as one strand; the change merely involved adding connecting links to the peripheral distributor roads and grading the three strands in different ways (chart 8.3). For two strands the land uses had to be rearranged: all the main centres of employment were placed between the two strands and the settlement became broader, shorter and more nearly rectangular (chart 8.3). Differences in the main road costs were not large. The primary–secondary–primary system of three strands would, in practice, have little to commend it unless the external strands were regional roads, since it would provide a slow speed road as a major link between homes and jobs.

4

Table 8.8. *Effect on road costs of the number of strands
in a road system*[a]   *£s, 1967 prices*

Number of strands	Grading of roads	Cost per head
1	Primary	121
2	Primary, primary	116
3	Secondary, primary, secondary	116
	Primary, secondary, primary	117
	Primary, primary, primary	119

SOURCE: NIESR estimates.

[a] In a linear decentralised settlement for 250,000 persons.

It could be argued that the current view on protecting environmental areas is incorrect, that more traffic could be accepted among them and that they could be smaller. The development of an electric town runabout would reduce noise and fumes, but only practical economic battery-propelled vehicles suitable for both long and short journeys, replacing petrol and diesel vehicles, would transform the situation. The problem of pedestrian safety would remain. However, if more traffic were acceptable around the environmental areas there would be greater freedom to plan more extensive and less restricted networks of main roads, which could be more evenly loaded. One possibility would be to make the shape of the secondary grids more regular, and interconnect them to provide a through network. The result would be something like the directional grid proposed by Buchanan. Some traffic would be transferred from the primary to the secondary roads. A more radical change would be to abolish the difference between primary and secondary roads, and redistribute the employment areas evenly over the whole system, to produce a grid of roads of equal importance. The mesh of the grid could be reduced by making the environmental areas smaller, but there would be no point in making it so fine that the roads operated substantially below their optimum capacity. The lane costs of such systems would probably be higher than those of the systems discussed above and many more pedestrian underpasses might be needed. On the other hand, interchanges would be much cheaper and it might even be possible to develop one-way systems using a stepped grid with minimal interchange costs. Such systems might not, therefore, differ greatly in total cost from those discussed.

Unfortunately there appeared to be no general studies of the economics of road patterns, although there were studies of the costs of road patterns for circular towns. Smeed and Holroyd showed that no road system is more economic than going direct, as the crow flies.[1] They found that the most efficient road pattern in terms of distance and road space was a combination of radial and ring roads. Reynolds, using as indicators total annual costs of the road system and travel costs, was also in favour of this type of system for circular towns.[2] His results suggested that replacing the arcs of the rings by straight lines might be a slight improvement. Care is necessary in interpreting such results, but it is clear that for a circular town a system based on interconnected radials is the most economic.

ROAD COSTS IN CLUSTER SETTLEMENTS

Main road costs were compared in five types of cluster (see chapter 5) each housing 250,000 people in five equal settlements. The more dispersed the constituent settlements the longer the average journey to work and the more costly the main road system, provided the length of the journey was no deterrent to travelling. Under these conditions, cluster settlements' main road systems were 20 to 30 per cent more expensive on average than the roads in individual settlements, and 40 to 50 per cent more expensive than in the type of individual settlement with the lowest main road costs (table 8.9). Of the cluster settlements, the form with the lowest main road costs (with $n = 0\cdot0$) was the cross, followed by the linear block (with one and two strands) and the linear line.

Once distance acted as a deterrent, interpretation of the results became more difficult. Since the workers' choice of employment area was influenced by distance, increasing the distance between the separate settlements resulted in fewer travelling to other settlements to work. The resultant savings on road capacity had to be set against the increased costs of longer connecting roads. The assumption that journey length was only a slight deterrent ($n = 0\cdot5$) reduced the costs of the main roads in individual settlements by about 4 or 5 per cent; for linear block clusters the reduction was about 15 per cent (table 8.9). A high deterrence ($n = 1\cdot0$) gave savings of up to 50 per cent (in linear line clusters).

Moderate changes in the distance between the settlements in a cluster made little difference to main road costs so long as the deterrent effect was high ($n = 1\cdot0$), because, again, the extra length of roads between settlements was largely offset by the reduction in journeys. Differences in costs with settlements 1, 2, 3 or 4 miles apart were only 2 or 3 per cent.

A full set of comparable road costs was available only for linear decentralised settlements (table 8.9). Where the deterrent effect of a

---

[1] Smeed and Holroyd, *Some Factors affecting Congestion in Towns.*
[2] Reynolds, *Urban Layout and Transport Systems.*

Table 8.9. Main road costs[a] and sub-regional form

£s per head, 1967 prices

Constituent settlements	Distance apart (miles)	Individual settlements[b] n 0·0	0·5	Linear block (1 strand) n 0·0	0·5	1·0	Linear block (2 strands) n 0·0	0·5	1·0	Linear line n 0·0	1·0	Cross n 0·0	1·0	Necklace n 1·0
Rectangular														
Decentralised	.	99[d]												
	1											131	92	
Partly centralised	−	114[d]	111											
Centralised	−										109			
	1												110	
Star														
Decentralised	−	123									111			
Partly centralised	.	119												
Linear[e]														
Decentralised	−	121	114							152	96			100
	½											142	104	
	1			140	126	102	132	119	100		98		106	101
	2						145				97		107	100
Partly centralised	−	117	113								98			
	2					99								
	3					98								
	4					100								
Centralised	−										119			
	1					121								
	2					125								
	3					124								
Average		116	113	140	126	110	139	119	100	152	104	137	104	100

SOURCE: NIESR estimates.

[a] All with modal split 1·6 and peaking factor 62%.
[b] For 250,000 persons.
[c] Each of five equal settlements for 50,000 persons.
[d] With 75 vertices only.
[e] With 1-strand road networks.

long journey was high ($n = 1·0$), the variation in costs was small and the form of the constituent settlements appeared more important. The figures for clusters of rectangular centralised settlements, after deducting £15 to £20 a head for additional costs of centralisation, confirmed that clusters of rectangular decentralised settlements had road costs (with $n = 1·0$) of about £95 a head, which was clearly lower than for clusters of other settlement forms. The only individual settlement tested with $n = 1·0$ had a non-standard PCU index and peaking factor (table 8.2), but, making a rough allowance for this, costs for an individual rectangular decentralised settlement for 250,000 persons would probably be under £90 a head, so that where the deterrent effect of distance was high the main roads seemed likely to be cheaper in individual settlements than in the corresponding clusters.

With a high deterrent ($n = 1\cdot0$) only about 10 per cent of workers from the peripheral settlements in clusters would work outside their own settlement. Adding settlements to the cluster would then make little difference to main road costs per person, and the increase in these costs with total population would probably be less rapid in clusters than in large individual settlements. Possibly there is a size of urban development, well above 250,000 persons, where clusters have cheaper main road systems than single large settlements. Tentatively, the road costs indicated that compact arrangements of the constituent settlements in the cluster were most economic, so that a series of rectangular decentralised settlements arranged in cross form might be cheapest. It will be appreciated that the form with the cheapest road network is not necessarily the optimum. Compactness implies that more jobs are easily accessible, and more movement results. Up to a point, small additional costs to accommodate this extra movement may be worthwhile.

The measurement of the workers' propensity to make long journeys to work by Tanner constants calculated for existing towns was not conclusive evidence of the level of this propensity in a new settlement. As pointed out earlier (chapter 7), with a purpose-designed, high-speed road system, journeys would take such a short time even in large towns that longer journeys would be less of a deterrent. However, the above analysis indicated that the greater the propensity to travel long distances to work by road, the greater the economies of compact settlements are likely to be.

CHAPTER 9

THE CAPITAL COSTS OF CONSTRUCTING
A SETTLEMENT

PRICE DATA

To estimate the costs of developing and redeveloping settlements from the projected requirements for facilities and land, prices were needed for construction work and land. Published price data were, of course, the easiest to obtain and consisted of typical prices published in builders' price books, descriptions and prices of building and works of particular interest published in trade journals, and published accounts of public developers such as new town Corporations. These were augmented by a few published papers which review price data and trends. Unpublished price data, consisting of the contract prices for various contracts and land, could sometimes be obtained by individual approaches to private and public developers and to government departments, but were usually available only in the strictest confidence. Price details for many developments were not obtainable either because the developers were unwilling to provide them, or because the contract was such that prices for the individual constructions could not be separated.

Prices varied widely with the specification and other conditions of supply, with the geographical area and over time, so that a complete knowledge of all the circumstances was important. However, there was no point in price data with a finer classification than was usable. For example, manufacturing space required can only be estimated for broad industrial groups, so that, although unit prices for factory space might vary widely within a group, only the average price could be used. Allowance for differences in time and location had to be made, but even then the price range was wide.

Prices will change in future with productivity and the competitiveness of the market, and with standards, but in a comparative study such as this it was unnecessary to attempt forecasts of these changes, and the mid-1967 price level was used. The effect of differential movements will be considered later in relation to the cost aggregates. Price changes resulting from changes in the value of money were not relevant since it was real resources that were under consideration.

THE COSTS OF DWELLINGS

Prices for housing were based on a detailed study of tender prices for public authority dwellings and on some price data for private dwellings.[1] Prices varied with the size, form and standard of dwellings and with region, but the base price in 1967 for a 5-bedspace public dwelling of one or two storeys,[2] from which all other prices could be calculated, was £2,900, including all works within the curtilage except a garage and hardstanding for a car.

The size distribution of dwellings required for 10,000 persons with the household distribution projected for a settlement at maturity was given in table 6.4. Relating the sizes to price indices gave a weighted price indicator (table 9.1), which, multiplied by £2,900 (the base price taken as 100 in the size price index), gave a total basic price of just over £8 million for housing 10,000 persons.

The actual cost of housing depends on the distribution between houses, low flats and high flats, which is primarily determined by the overall density of the residential areas. The three main values used – 30, 37 and 50 persons per acre – were converted to 41, 51 and 68 habitable rooms per acre on the basis of the average occupancy ratio, 0·73 (see table 6.4). These densities could be achieved as follows:

41 habitable rooms per acre with all households in houses;[3]

51 habitable rooms per acre with 80 per cent of households in houses and 20 per cent in low flats;[4]

Table 9.1. *Basic costs of dwellings per 10,000 persons*

Dwelling size (habitable rooms)	No. of dwellings	Price index	Weighted price indicator
1	13	60	780
2	116	69	8,004
3	332	80	26,560
4	838	93	77,934
5	1,061	100	106,100
6	374	109	40,766
7	132	117	15,444
8+	60	123	7,380
Total	2,926	—	282,968

SOURCES: table 6.4; Stone, *Urban Development in Britain*, vol. 1, table 7.9.

[1] Stone, *Urban Development in Britain*, vol. 1.
[2] Built in England and Wales, outside London.
[3] Houses here include any single dwelling of one or two storeys.
[4] Two to four storeys, with an average height of three storeys.

Table 9.2. *The costs of dwellings per 10,000 persons by density*

	Density per acre		
	30 persons, 41 rooms	37 persons, 51 rooms	50 persons, 68 rooms
Housing form[a]	100:0:0	80:20:0	60:30:10
	(£ thousands, 1967 prices)		
Basic cost	8,000	8,000	8,000
Extra for low flats	—	192	288
Extra for high flats[b]	—	—	577
Basic garage costs	658	658	658
Total (inc. 10% extra for higher quality)[c]	9,520	9,730	10,470

SOURCE: NIESR estimates.

[a] Percentages of houses:low flats:high flats.
[b] Including extra garage costs.
[c] Rounded to nearest £10,000.

68 habitable rooms per acre with 60 per cent of households in houses, 30 per cent in low flats and 10 per cent in high flats.[1]
Compared with houses, low flats cost 12 per cent extra and high flats 68 per cent extra.[2] Garages were assumed to cost an additional £225 each for houses and low flats, but £338 for high flats.

Allowance was also necessary for a proportion of better quality dwellings. The recommendations of the Parker-Morris Committee[3] are usually accepted as setting the standards for low cost housing, although they have not always been fully implemented. Much privately constructed housing is built to about the same standard, but about 20 per cent of private dwellings are built to higher standards, and, on average, these are about 50 per cent more expensive. Thus if new settlements were developed with a similar mixture of standards to that found nationally, average prices would be about 10 per cent higher than those of low cost dwellings.

The total building cost of dwellings for 10,000 persons was about £10 million (table 9.2). Development costs of housing areas would be additional. Clearly the costs for housing at other densities and in other combinations of houses and flats could be estimated in the same way. The costs for particular regions could be obtained by using regional indices which vary also with the form of dwelling.[4] Some examples are worked out in table 9.3.

[1] Five storeys or more, with an average height of thirteen storeys.
[2] Stone, *Urban Development in Britain*, vol. I, table 7.11.
[3] Ministry of Housing and Local Government, *Homes for Today and Tomorrow*, London, HMSO, 1961.   [4] Stone, *Urban Development in Britain*, vol. I, table 7.12.

Table 9.3. *The costs of dwellings per 10,000 persons
by density and region*

Housing form[a]	Density per acre			Price indices[b]		
	50 persons, 68 rooms	75 persons, 102 rooms	100 persons, 137 rooms		Low	High
	60:30:10	20:50:30	0:25:75	Houses	flats	flats
	(£ millions, 1967 prices)					
Midlands	10·47	11·95	14·54	*100*	*100*	*100*
South East	10·98	12·42	14·94	*105*	*105*	*102*
North	9·57	11·15	13·90	*91*	*91*	*97*

SOURCE: Stone, *Urban Development in Britain*, vol. I, table 7.12.
[a] Percentages of houses:low flats:high flats.
[b] Average price in England and Wales outside London = *100*.

THE COSTS OF OTHER BUILDINGS

Price data for buildings other than dwellings were obtained from other studies,[1] from trade journals, from the Royal Institute of Chartered Surveyors' cost information service and from new town Development Corporations. The range of the prices was examined and in most cases they were found to be distributed normally, the mean and the median having similar values, and to be in close agreement with prices from builders' price books.[2] For purposes of this study the prices were inflated to mid-1967 levels and combined with the floor area requirements from chapter 6 to give total costs.

At 1967 prices, floor space for retailing and most other retail service

Table 9.4. *The costs[a] of buildings for retail and other service trades
per 10,000 population*

	Floor area	Price	Total cost
	(sq. ft. 000s)	(£ per sq. ft.)	(£000s)
Shopping[b]	83	5·6	465
Motor trades	63	8·1	510
Other service trades	7	5·6	39
Total	153		1014

SOURCES: tables 6.7 and 6.8; Stone, *Urban Development in Britain*, vol. II.
[a] At 1967 prices.
[b] For a settlement of average status.

[1] See Stone, *Urban Development in Britain*, vol. II.
[2] *Spon's Architects' and Builders' Price Book*, 1964–5.

Table 9.5. *Building and development costs[a] of schools per 10,000 population*

	Building prices	Building and development costs		
		Public	Private	Total
	(£ per sq. ft.)	(£ thousands)		
Nursery schools	5·60	14·2	2·9	17·1
Primary schools	5·60	278·1	6·9	285·0
Secondary schools	5·85	508·3	33·7	542·0
Total		800·6	43·5	844·1

SOURCE: table 6.10.

[a] At 1967 prices.

Table 9.6. *The costs[a] of factory floor space per 10,000 population*

		Area	Price	Total cost
		(sq. ft. 000s)	(£ per sq. ft.)	(£000s)
III	Food, drink and tobacco	25·7	5·1	131
IV	Chemicals and allied industry	41·0	5·1	209
V	Metal manufacture	16·9	4·3	73
VI	Engineering and electrical goods	216·7	4·3	932
VIII	Vehicles	77·8	4·3	335
IX	Metal goods n.e.s.	18·1	4·3	78
X	Textiles	3·4	3·6	12
XI	Leather, leather goods and fur	0·9	3·6	3
XII	Clothing and footwear	8·2	3·6	30
XIII	Bricks, pottery, glass and cement	31·2	4·3	134
XIV	Timber and furniture	13·6	3·6	49
XV	Paper, printing and publishing	18·5	3·6	67
XVI	Other manufacture	14·3	3·6	51
	Total	486·3		2104

SOURCES: table 6.16; Stone, *Urban Development in Britain*, vol. II.

[a] At 1967 prices.

Table 9.7. *The costs^a of buildings for other service industry^b per 10,000 population*

	Floor area	Price	Total cost
	(sq. ft. 000s)	(£ per sq. ft.)	(£000s)
Offices	112·6	5·85	659
Workshops and stores	22·8	4·30	98
Warehouses etc.	20·0	3·90	78
Total	155·4		835

SOURCES: table 6.17; Stone, *Urban Development in Britain*, vol. II.

^{a} At 1967 prices.

^{b} Construction, transport and communications, wholesale distribution, insurance, banking and finance, professional and scientific services, public administration.

trades would cost about £5·6 a square foot, but for the motor trades the appropriate figure was about £8·1; the latter included costs of sinking storage tanks and providing large areas of concrete. Total costs per 10,000 persons in a settlement of average shopping status would be just over £1 million (table 9.4).

For nursery, primary and secondary schools, cost limit and price data were obtained from the Department of Education and Science, costs were adjusted to mid-1967 levels, and development costs, at £5,000 per acre for hard surfaces and £650 per acre for playing fields, were added to building costs. The totals were estimated separately for public and for private schools (table 9.5). The 1967 unit price for a college of further education was estimated at about £5·85 a square foot,[1] so that on the basis of the areas given in chapter 6 and including development, its cost in a settlement for 100,000 persons would be about £1,342,000 and in a settlement for 250,000 persons about £3,356,000.

In many cases price data for factories could not be analysed by trade because no information was available on the purpose of the buildings. However, some trades require more costly buildings than others, so that some price differentiation was necessary. These differences were estimated on the basis of specialised needs: for example, trades which need buildings with a large span, with high clearance, with a heavy structure, or with high-class insulation and finishes. Mean prices were adjusted accordingly with reference to cost studies.[2] Total costs of factory buildings per 10,000 persons calculated on this basis were just over £2 million (table 9.6).

[1] See Stone, *Urban Development in Britain*, vol. II.

[2] DSIR, *The Economics of Factory Buildings* by P. A. Stone, and *Structural Frameworks for Single-Storey Factory Buildings*, by H. V. Apcar, London, HMSO, 1960; *Spon's Architects' and Builders' Price Book*, 1964–5.

Table 9.8. *The costs^a of minor building facilities
per 10,000 population*

	Floor area			Cost		
	Town centre	Sub-centre	Price per sq. ft.	Town centre	Sub-centre	Total
	(sq. ft. ooos)		(£)	(£ thousands)		
Court house	3·5	—	8·45	30	—	30
Libraries	1·2	4·0	7·30	9	29	38
Police, fire, ambulance stations	5·0	—	6·50	32	—	32
Post Office	3·6	—	5·85	21	—	21
Museum/Art gallery	2·0	—	9·00	18	—	18
Concert hall/Theatre/Cinemas	2·0	—	6·75	13	—	13
Dance hall/Amusement centre	5·5	—	5·75	32	—	32
Churches	0·5	20·0	7·55	4	151	155
Hotels	3·5	—	8·75	31	—	31
Bus station	5·0	—	4·00	20	—	20
Market	0·5	—	3·60	2	—	2
Public conveniences	0·1	0·6	8·10	1	5	6
Public houses	—	8·0	6·50	—	52	52
Residential institutions	—	10·5	5·60	—	59	59
Community centres/Clubs	—	9·0	5·40	—	49	49
Health centres/Surgeries	—	5·0	5·60	—	28	28
Total	32·4	57·1		213	373	586
Buildings in open space^b				n.a.	n.a.	105
Refuse disposal plant (in industrial area)				n.a.	n.a.	20
Total						711

SOURCES: table 6.19; Stone, *Urban Development in Britain*, vol. II.

^a At 1967 prices.
^b Floor area 15,000 sq. ft. @ £7.00 per sq. ft.

The costs of buildings for retail distribution and miscellaneous retail services have already been considered. The floor areas for service industries set out in table 6.17 could be grouped into offices, workshops and stores, and warehouses etc., which were costed at £5·85, £4·30 and £3·90 a square foot respectively. Total costs per 10,000 persons for these categories amounted to about £835,000 (table 9.7).

Hospital floor areas required for 10,000 persons were estimated at 42,930 square feet in general hospitals and 11,740 square feet in psychiatric hospitals (see table 6.18). Price data for hospital buildings were difficult to interpret as they related mainly to contracts for phases of development and large extensions, and hence not necessarily to balanced building complexes. Neither Ministry of Health cost allowances nor Spon's prices were directly usable; a comparative average was taken for general hospitals of £9·0 a square foot at 1967 prices, and the Spon's price (inflated to 1967) of £5·6 a square foot for psychiatric hospitals, so that about £452,000 was the total cost per 10,000 persons.

The floor areas per 10,000 persons given in table 6.19 for minor building facilities multiplied by the costs per square foot for each type gave a total of £711,000 (table 9.8). As well as commercial and social buildings, which may be in the town centre or sub-centre or in the residential areas, this figure included miscellaneous recreational buildings in the area allocated for open space, and a refuse disposal plant – the only separable item in public utility costs – which would be sited in an industrial area.

NOISE AND BUILDING COSTS

Price levels related to typical current standards, but by 1989 standards might be substantially higher. If standards rose unevenly the relative costs of different facilities would alter, but probably not enough to invalidate the conclusions on the relative economics of urban form. Completely new standards might, however, be introduced, resulting in substantial differences in costs. A high standard of insulation against noise could be of this type,[1] so that it appeared worth considering as an example of the effect on costs of a change in standards.

Noise is measured in decibels, with doubling of noise equivalent to 10 decibels. Traffic noise increases with the volume of traffic up to 80 or 90 decibels and then becomes more continuous rather than more intense.[2] The noise level along any fully loaded main road would be of this order, and so would the noise from aircraft in the immediate vicinity but, except around airports, the latter is intermittent.[3] It is not possible to hear the telephone where the noise is more than about 50 decibels.[3]

There are a number of ways of reducing traffic noise. It can be reduced at source, but not a great deal in the internal combustion engine. Electrically propelled vehicles are much quieter, but not yet technically feasible except to a limited extent. Barriers 10 feet high built along the side of a road, or some distance between the road and the nearest buildings will reduce noise by about 10 decibels.[2] Elevated roads need to be about 180 feet away for such a reduction, but the distance is much lower for roads in cuttings. A further reduction of 10 decibels needs about a five-fold increase in distance.

[1] The Road Research Laboratory estimated that about 20 per cent of the urban population lives beside roads with noise levels judged to be undesirably high. In ten years time the increase in traffic could raise this figure to 30 per cent.

[2] Goldstein, *Motorway Route Location Studies*.

[3] T. W. Parker, 'Noise problems in buildings', *Royal Society of Health Journal*, no. 2, March 1961.

Thus, even in a planned settlement, insulation from traffic noise is difficult. Residential areas can be given some protection by siting open space between the distributor roads and the dwellings, but without some earth banks and planting the protection would usually be inadequate, and open space used in this way is itself unpleasantly noisy in peak periods. Industrial areas can be similarly protected, but the noise inside some industrial buildings makes traffic noise unimportant. Such buildings could be used to shield others from traffic noises. Noise is more of a problem in commercial areas which themselves generate large volumes of traffic. Again some relief can be obtained by placing car parks between the distributor roads and the buildings, and buildings can be used to create sound barriers. One solution is to build an unbroken wall of buildings around a traffic free precinct. Clearly it would be more difficult to adopt these solutions in existing areas than in those still to be planned.

The walls of traditional buildings usually provide adequate insulation against external noise, which enters mainly through the windows. To reduce this by 40 decibels requires sealed 6-inch double glazing,[1] and, in consequence, mechanical ventilation. Even without full air conditioning, prices per square foot of floor area would be increased by about 25 per cent, and running costs would also be substantially higher. Some savings are possible, however, from rearrangement of the buildings. If they are detached, noise circulates round them and the whole of every building, except perhaps storage areas, needs soundproofing, but with a solid wall of buildings fronting the distributor roads, only the exposed side, perhaps a quarter or even less of the floor area, needs insulation and other buildings within the precinct would generally be adequately protected. Even some protection is worthwhile; ventilated baffles costing about half as much as full protection could be designed to reduce noise by about 20 decibels.[1]

The arrangement of buildings is little help in dealing with aircraft noise, but airports and flight paths can sometimes be planned to avoid interfering with nearby settlements. Residential buildings are generally less satisfactorily insulated and less easy to adapt for insulation than office buildings. Protection against aircraft noise would be very expensive: the capitalised initial and running costs of insulating the buildings in a square mile of an existing city against aircraft noise were estimated in 1960 at about £90 million,[1] and would have been some 30 per cent higher in 1967.

[1] Parker, 'Noise problems in buildings'.

SITE DEVELOPMENT COSTS

Suitable data on the costs of developing sites were difficult to find. This arose mainly from the way in which site development work is contracted: often specifications, area plans and price levels change substantially while work is in progress, and frequently contracts are related to several types of site (for example, housing and commercial areas), or include only part of the development work – main road construction, and the installation and movement of trunk public utility services are frequently included in estate development contracts. Site development prices could not therefore be ascertained with the same precision as building prices. In the case of housing they have been found to be related logarithmically to density.[1]

The costs per acre for site development – clearance and levelling, the provision of estate roads, sewers, lighting and street furniture, and landscaping – depend, in addition to density of development, on the standard and the form. Estate development for medium density housing probably cost in 1967 between £3,000 and £4,000 per acre of estate area, where the area actually developed, that is the area outside the curtilage, varied from about a tenth to about a sixth. A figure of about £4,000 per acre also seemed appropriate for neighbourhood facilities, other than the shopping and service core, and perhaps £6,000 for industrial estates, where the roads would take greater loads. In both cases areas of playing fields and landscaping would be excluded and about a sixth of the area would be developed with roads and paving. The costs per acre of shopping and service cores developed at ground level were estimated at about £13,000, allowing for access roads behind the premises, and paving and access to their fronts. (About half the total area might be developed with roads and paving, but standards would be higher than in other areas.) All these figures would be about 50 per cent higher if the development took place on land which had been developed previously. The need to move existing services, to operate with services already in the ground, to remove existing paved areas and other works, and to develop on made-up ground, would all add to the cost.

Decked shopping and service cores were about five times as expensive as cores developed on the ground, that is they cost about £65,000 per acre at 1967 prices.[2] The largest additional cost was, of course, the concrete deck which carries the shopping, service and circulation space. Paved surfaces, lighting and screen walls have also to be provided on

[1] Stone, *Housing, Town Development, Land and Costs.*
[2] This was based on confidential information and was consistent with such published data as were available; see R. Steel, 'Town development: roads and economics', *Journal of the Institution of Highway Engineers*, vol. 12, March 1965 and London County Council, *The Planning of a New Town*, London, 1961.

Table 9.9. *The costs of car parks in central areas
per 10,000 population*

	Form of parking			Parking places
	Ground-level	Multi-storey	Decked	
Cost per place	£50	£500	£300	
	(£ thousands, 1967 prices)			
Fully centralised	60	599	359	*1197*
Partly centralised				
Town centre	12	119	71	*237*
District centres	44	440	264	*879*
Decentralised				
Town centre	40	399	239	*798*
Neighbourhood centres	17	..	..	*336*

SOURCES: table 6.20; NIESR estimates.

Note: Decked parking implies a main deck carrying shops with parking on sub-decks.

and under the decks, and vertical circulation between the ground and
the decks. There would, of course, be space available under the main
deck for parking.

Numbers of parking spaces estimated for the three systems of central
area provision were shown in table 6.20. An area of 250 square feet is
adequate for each car including standing space and access. The price
depends on the form of parking (table 9.9): for hardstanding in 1967
it was about £50 per vehicle; for multi-storey parking an average figure
of £500 seemed reasonable, unless extra space under decks could be
obtained by building sub-decks, which would reduce average costs per
car to about £300.

The larger the settlement and the more facilities there are within the
core of the town centre, the greater the area of development and the
further ground-level car-parking would be on average from the shopping
core; the distance to walk might be up to a quarter of a mile depending
on the size and form of the settlement. Multi-storey car parks, or parking
under decked shopping and service cores, would reduce this distance –
the former at least four-fold, while the latter would enable all cars to be
parked beneath the shopping and service core. Although multi-storey
car parks cost about ten times as much as hardstanding on the ground,
they occupy only about a fifth of the land. Thus the cost per acre of land
saved is about £100,000, and the figure for decking and two-level car-
parking is similar.

THE COSTS OF LAND

The price of land is determined by the use to which it can be put, its location, physical quality and existing development. The price of an acre of residential land is related linearly to density and exponentially to the distance from the centre of the region. In the South East, where the central area of London is dominant, density and distance accounted for 90 per cent of the variation in price per acre recorded for the period 1960–2.[1]

Under the Town and County Planning Act, 1959, authorities acquiring land would pay the open market price – the price the land would fetch in its current use or with the planning consent deemed obtainable, whichever is the greater – but no account would be taken of proposed development such as new towns or similar comprehensive schemes. The price would thus vary considerably with the location of the settlement. In a rural situation, undeveloped land, even with planning consent, if some miles from a substantial centre of employment and without good communications or main services, was probably not worth more than £500 an acre in 1967, that is not much more than its agricultural value. This would probably be an appropriate figure for a town built in a greenfield situation. In a village near a prosperous but not large centre of employment, for example, a free-standing town of something over 100,000 population in a rural part of the country, sites ripe for development along existing roads with services might have sold for £5,000 an acre, but a large proportion of the land to be acquired for town development would not have access to roads or services, and would be worth little more than its agricultural value. Thus, overall, £2,000 an acre might be appropriate. In an urban situation, in a prosperous area where the demand for sites was heavy, the cost of acquiring land would be much higher. Most land would be valued as though it were ripe for development, and the overall price in 1967 might have been about £5,000 an acre.[2]

The amount of land required was 557 acres per 10,000 persons (table 5.1). In a rural situation this would cost £279,000, in a semi-rural or village situation it might cost £1,114,000, and in an urban situation £2,790,000. To these figures 10 per cent would have to be added for fees etc.

[1] P. A. Stone, 'The price of sites for residential building', *The Property Developer*, 1964.

[2] Where existing urban areas were to be incorporated in planned development some built up development would have to be acquired. Areas of sound housing might have cost, in 1967, about £40,000 an acre, areas of industry might have cost twice as much, while areas of commerce could have cost three or four times as much – depending, of course, on their future potential.

RESIDENTIAL AREAS

Housing density is one of the major factors of town form through its effects on the costs of dwellings. Whereas blocks of flats and maisonettes can be developed at any density, houses become less practical as density increases. Generally, the higher the density the greater the proportion of flatted dwellings, and particularly of high flatted blocks. However, detached houses cost more than terraced houses, and low-density housing is likely to be of a higher standard, so that the curve of costs per dwelling plotted against density may be U-shaped. At the occupation rates assumed, the building costs of housing increase more than proportionately to density – for an increase from 30 to 50 persons per acre by about 10 per cent, and from 50 to 75 persons per acre by about 14 per cent, with a further 22 per cent from 75 to 100 persons per acre (table 9.10).

Table 9.10. *Housing: land and capital costs[a] per 10,000 persons*

Density per acre		Housing form[b]	Building costs	Site area	Development cost	Land cost[c]	Total capital costs
Persons	Rooms						
			(£m)	(acres)	(£m)	(£m)	(£m)
30	41	100 : 0 : 0	9·52	333	1·11	0·67	11·30
37	51	80 : 20 : 0	9·73	270	0·97	0·54	11·24
50	68	60 : 30 : 10	10·47	200	0·76	0·40	11·63
75	102	20 : 50 : 30	11·95	133	0·50	0·27	12·72
100	137	0 : 25 : 75	14·54	100	0·42	0·20	15·16

SOURCES: tables 9.2 and 9.3; NIESR estimates.
[a] At 1967 prices.
[b] Percentages of houses:low flats:high flats.
[c] At £2,000 an acre.

Corner-shops are usually provided in the residential areas at a rate varying with the development policy. It was assumed for these studies that there would be 1 square foot per resident, so that costs per 10,000 persons would be £56,000 for buildings and £3,000 for development, making a total of £59,000 to be added to the figures in the table in calculating total capital costs of residential areas.

As density increases, although building costs rise the costs of estate development fall; the fall was from £1·11 million per 10,000 at 30 persons per acre to £760,000 at 50 persons per acre (table 9.10). The amount of land required also falls as density increases, but this does not normally result in a proportionate fall in land costs, because land is usually purchased with planning consent for the erection of a given number of dwellings and the price per acre depends on this consent;[1]

[1] Stone, 'The price of sites for residential building'.

with increases in density the price per acre increases linearly and site costs per dwelling fall hyperbolically. However, the net effect is not big; for example the price per dwelling would fall by only about 20 per cent between densities of 15 and 40 dwellings per acre. Location is the major cause of varying land prices, which may be from £500 to £5,000 an acre without any standing development (see page 113 above). Taking £2,000 per acre and varying the housing density from 30 to 100 persons per acre resulted in a range of land costs as shown in table 9.10.

SCHOOLS AND COLLEGES

Costs of site development were included with building costs for schools and colleges (table 9.5). At this point it was therefore only necessary to add on land costs, which at £2,000 per acre would be £82,000 per 10,000 persons for all schools. The land for a college of further education would cost an extra £14,000 in a settlement for 100,000 persons, and £35,000 in a settlement for 250,000. Thus in the two larger settlements total capital costs of educational facilities per 10,000 persons would be about £1,062,000.

INDUSTRIAL AREAS

Most manufacturing industry, all warehousing, the offices and work-

Table 9.11. *Industrial areas: land and capital costs[a]*
per 10,000 population

	Site area (acres)	Costs (£000s)
Buildings		
Manufacturing (part)[b]	⎫	⎧ 1926
Workshops and stores[c]	⎬ 28	⎨ 98
Warehouses[c]		78
Offices[d]	⎭	⎩ 36
Public utilities	21	20[e]
Total	49	2158
Roads	8	.. [f]
Land @ £2,000 per acre		114
Development @ £6,000 per acre		342
TOTAL	57	2614

SOURCES: tables 5.1, 9.6 and 9.7.
[a] At 1967 prices.
[b] Part only, balance in central area.
[c] For other service industry as defined in table 9.7.
[d] See text.
[e] Refuse disposal plant, also included in table 9.15.
[f] Land and development costs for roads included in the overall figures for the area.

shops of construction firms, and of transport and communication firms and organisations, and the workshops and stores of the local authority were assumed to be located in the industrial areas; also terminal works for the public utilities. The cost of buildings included hardstanding for workers' cars (0·62 cars per worker, see table 6.20). Except for the refuse disposal plant, separate costs of buildings and works for the public utilities were not obtainable. The total cost per 10,000 persons was £2,614,000 (table 9.11).

CENTRAL AREAS

The central area facilities were defined as all those not expressly considered elsewhere. They were of two kinds, facilities which were essentially central and those which could be provided in the residential areas. The first group comprised the central core of shopping and service trades, public buildings, offices and other central employment facilities, central parking facilities, access roads and perhaps public gardens. The second group consisted of social and communal buildings such as churches, social clubs and youth centres, residential institutions, hotels and similar buildings, electric sub-stations, open space and incidental landscaped areas and the roads serving them. No hard and fast division was possible: the form of settlement and local requirements would determine the distribution in each case.

It was assumed that a given population would require the same amount of goods and services irrespective of the locations in which they were supplied. Overall floor areas for each facility would change only with a change in the output per square foot of floor area. This might occur if buildings were not sufficiently adaptable to changing needs and is probably more likely for shopping than for other types of central area function. Clearly, there is a practical minimum to the size of a shop, below which floor area cannot be scaled down with turnover, so that in smaller shopping centres, after the possibilities of combining a greater range of goods have been exhausted, turnover per square foot is likely to be lower. Moreover, it is possible to use more efficient methods in larger shops. Probably therefore less floor area of shopping would be needed in settlements where it was organised in larger centres, although this potential would only be realised if the shop operators possessed managerial ability and capital.

No operational studies have been carried out, so no measure of these potential differences was available. Rents and other indicators of turnover per square foot reflect present and historical conditions rather than potential. Total floor areas and costs were therefore distributed between the different centres on the basis of the best data available (chapter 6). The major effect of different arrangements would be on the

Table 9.12. *Central area facilities: land and capital costs[a]*
per 10,000 population

	Building costs	Fully central-ised	Partly centralised		Decentralised	
			Town centre	District centre	Town centre	Neighbourhood centre
	(£000s)			(acres)		
Central area						
Shopping	409					
Services	548	17·1	2·0	15·1	5·1	12·0
Offices	623					
Other buildings[b]	464					
Parking[c]	—	6·9	1·4	5·1	4·6	1·9
Roads	—	5·0	0·5	3·8	1·0	3·0
Gardens	—	1·0	0·1	0·9	0·1	0·9
Residential area						
Social buildings		3·6		3·6		3·6
Residential institutions,	298					
hotels, etc.		4·0		4·0		4·0
Electricity substations	—	1·0		1·0		1·0
Open space	—	4·0		4·0		4·0
Roads	—	5·0		5·5		6·0
Incidental space	—	2·4		3·0		2·8
Total	2342	50·0		50·0		50·0
				(£ thousands)		
Land costs		100		100		100
Development costs						
Basic		200		200		200
Additional						
Central cores		199	23	170	55	135
Parking[c]		60	12	44	40	17
Central gardens		1	—	1	—	1
Open space		5		5		5
Total		465		455		453
Total capital costs		2907		2897		2895

SOURCES: tables 9.4, 9.7 and 9.8; NIESR estimates.

[a] At 1967 prices.
[b] Including £177,000 for manufacturing buildings not in the industrial area.
[c] Car-parking assumed at ground level.

use of cars for shopping: with more shopping close to home, cars would be used less, and costs of car parks would be lower (table 9.12).

The figures in table 9.12 relate to a settlement of average status, but if it had only subordinate status less service industry and offices would be attracted. The effect is difficult to quantify, but variations in costs,

Table 9.13. *The effect of status on costs of central area facilities*[a]
per 10,000 population

£ thousands, 1967 prices

	Subordinate	Average	Predominant
Building costs			
Shops[b]	252	465	638
Service trades[c]	438	548	658
Offices[c]	500	623	748
Development costs			
Basic[d]	90	120	150
Central core[d]	150	199	250
Parking[e]	42	60	75

SOURCES: tables 6.7 and 9.12; NIESR estimates.

[a] Only those costs are shown for which an assumption about the variation with status has been made.
[b] Including corner-shops in housing areas.
[c] Variation assumed to be ±20%, see text.
[d] Variation assumed to be ±25%.
[e] In proportion to assumed variation in number of cars.

assuming that service trades and offices were reduced by 20 per cent, are shown in table 9.13, together with the comparable figures for a new settlement which became the predominant shopping and commercial centre in its area and thus attracted more service industry and offices. Most of the difference would be absorbed by the town centre, but some effects might spill over to the district centres. Certain other differences would be caused in the settlement structure: for example, the number of workers employed in shops, service industry and offices would interact with the numbers employed in other activities; the flow of commuters and of visitors into and out of the settlement would also change, and affect the size of the primary road network. Of course, the national effect might be quite small; additional facilities in one settlement would be largely offset by a reduction in another – only their location would be changed.

HOSPITALS AND INSTITUTIONS

An allowance was made for land for general and psychiatric hospitals at the rate of 7 acres per 10,000 persons. Total costs including site development were estimated at £469,000 per 10,000 persons. Only the two larger sizes of settlement have provision for such facilities and these would, in practice, cater for small settlements in the region around. Thus, nationally, the effect on these costs of varying settlement sizes would be small.

OPEN SPACE

Open space was assumed to include facilities for all types of recreation which take place in the open air and all land not developed with buildings or for transport or public utility services. This space would be sited in various parts of the settlement, with a total area of 100 acres per 10,000 persons, 5 acres of which were in central areas (table 9.14). The capital cost excluding the part in central areas would be about £175,000 per 10,000 persons for buildings and development and £190,000 for land. In addition, there would be another £6,000 for development in the central area, and £10,000 for a further 5 acres of land, which are already included in the costs in table 9.12.

Table 9.14. *Open space: land and capital costs*[a]
per 10,000 population

	Building cost	Site area	Land cost[b]	Development cost[c]	Total capital costs
	(£000s)	(acres)	(£000s)	(£000s)	(£000s)
Golf courses	3	10	20	7	30
Parks and public gardens[d]	3	7	14	9	26
Stadium, hall, swimming bath	90	3	6	4	100
Playing fields					
In residential areas	6	37	74	24	104
In industrial areas	3	18	36	12	51
Landscaped areas					
In residential areas	—	10	20	7	27
In industrial areas	—	10	20	7	27
Total	105	95	190	70	365

SOURCE: NIESR estimates.

[a] At 1967 prices.
[b] At £2,000 an acre.
[c] At £1,300 an acre for parks and public gardens, and stadium etc.; at £650 an acre for landscaped areas, playing fields and golf courses.
[d] Excluding 5 acres of public gardens included in the central area.

PUBLIC UTILITIES

It could be argued that the distribution networks of the public utility services should be included in estate development. However, these costs are only borne by the developer in special cases; normally the public utility organisations pay and recover the costs through their charges to the consumers. The organisations are therefore not very interested in the costs of installing each part of their system; their annual capital

Table 9.15. *The capital costs of public utility services per 10,000 population*

£millions, 1967 prices

Electricity	0·78
Gas	0·12
Telephone	0·13
Refuse disposal	0·02
Sewerage	0·30[a]
Water	0·25
Total	1·60

SOURCE: NIESR estimates.

[a] Excluding estate sewers, included in development costs.

expenditure is determined largely by the expected level of demand, rather than by cost considerations.

Public utility systems can be divided into national (or at least regional) terminal works and supply grids, local terminal works and mains, and estate distribution services. Electricity, gas and telephone services are all supplied nationally or regionally by means of grids. While water is sometimes obtained from a distant source, generally there is a local supply. Sewage is also treated locally. The form of development is unlikely to have any effect on national and regional costs, although location might affect grid costs. Costing for the purposes of this study therefore commenced at the local terminals.

Clearly the planning of public utility networks is complex and it was not feasible to study it in detail. The plans of the model settlements were discussed with the public utility organisations, who planned and costed systems for electricity, gas and telephones in a range of sizes and forms of settlement. However, costs were thought to depend mainly on the standard of provision, and it was agreed to assume that in 1989 half the households would have electric central heating and half gas, and industrial loads would be double the current level. Allowance was made for a telephone to each dwelling and for the equivalent of one business line to every five domestic lines.

An average cost per head was accepted in all cases (table 9.15). For electricity services the maximum difference in costs per person between different forms and sizes of settlement was less than 3 per cent, which was thought to be within the margins of error. The variations in costs per head for gas services were larger, up to 5 per cent, but again lacked consistency and could be regarded as insignificant since the total cost per head was so small. The telephone authority was unable to establish any cost difference per head over the range of settlements.

Costs per head for drainage and for sewerage fall sharply with increases in capacity from 1,000 to 5,000 persons but then flatten out. For larger districts, over 50,000 persons, costs per head change very little.[1] The situation for water supply is not dissimilar. Thus, except for very small districts, costs per head are not significantly affected by size, and since small settlements often combine to operate joint works and obtain the economies of scale, again a single figure seemed appropriate (table 9.15).

For all utilities, costs of estate services would be affected by density, but the differences over the range of densities considered in this study would be small – not more than about £3 per head for an increase in net residential density of 5 persons per acre.

The land required for public utility services had already been accounted for in the separate areas. The total costs per 10,000 persons for all public utility services were estimated at £1·60 million (table 9.15).

TOTAL CAPITAL COSTS

The total costs of buildings per head of population were about £1,580 (table 9.16), nearly two thirds of it accounted for by housing. If the housing was developed at 100 instead of 37 persons per acre its cost would increase by about 50 per cent, and the total cost of buildings would rise by a third, with housing increased to three quarters of the total. The costs of civil engineering work for the same population would be about £4·6 million, in which the main road network is the most variable item. The form and costs of main roads, that is the distributor roads, were discussed in detail in chapter 8. While they could generally be accommodated in an area of 37 acres per 10,000 persons, their costs would be very variable, ranging from about £60 to £150 per head (table 9.16). However, an internal railway system could be twice as expensive (see chapter 11 below), and could increase civil engineering costs by 50 per cent or the total construction costs by over 10 per cent. Land costs were also very variable, adding from a little over 1 per cent to about 15 per cent to the total costs of a settlement.

An examination of the incidence of fees, design and administrative costs, and interest during construction suggested that about 10 per cent was appropriate. This was added to total construction and land costs, and gave total capital costs which were estimated at between £2,329 and £2,577 per person (table 9.16). The sources of this variation were

---

[1] C. B. Townsend, 'The economics of waste water treatment', *Proceedings of the Institution of Civil Engineers*, vol. 15, no. 3, March 1960.

Table 9.16. *Total capital costs of constructing a new settlement*

£s per head, 1967 prices

	Residential areas[a]	Industrial areas	Central areas	Other areas	Total
Buildings					
Housing	973^{-21}_{+74}	—	—	—	973^{-21}_{+47}
Shops and retail services	6	—	96^b	—	102
Other commercial	—	23	91^c	—	114
Social and institutional	—	—	30^d	—	30
Factories	—	192	18	—	210
Schools and colleges	30	—	—	68^e	98
Recreational	—	—	—	10	10
Hospitals	—	—	—	45^f	45
Total	1009^{-21}_{+74}	215	235	123	1582^{-21}_{+74}
Civil engineering					
Residential development	97^{+14}_{-21}	—	—	—	97^{+14}_{-21}
Non-residential development	3	36	46^g	2	87
Main roads	—	—	—	115^h	115^h
Public utilities	—	—	—	158	158
Total	100^{+14}_{-21}	36	46	275	457^{+14}_{-21}
Total construction	1109^{-7}_{+53}	251	281	398	2039^{-7}_{+53}
Fees and interest[i]	111^{-1}_{+5}	25	28	40	204^{-1}_{+5}
Land (including fees and interest thereon)[j]	73^{+144}_{-58}	19^{+28}_{-14}	11^{+17}_{-8}	20^{+30}_{-15}	123^{+219}_{-95}
TOTAL CAPITAL COSTS	1293^{+136}_{-0}	295^{+28}_{-14}	320^{+17}_{-8}	458^{+30}_{-15}	2366^{+211}_{-37}

SOURCES: tables 9.10, 9.11, 9.12, 9.14 and 9.15.

[a] At density 37 ppa, with top differences for 30 ppa and lower differences for 50 ppa.

[b] Would be divided between town centre and others, 17:79 in a partly centralised settlement, 57:39 in a decentralised settlement.

[c] Would be divided between town centre and others, 37:54 in a partly centralised settlement, 67:24 in a decentralised settlement.

[d] Though classified as 'central area facilities' could actually be located in the residential areas; see table 9.12.

[e] Includes a college of further education as for a 100,000 person settlement.

[f] Includes a hospital as for a 100,000 person settlement.

[g] For a partly centralised settlement: would be £1 a head higher in a centralised settlement or lower in a decentralised settlement.

[h] Would vary with all the factors of settlement form, possibly by +37 or −55.

[i] At 10% of total construction.

[j] At £2,000 per acre, with top differences for £5,000 per acre and lower differences for £500 per acre.

the price of land and the density and form of the component areas of the settlement. The interactions between the size and form of the settlement and the main road networks could cause additional variations to perhaps a range of £2,270 to £2,610. Variations might also arise from the size and form of the settlement in relation to the facilities, from differences in regional status, from variations in the structure and activities of the population at maturity, and from prediction errors.

CHAPTER 10

THE COSTS OF TRAVELLING TO WORK

OPERATING COSTS OF PRIVATE CARS

In 1967 when the estimates were made, the typical private vehicle was a car of 1,000 cubic centimetres engine size, with standing charges of about £170 a year made up as follows:[1]

Licence	£17.50
Insurance	24.00
Driving licence	0.50
Amortisation	80.00
Rates on garage	22.00
Garage rent	26.00
	£170.00

The average annual mileage was 7,400,[2] giving standing costs per mile of 2.3p. Typical running costs were 1.25p per mile, of which over half was for petrol and more than a third for servicing and repairs;[1] thus the total cost per mile was about 3.55p. At an average occupancy rate of 1·3 persons per car (chapter 7) and an average overall speed of 30 miles per hour (as assumed for cars on the roads of the model settlements), the cost per head would be about 82p an hour. Average earnings were then about 40p an hour, so that if the time spent travelling was valued at the same rate as time spent working,[3] the cost per head for the vehicle and travelling time would be £1.22 an hour—just over 2p a minute.

The total operating costs of private cars cannot be determined exactly: they depend on the purpose of the journey and on the way the drivers and passengers value their costs. If a private car is regarded as an essential for satisfactory living, the standing charges should not be included in the costs of the journey to work and the hourly vehicle costs per head would be 29p instead of 82p. Some studies of the way travellers save time on their journey to work suggest that travelling

[1] Hamlyn Group, *Commercial Motor Tables of Operating Costs for Goods and Passenger Vehicles*, 1967.
[2] DSIR, *Factors affecting the amount of Travel.*
[3] M. E. Beesley, 'The value of time spent in travelling: some new evidence', *Economica*, vol. 32, no. 126, May 1965.

time is valued at only half the earning rate,[1] or drivers might value time spent driving their own vehicle at less than time travelling on public transport. Moreover, car owners are likely to earn more than the average wage.

OPERATING COSTS OF BUSES

The largest size of bus shows considerable economies in operating costs, which are only doubled by a five-fold increase in capacity.[2] None of the cost elements increases in proportion to size and the largest, the crew, is constant except with conventional operation for very small buses. (Buses of all sizes can be operated with a crew of only one, although boarding times tend to increase with size.) Peak demand determines the capacity required and a few large buses are likely to meet requirements more cheaply, despite low use in off-peak periods, than more, smaller buses. Smaller buses would, of course, allow an improved service, but the frequency feasible with large buses was adequate in the model settlements, except perhaps when used by only 10 per cent of workers.

Weekly mileage was estimated at about 500, and for a 70-seat bus weekly operating costs would be about £94, or £132 including administration.[2] Total costs per mile would therefore be 26.4p and, at a typical speed of 10.9 miles per hour during the peak period, costs per hour would be £2.88. About 28 passengers on average would be carried per bus, so that for each passenger these costs would be about 10.3p per hour, or 50.3p with travelling time valued at the earnings rate (1.2p less if there was no conductor).

COMPARATIVE TRAVELLING COSTS

In London and other conurbations the speeds of buses and of private cars are not very different, but in the model settlements cars would travel about three times as fast. It would take longer to walk to a bus stop than to reach that point by car, and some waiting for buses would be unavoidable. It is unlikely to be much quicker to walk from the bus stop than to park and walk from a conveniently sited car park. Hence, unless buses were deliberately favoured, for example by bus routes shorter than the roads, or by siting car parks away from homes and jobs, bus journeys would probably take rather over twice the time by car. If travelling time was valued as time at work, travelling by bus would at best break even with travelling by car. The lower travelling time was valued, the more favourable to buses would be the comparison but, if running costs only were used for cars, they would be cheaper than buses even if time had little value.

[1] Beesley, 'The value of time spent in travelling'.　　[2] *Commercial Motor Tables*, 1967.

Table 10.1. *Annual travelling costs in individual settlements*

Settlement	Traffic Tanner n	Modal split[b]	Peaking factor	Travelling costs[a] in settlements for: 50,000 persons	100,000 persons	250,000 persons 75 vertices	149 vertices
Rectangular[c]			(%)	($£$s per head, 1967 prices)			
Decentralised[d]	0·0	1·6	62	35[e]	41	60	..
	0·0	1·4	73	39	47	70	..
	0·5	1·4	62	36	45	65	..
	0·5	1·4	73	36	45	65	..
	1·0	1·4	73	30	41	56	..
Partly centralised[f]	0·0	1·6	62	..	46	68	..
	0·5	1·6	62	..	42	63	..
Centralised[f]	0·0	1·6	62	38	47	..	..
Star[g]							
Decentralised	0·0	1·6	62	40	54	..	75
Partly centralised	0·0	1·6	62	..	50	..	76
	0·5	1·6	62	..	47	..	70
Centralised	0·0	1·6	62	40	50	..	..
Linear[h]							
Decentralised	0·0	1·6	62	42	57	97	84
	0·5	1·6	62	..	..	88	75
Partly centralised	0·0	1·6	62	39	55	..	81
	0·5	1·6	62	..	52	..	73
Centralised	0·0	1·6	62	40	52	..	..
	0·5	1·6	62	..	51	..	..

SOURCE: NIESR estimates.

[a] Including costs of vehicle and of travelling time, and terminal costs only within the settlement.

[b] PCU index.

[c] Rectangular settlements have grid road systems.

[b] For sub-form (B) of a rectangular settlement (see chart 5.4).

[e] The corresponding cost using sub-form (A) would be £33.

[f] For sub-form (A) of a rectangular settlement (see chart 5.4).

[g] Star settlements have radial road systems.

[h] For 1-strand roads only: costs for 2 and 3 strands in table 10.6.

The above comparisons are not, of course, conclusive, since if fewer cars were used there would be savings on road construction and parking costs. Moreover, the costs include transfer items, for which an allowance is necessary.[1] Total costs of public and private transport are compared in chapter 11.

[1] The figures given are at market prices, containing various elements – purchase tax, fuel tax, road tax and local rates – which must be removed to obtain the costs in terms of resources. This reduces total costs per head of travelling by car to 49p an hour (or 18p for running costs only) as compared with market costs of 82p and 29p respectively. For buses, hourly operating costs, including administration, would be 9·2p per passenger as compared

COSTS OF THE JOURNEY TO WORK

The total cost of the journey to work by car was taken as £1.22 per hour.[1] The corresponding figure for the journey by bus was taken as 50.3p per hour.[2] The EGTAC programme could only cost journeys expressed in PCU–miles, so that the meaning of the cost varied with the modal split. These travelling costs per hour imply, with a modal split index of 1·6, that travelling time was valued at about 70 per cent of average earnings; with a modal split index of 4·0 the implication was that travelling time was valued at only 25 per cent of average earnings. The journey to work would cost only 48.7p an hour, less than half the figure generally used in this study, if the car was valued at marginal cost and time at half average earnings.

On the costing basis set out above, the annual costs per head of the journey to work varied from about £35 to £90 (table 10.1). These figures included an allowance for journeys on the access roads and hence gave a door-to-door cost. The variation was much greater than in road construction costs and, as annual costs would need to be multiplied by a factor of between 16 and 20 to convert them to their equivalent capital costs, travelling costs, even at marginal rates, would be 8 to 10 times as important as road construction costs. It will be appreciated that, as these figures were for the journey to work, they applied only to working members of the population and not to all the inhabitants of the settlement. The other inhabitants and workers on non-work journeys would have their own travelling costs.

SETTLEMENT SIZE AND TRAVELLING COSTS

The results of the model studies were remarkably consistent (chart 10.1). Travelling costs rose much more steeply with the size of settlement than road construction costs, but for both the rate of increase declined with size. In interpreting the figures it must be remembered that the number of employment areas does not increase in proportion to the size of settlement. Average travelling costs per head were 22 per cent lower in settlements for 50,000 than in those for 100,000, and nearly 50 per cent higher in settlements for 250,000 (table 10.2). The costs rose most with size in linear settlements and least in rectangular ones; also least in centralised settlements and most in partly centralised ones.

with 10·3p, so that travelling by car compares even more favourably with buses at factor cost than at market prices.

[1] The journey to work implies journeys both to and from work, and this cost is calculated at market prices, with time valued at 40p an hour.

[2] The costs of a journey to work would be about the same by bus or by car because the former would take more than twice as long as the latter.

Chart 10.1. *Travelling costs and settlement factors*

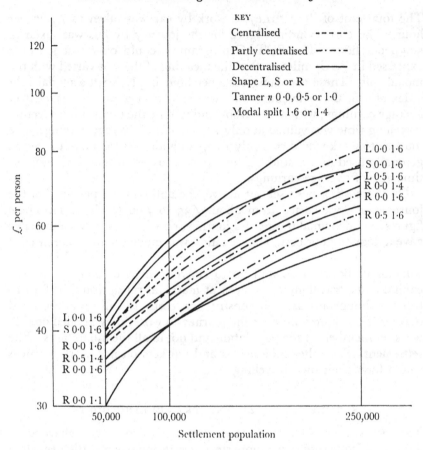

SOURCE: table 10.1.

Note: Costs at 1967 prices; shapes – L = linear, S = star, R = rectangular.

The number of vertices used in the traffic programme had more effect on travelling costs than on road construction costs: travelling costs fell about 13 per cent in two linear, 250,000 person settlements when the number of vertices was increased from 75 to 149 (table 10.1). In the largest rectangular settlements there was probably a substantial upward bias due to the shortage of vertices in those tests, so that the increase in travelling costs was probably considerably less for rectangular settlements than for other shapes. It also seems likely that rectangular settlements would retain their advantage in much larger sizes than those examined here.

Table 10.2. *Settlement size and annual travelling costs*

Settlement	Traffic			Variations of costs in settlements for:			
	Tanner *n*	Modal split	Peaking factor	50,000 persons	100,000 persons	250,000 persons	
						75 vertices	149 vertices
			(%)		(*percentages*)		
Rectangular							
Decentralised	0·0	1·6	62	85	100	146	..
	0·0	1·4	73	83	100	149	..
	0·5	1·4	62	80	100	144	..
	0·5	1·4	73	80	100	144	..
	1·0	1·4	73	73	100	137	..
Partly centralised	0·0	1·6	62	..	100	148	..
	0·5	1·6	62	..	100	150	..
Centralised	0·0	1·6	62	81	100	..	..
Star							
Decentralised	0·0	1·6	62	74	100	..	139
Partly centralised	0·0	1·6	62	..	100	..	152
	0·5	1·6	62	..	100	..	149
Centralised	0·0	1·6	62	80	100	..	..
Linear							
Decentralised	0·0	1·6	62	74	100	170	147
Partly centralised	0·0	1·6	62	71	100	..	147
	0·5	1·6	62	..	100	..	140
Centralised	0·0	1·6	62	77	100	..	..
Averages							
Decentralised settlements				78	100	144	
Partly centralised settlements				71	100	148	
Centralised settlements				79	100	..	
Rectangular settlements				80	100	145	
Star settlements				77	100	147	
Linear settlements				74	100	149	
Overall				78	100	146	

SOURCE: table 10.1.

The greater the deterrent effect of distance, the less travelling costs rose with the size of the settlement: with Tanner *n* = 0·5 they rose between settlements for 100,000 and 250,000 persons about 4 per cent less on average than with *n* = 0·0; when *n* = 1·0 they rose about 7 per cent less than with *n* = 0·5 (table 10.2).

SETTLEMENT SHAPE AND TRAVELLING COSTS

As would be expected travelling costs were lowest in rectangular settlements and highest in linear ones (table 10.3). In star settlements, average costs were 14 per cent higher than in rectangular ones; in linear settlements they were 23 per cent higher. These increases reflected the greater distances travelled in the less compact shapes. The decentralised form of star and linear settlements compared particularly unfavourably with the corresponding rectangular form because the grid road network in sub-form (B) of the rectangular settlements was more economic than the open box network in sub-form (A) (table 10.1; chart 5.4). The advantages in travelling costs of rectangular settlements over the others increased with the size.

Table 10.3. *Settlement shape and annual travelling costs*

Settlement	Tanner n^a	Variation of costs		
		Rectangular	Star	Linear
		(percentages)		
50,000 persons				
Decentralised	0·0	100	114	120
Centralised	0·0	100	105	105
100,000 persons				
Decentralised	0·0	100	132	139
Partly centralised	0·0	100	109	120
	0·5	100	112	124
Centralised	0·0	100	106	111
250,000 persons				
Decentralised	0·0	100	125	152[b]
Partly centralised	0·0	100	112	119
	0·5	100	111	116
Averages				
Settlements for				
50,000 persons		100	110	113
100,000 persons		100	115	124
250,000 persons		100	116	129
Decentralised settlements		100	124	137
Partly centralised settlements		100	111	120
Centralised settlements		100	106	108
Overall		100	114	123

SOURCE: table 10.1.

[a] Only results for standard modal split (1·6) and peaking factor (62%) included in this table.
[b] Average of results with 75 and 149 vertices on the EGTAC programme.

DEGREE OF CENTRALISATION AND TRAVELLING COSTS

The effects of centralisation on travelling costs were not as simple as those of size and shape, partly because of interactions, partly because differences in form were not as distinctive as in size and shape, and partly because of the different road networks in the sub-forms of rectangular settlements. A simple theoretical analysis illustrated the relation between centralisation of employment areas and the average length of the journey to work.

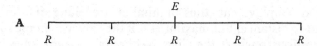

If the workers' homes were equally divided between five centres arranged linearly 1 mile apart and all employment was concentrated in the middle centre, the average journey to work would be

$$\tfrac{1}{5}(2+1+0+1+2) = 1\cdot20 \text{ miles.}$$

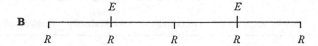

If the residential areas were as in A, but employment was in two centres as illustrated:

(i) if workers were employed in the nearest centre to their homes, the average journey to work would be

$$\tfrac{1}{5}(3 \times 1 + 2 \times 0) = 0\cdot60 \text{ miles;}$$

(ii) if workers were equally likely to be employed in any centre, the average journey to work would be

$$\frac{1}{5}\left(2 \times \frac{1+3}{2} + 2 \times \frac{0+2}{2} + \frac{1+1}{2}\right) = 1\cdot40 \text{ miles.}$$

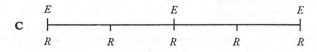

If the residential areas were as in A, but employment was in three centres as illustrated:

(i) if workers were employed in the nearest centre to their homes, the average journey to work would be

$$\tfrac{1}{5}(3 \times 0 + 2 \times 1) = 0\cdot40 \text{ miles};$$

(ii) if workers were equally likely to be employed in any centre, the average journey to work would be

$$\frac{1}{5}\left(2 \times \frac{0+2+4}{3} + 2 \times \frac{1+1+3}{3} + \frac{2+0+2}{3}\right) = 1\cdot73 \text{ miles.}$$

Centralised employment thus minimises travelling if workers are indifferent to distance, but maximises it if they always choose to work as close as possible to where they live. Neither of these extremes is true in practice; usually the longer the journey to work the fewer people are prepared to make it. Hence in smaller settlements centralisation is more

Table 10.4. *Degree of centralisation and annual travelling costs*

Settlement[a]	Variation of costs		
	Decentralised	Partly centralised	Centralised
50,000 persons			
Rectangular	100	..	109
Star	100	..	100
Linear	100	93	95
100,000 persons			
Rectangular	100	112	115
Star	100	93	93
Linear[b]	100	96	91
250,000 persons			
Rectangular	100	113	..
Star	100	101	..
Linear	100	96	..
Averages			
Settlements for			
50,000 persons	100	93	101
100,000 persons	100	100	100
250,000 persons	100	103	..
Rectangular settlements	100	113	112
Star settlements	100	97	97
Linear settlements	100	95	93
Overall	100	101	101

SOURCE: table 10.1.

[a] Only results for standard traffic conditions ($n = 0\cdot0$, modal split $= 1\cdot6$, peaking factor $= 62\%$) included in this table.

[b] With 149 vertices.

likely to minimise travelling costs, but the best arrangement in a particular case can only be found if the probabilities of workers travelling various distances are known. Also, centralisation implies a tidal flow of traffic to work and a network designed to operate such a system may not be convenient for other types of journey.

The centralised settlements' average costs for different shapes and overall were misleading because they did not include figures for the largest settlement (table 10.4). The size averages showed no significant variations, since in those for 50,000 persons the partly centralised average was based on a result for the linear shape only, and there was no variation by form in the average for 100,000 persons. The only shape that showed a consistent variation was rectangular, where in models for all sizes the decentralised form had lower costs than partly centralised or centralised, again probably because of the advantages of a grid road network over an open box type (chart 5.4). The physical difference between decentralised and partly centralised models lay, of course, in the location of central area employment and in the grouping of the residential areas; industrial areas were in the same positions in both forms.

DENSITY AND TRAVELLING COSTS

Uniform changes in density had an inverse effect on travelling costs, and this could be measured roughly by the percentage change in road lengths, even though traffic was not spread uniformly over all roads. Road lengths were found to vary by about 4 per cent for density changes from 37 persons per acre to either 30 or 50 persons per acre (chapter 8). The savings would be higher if densities increased more around the employment centres and less elsewhere, but unless densities around

Table 10.5. *Effect on travelling costs of eliminating neighbourhoods*

Size of settlement[a]	Neighbourhoods		Adjusted density[b]	Travelling costs[c]	
	Standard	Adjusted		Standard	Adjusted
(persons)			(ppa)	(£s per head)	
100,000	10	8	46·25	57	53
250,000	25 {	21	44·00	84[d]	81
	{	17	54·41	84[d]	86

SOURCE: NIESR estimates.

[a] Linear decentralised settlements.
[b] Standard density is 37 persons per acre.
[c] At 1967 prices.
[d] With 149 vertices.

the employment areas were very high the overall savings would be small.

The decrease in travelling costs from using higher densities to reduce the number of residential areas was also moderate (table 10.5). As with road construction costs, travelling costs actually increased when eight neighbourhoods were eliminated from a 250,000 person settlement, because this increased the average distance between homes and jobs.

THE ROAD NETWORK AND TRAVELLING COSTS

A single-strand primary road in a linear model lay some distance from the outer areas of the settlement. This could be improved by building multi-strand roads. Of the alternatives examined, two strands had much the lowest travelling costs (table 10.6). It seemed probable, however, that the saving resulted more from altering the shape of the settlement, which became more nearly rectangular, than from introducing a second strand (chart 8.3).

Table 10.6. *Effect on travelling costs of the number of strands in a road system*[a]

£s, 1967 prices

Number of strands	Grading of roads	Travelling costs per head
1	Primary	84
2	Primary, primary	70
3	Secondary, primary, secondary	81
	Primary, secondary, primary	85
	Primary, primary, primary	77

SOURCE: NIESR estimates.

[a] In a linear, decentralised settlement for 250,000 persons.

TRAVELLING COSTS IN CLUSTER SETTLEMENTS

If the length of the journey to work was no deterrent, and this might be nearly so in planned settlements of the future, annual travelling costs in developments for 250,000 persons would lie between £60 and £84 per head (table 10.7). With different assumptions for the costs of vehicles and of time these figures could be substantially lower (page 124 above), but the relative differences between the various settlements would be unchanged. Travelling costs varied much less between sub-regional forms than capital costs of main roads, but again the rectangular

Table 10.7. *Annual travelling costs[a] and sub-regional form*

£s per head, 1967 prices

Constituent settlements	Distance apart (miles)	Individual settlements[b] n		Clusters[c] Linear block (1 strand) n			Linear block (2 strands) n			Linear line n		Cross n		Neck-lace n
		0·0	0·5	0·0	0·5	1·0	0·0	0·5	1·0	0·0	1·0	0·0	1·0	1·0
Rectangular														
Decentralised	.	60[d]												
	1											68	32	
Partly centralised	–	68[d]	63[d]											
Centralised	–										33			
	1												31	
Star														
Decentralised	–	75									33			
Partly centralised	.	76												
Linear[e]														
Decentralised	–	84	75							77	29			32
	½											71	32	
	1			78	61	34	66	54	34		30		33	33
	2						77				29		33	32
Partly centralised	–	81	73								26			
	2					28								
	3					27								
	4					26								
Centralised	–										32			
	1					37								
	2					37								
	3					36								
Average	.	74	70	78	61	32	72	54	34	77	30	70	32	32

SOURCE: NIESR estimates.

[a] All with modal split 1·6 and peaking factor 62%.
[b] For 250,000 persons.
[c] Each of five equal settlements for 50,000 persons.
[d] With 75 vertices only.
[e] With 1-strand road networks.

decentralised form, particularly when it was an individual settlement, had the lowest costs. Among the clusters the cross and the two-strand linear block were marginally cheapest, which was to be expected since they had the shortest centre-to-centre di tances. The average estimates for some individual settlements were biased upwards by the limited number of vertices on which they were based. Similarly, the averages for linear block clusters reflected the higher costs of their linear constituent settlements. Nevertheless, since the differences were so small, clusters of suitable forms might exist with travelling costs little or no greater than individual settlements of the same size, even with no distance deterrent.

The influence on travelling costs of the deterrent effect of long journeys to work was greater in clusters, where inevitably a large proportion of jobs were some distance from home, than in individual settlements. In clusters, travelling costs fell by about 25 per cent when Tanner n increased from 0·0 to 0·5 and by over 50 per cent when n increased to 1·0 (table 10.7). The corresponding figures for individual settlements for 250,000 were 8 and 20 per cent (table 10.1). Thus the greater the deterrent effect of distance, the more the comparison of travelling costs would favour clusters.

When the deterrent was high (Tanner n = 1·0), travelling costs varied little between one form of cluster and another (table 10.7); a linear line cluster had slightly lower travelling costs than the other forms. The advantage depended on the distribution of journey lengths more than on the average journey, because the greater the reluctance to travel far the more short journeys would be substituted for long ones; the greater the dispersion of jobs and the more workers disliked long journeys, the more they would tend to work locally. In some cases when distances between constituent settlements increased, the fall in the number of long journeys more than compensated for the increased length of those still made to other settlements, and travelling costs fell (table 10.7).

Where the length of journey had a deterrent effect, clusters of the size examined had lower travelling costs than individual settlements, but also fewer accessible jobs. If the numbers prepared to work outside their own settlement were low, additional settlements could be added to the clusters without much effect on travelling costs per head. Since travelling costs in individual settlements rose strongly with size, even where the reluctance to travel was only slight, travelling costs would be less in large clusters than in large individual settlements. However this type of cluster would provide a narrower choice of jobs unless each settlement had a specialised range of employment and this might, if carried too far, produce economic instability.

CHAPTER 11

THE COSTS OF PUBLIC TRANSPORT:
BUSES AND RAILWAYS

PUBLIC TRANSPORT REQUIREMENTS

In comparisons between the costs of different forms of transport, it was necessary to combine costs of the track, whether roads or railways, costs of operating vehicles, including wages, and the value of passenger time. The use of public rather than private transport changes not only the form of transport but also the road requirements. The cost of transport depends, of course, on the way it is used and no comparison could be made without considering the pattern of the various uses.

Some people are prevented from driving a car by physical or legal factors, and some are disinclined to drive, or feel unable to afford a car of their own. These people may travel to work on foot, by bicycle, or on public transport. Even with considerable increases in car owner- ship, by 1989 at least 10 per cent of journeys to work would still probably be made by public transport (chapter 7), and a suitable service for this proportion of workers would be socially necessary. Public transport is subject to economies of scale, but costs per passenger do not necessarily fall with increases in the proportion of workers carried. The number of vehicles is usually determined by the peak load of the journey to work, so that the greater this is in relation to off-peak requirements, the lower the occupancy rate in off-peak periods and the higher the average costs per passenger. Usually the same fares are charged for peak and off-peak journeys, so that increases in peak loads normally result in a more frequent service rather than lower fares. However, while changes in the use of public transport may not have much effect on its running costs, they do affect the costs of the road network and of parking facilities.

The upper limit for the proportion of workers using public transport will be far below 100 per cent. Some will walk or cycle; others will need their cars for the journeys during the day, or to travel direct from work to other activities; others will consider it worth the cost to drive to work. Probably never more than 50 per cent of journeys to work will be by public transport.

BUSES AND THE ROAD NETWORK

The extent to which a bus service is used depends on its convenience, safety and cost. Distance and amenity of the walk to board a bus, the frequency of the service and the directness of the bus route all affect convenience, which is judged in comparison with the corresponding journey by car. It has been suggested that the comparative convenience of buses relative to cars should be increased by, for example, siting parking facilities as far away as bus stops, limiting parking and arranging bus routes far shorter than car routes. Such arrangements would, however, have a negative as well as a positive effect on the value of the settlement.

There are three ways in which bus routes can be provided: on the road system developed for general transport, on ordinary roads but with the routes shortened by special bus-only links, or on bus-only roads reserved entirely for buses. The convenience of bus routes and their use could be increased by designing the settlement to meet that end, but overall costs of the settlement might increase in consequence. In this study no attempt was made in planning the settlements to take account of the requirements of bus routes; rather bus routes were planned to meet the needs of the settlements already designed.

In the small settlements two continuous inter-linking bus routes appeared adequate. In large settlements where more routes were necessary, they were planned at right angles to each other or linking through the centre, so that no journey involved more than one change. The routes as far as possible avoided primary roads, on which there would be no stops, and passed through, or at least near, the commercial centres and other traffic generation points, such as industry, schools and hospitals (chart 5.5). Usually convenience could be improved by using the estate spine roads, and connecting their cul-de-sac ends by short narrow link roads (about 40 yards long). These links would cross the pedestrian ways, but safety could be maintained by treating the crossings as bus stations and preventing other traffic from using the links. These bus stations would be valuable interchange points between the pedestrian ways and the spine roads. Alternatively, special bus-only roads could be planned, which would avoid the use of estate roads by buses and provide a more convenient bus system. However, in most settlements, particularly those of any size, frequent crossings of the pedestrian ways and of minor and major roads would be unavoidable. The buses would generally not be so frequent (a maximum of 50 per hour in peak periods) as to justify crossings at grade for pedestrians or vehicles on minor roads. Crossings at grade would, however, be necessary for primary roads.

Conceivably a works or Peoria-type bus service could be developed, but this would have few advantages where each main employment area contained a large number of employers.

BUSES AND THE COST OF MAIN ROADS

Since cars on the journey to work carry on average only 1·1 to 1·3 persons, whilst a bus could carry about 70 and occupies only three times the road space required by a car, it is the proportion of people travelling by car, rather than by bus, which determines the road capacity required. If the proportion using cars fell from 80 to 25 per cent, with some increase in walking and cycling and a five-fold increase in the proportion travelling by bus, the PCU index for the modal split would increase from 1·6 to 4·0 (table 7.4). The effect on road capacity of how many walked or cycled would be small, and the same PCU index would be obtained with 27 per cent travelling by car and 63 per cent by bus.

The effect of a change in the modal split on the capital costs of the road system depends on the size and form of the settlement and on how far road capacity is fully utilised. In some settlements, particularly the smaller ones, the traffic on some routes would not utilise the capacity even of a two-lane road. In such circumstances, or if greater capacity was required for types of journey other than the journey to work, reductions in traffic to work by car might not decrease road specifications or costs.

In theory, savings on the capital costs of main roads of between £20 and £50 per head could be achieved by reducing the proportion travelling to work by car from 80 to 25–7 per cent (table 11.1). The savings tended to increase with the size of the settlement. These estimates were based on the assumption that the length of journey did not affect the choice of employment area. The greater the deterrent effect of a long journey, the lower the main road costs and the smaller the savings. The extent to which the road network could be reduced is, of course, limited by the capacity needed for other types of journey.

If fewer people used cars for the journey to work, the need for car parks and their costs would also be lower. A fall in the proportion of car users from 80 to 27 per cent would reduce from 62 to 21 the number of parking spaces required per 100 workers. In the industrial areas the direct saving of land would be 33, 66 and 164 acres in settlements for 50,000, 100,000 and 250,000 persons respectively. In addition small savings would arise from a tighter layout, making a total of between £12 and £15 per head. In the central areas more parking would be saved during the week than on Saturdays and the Saturday peak would now determine the parking required (table 6.20). The reduction would

Table 11.1. *The use of cars and buses for the journey to work:
effect on capital costs per head[a] of main roads*

Settlement[b]	Costs with modal split (PCU)		Reduction in costs[e]	
	1·6[c]	4·0[d]		
	(£)	(£)	(£)	(%)
50,000 persons				
Linear	80	58	22	28
100,000 persons				
Linear	101	68	33	33
Star	107	83	24	22
250,000 persons				
Linear	121	74	47	39
Rectangular	99	54	45	45

SOURCE: NIESR estimates.

[a] At 1967 prices.
[b] All decentralised with Tanner constants $\lambda = 0\cdot0$, $n = 0\cdot0$.
[c] 80% by car, 10% by bus, 10% walking or cycling.
[d] Either 25% by car, 50% by bus, 25% walking or cycling; or 27% by car, 63% by bus, 10% walking or cycling.
[e] No allowance for minimum road requirements for other journeys.

be 456 parking places per 10,000 persons, which would save about 2·6 acres and hence between £5 and £6 per person, or about five times as much on multi-storey parking. The theoretical overall savings on car parks would be of the order of £20 per head. Not all of this would be realised in practice, since without a land reserve created by the large areas used for parking, special reservations would be needed in case of changing requirements.

COSTS OF BUS LINKS AND BUS-ONLY ROADS

It was not possible to examine the provision of bus routes in detail for all the model settlements, but three different shapes of decentralised settlements for 50,000 persons were taken as examples.

If bus links were used, their total length would vary from 0·9 to 1·9 miles, costing about £50,000 to £120,000, or between £1 and just over £2 per head. Clearly this cost was small in relation to the possible savings from fewer workers using their cars.

The costs of bus-only roads (with two lanes and costing about £120,000 a mile) were estimated for the same model settlements. The lengths of the bus routes would be about 11, 12 and 16 miles in the three models (table 11.2), and these compared quite well with the figure of

Table 11.2. *Bus-only roads: capital costs per 10,000 population*

£ thousands, 1967 prices

Settlement	Cost of road[a]	Cost of crossings[b]	Total cost
Star[c]	372	78	450
Linear[c]	283	59	342
Rectangular[c]	266	78	344
Runcorn[d]	265	111	376

SOURCES: Ministry of Housing and Local Government, *New Towns Act 1965. Reports of the Development Corporations to March 31, 1970*; NIESR estimates.

[a] Two lanes at £119,260 per mile (see table 8.1).

[b] At £75,000 each for underpasses on crossings with primary roads and £6,260 each for traffic signals on other crossings.

[c] Model settlements, decentralised, for 50,000 persons.

[d] Population 90,000.

2·2 miles per 10,000 persons for Runcorn, which was designed for bus transport.[1] The bus road would cross the primary road in three or four places and there underpasses or bridges would be necessary; other crossings would be light-controlled. Total costs per person would vary from £34 to £45. While the Runcorn bus road is at the lower end of the range in length, it crosses the primary roads eleven times, making its overall cost £38 per head.

Thus, in the smaller settlements, the cost of a bus-only road would be similar to the savings obtained from reducing the use of cars for the journey to work by about two thirds. The bus-only roads would generally reduce traffic on ordinary roads too little to result in any saving in their construction costs. Of course, the bus-only road could be built as one lane only with passing places, which would save up to about a third of the cost, but this might not be very convenient and would probably reduce the speed of the buses.

THE ECONOMICS OF BUSES

If a worker owned a car in any case, so that only running costs were relevant in the comparison, he would be likely to find it cheaper to go to work by car than by bus (chart 11.1). This would be true even if he attached no value to the time spent in getting to work. If the car was purchased especially for the journey to work, which is not likely in many cases, the bus would be cheaper unless a very high value was put

[1] Ministry of Housing and Local Government, *New Towns Act 1965. Reports of the Development Corporations to March 31, 1970*, HC 64, London, HMSO, 1970.

Chart 11.1. *Comparative travelling costs^a of journeys by car and by bus*

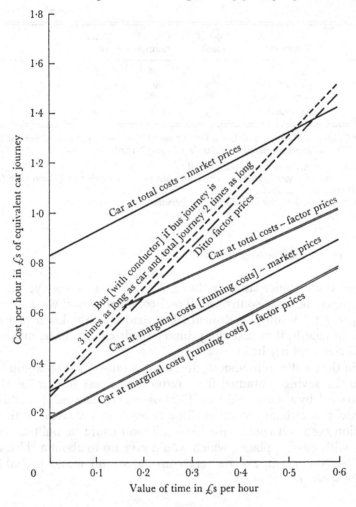

SOURCE: NIESR estimates.

^{a} At 1967 prices.

on travelling time. Bus fares could be reduced and buses made economic to more people by a subsidy, but this would only be justified economically if the total real costs of using buses were less than those of using cars.

If buses operated along the ordinary roads with short bus links, and the use of cars for the journey to work was reduced from 80 per cent to about a third of that level, then, assuming people were not deterred by the length of the journey to work, savings on construction of roads and car parks, and in land, might amount to between £40 and £70 per head. These would be maximum savings, the higher figure being for larger settlements, and their annual equivalents would be between £2 and £4. There would also be some savings on costs of road maintenance and servicing, and of accidents, and marginally less noise and fumes. In the absence of a detailed study, rough estimates suggested that these savings would be well under £1 a year per head. Thus total savings per head from the greater use of buses could not be higher than about 2p a day, or about 5p an hour actually spent on the journey to and from work, which by car is likely to average about 20 minutes a day. Buses are already subsidised at about twice this rate by the incidence of taxation (chapter 10), so that in real terms costs would be about the same for buses and cars if 50 per cent of workers travelled by bus. However even a subsidy of 5p a day would not compensate a car user charging only running costs unless he valued his time at less than 5p an hour.

Clearly the estimates were all far too tentative for conclusions to be drawn with much confidence. It appeared, however, that any economic advantages which buses might have over cars for the journey to work were likely to be minimal. A more intensive use of buses for the journey to work would enable a better service to be provided, which would make it more attractive, but costs and hence fares might be increased. Extra road capacity has the advantage of flexibility to absorb unexpected increases in traffic. Once the road system is established, it might perhaps be more economical to increase bus services than road capacity.

The problem in a new settlement is naturally very different from that in an existing town. In planning a new settlement the major traffic generators can be spread out to eliminate points of heavy traffic concentration, and roads and parking space can be provided for little more than their construction costs. Many existing towns, however, have developed in a highly centralised form with most of the large traffic generators concentrated in the middle. The amount of road and parking space required to meet current needs would cut heavily into space in the central area, so that either very expensive multi-storey redevelopment or the large-scale movement of existing users to other sites becomes necessary. This makes the real cost of roads and parking space probably five to six times as great as in a new settlement. Generally the additional costs of operating public transport rather than private cars would be far less than this. Of course, in the long run, existing buildings and development become obsolete, and it then becomes cheaper to resite the major traffic generators. The land released can be redeveloped so as to balance road capacity with the traffic likely to be generated in the area.

RAILWAY SYSTEMS IN DIFFERENT SETTLEMENTS

There appeared to be only two systems of tracked transport suitable for passenger transport in the settlements, either monorails or duorails. These can be compared with cars and buses if they are designed to provide services comparable in convenience, frequency and comfort. Convenience requires that the pick-up and setting down points should be close to homes and destinations; in the models as designed this implied a complex system of parallel tracks with interchange points, but convenience would be greater with a single loop of track with the developed areas arranged close around it.

The model settlements were examined to determine the track layout most suitable for each. Only settlements for 250,000 persons were considered, so that the alternative forms were partly centralised or decentralised. The former seemed the most appropriate for this exercise and in it three shapes of individual settlement (rectangular, star and linear) and a settlement cluster were examined. The rectangular shape was the most difficult to handle: in fact, it was found impossible to design a practical rail system for it. More success was achieved for the star shape, but to ensure that no one would live more than a quarter of a mile from a station (taken as a 5-minute walk) which was the standard adopted, four parallel routes had to be provided in each arm of the star, all linked through the settlement centre (chart 11.2). Similarly, in a linear settlement four parallel routes were necessary and, because of the length of a linear settlement of this size, seven cross-settlement links were also needed. Two parallel routes were adequate for a settlement cluster.

Clearly, better results could be obtained from a railway system if its form was determined first and the settlement planned around it. Under these conditions, a railway in the shape of figure of eight would make the maximum contribution to the movement of people with a minimum length of track and only one interchange station (chart 11.2). However, such a settlement would have to have much longer primary roads with many more junctions than the standard models.

A rail system of any kind would inevitably change the amenities of the settlement. Unless it was completely underground, it would be noisy and unsightly. Most monorails are overhead systems and these must intrude at least visually.

A railway built on the ground tends to divide the settlement into sectors unless frequent road and footpath crossings are provided. Level crossings reduce safety as well as the efficiency of all transport affected. Crossings under the track need greater clearance than bridges and use more land. If the noise is to be kept at an acceptable minimum, either

Chart 11.2. *Railway systems in various settlements[a]*
and a settlement cluster

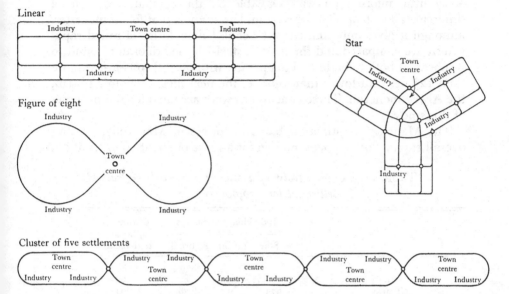

[a] All partly centralised for 250,000 persons.

considerable open space must be left between the railway and other development, or noise deflectors and absorbants, such as earthworks, must be provided around the track.

A railway in a cutting interferes less with roads and footpaths and creates fewer problems of noise, but still divides the settlement. Unless expensive retaining walls are built, the cutting takes about twice as much land as a track at ground level. Bridges over a cutting would be a little cheaper and would use less land; on the other hand, drainage would be expensive and public utility networks would be interrupted.

An overhead railway, although most expensive to build, requires least land and interferes least with freedom of access. On the other hand such a system is most intrusive visually and as a source of noise. It is difficult to alleviate the visual intrusion and, while the noise could be reduced by enclosure, this would be both expensive and an additional visual nuisance.

CAPITAL COSTS OF RAILWAYS

Very little information was available on the comparative costs of different rail systems. The most complete study is that for Manchester, although it gives only limited cost details.[1] Four forms of railed rapid transit are compared and the normal steel-wheeled duorail is found to be cheapest both to build and to operate, with overall costs-in-use more than 12½ per cent lower than those of the next most economic system, the Alweg monorail. These conclusions were accepted for the purposes of this study.

The Manchester estimates, based on prices in May 1967, give an overall capital cost of £53·6 million for a route of about 16 miles and a

Table 11.3. *Capital costs*[a] *of a railway in a partly centralised settlement for 250,000 persons*

	Individual settlements			Cluster of 5 linear settlements
	Star	Linear	Figure 8	
	(£ millions)			
Land[b]	1·35	1·23	0·87	1·02
Track[c]	37·61	33·57	26·36	27·04
Bridges	4·98	4·73	2·35	4·20
Yards and repair shops	2·52	2·52	2·52	2·52
Stations[d]	2·58	2·52	1·05	2·34
Signal equipment	6·47	5·78	4·54	4·65
Power supply	2·02	1·80	1·42	1·45
Total net cost	(57·53)	(52·15)	(39·11)	(43·22)
Engineering design[e]	6·90	6·26	4·69	5·19
Rolling stock	4·92	4·92	4·92	4·92
Total cost	69·35	63·33	48·72	53·33
	(£)	(£)	(£)	(£)
Capital costs per head	*277*	*253*	*195*	*213*
Capital costs per head				
excluding rolling stock	*258*	*234*	*175*	*194*

SOURCE: NIESR estimates.

[a] At May 1967 prices.

[b] At £2,000 per acre, including land for bridge approaches.

[c] In open cuttings. Route lengths: star 59 miles, linear 49 miles, figure of eight 38 miles and cluster 39 miles.

[d] At £30,000 each, and £60,000 for interchange stations, as follows:

	Star	Linear	Figure 8	Cluster
Stations	62	64	33	70
Interchange stations	12	10	1	4

[e] At 12% of total net cost.

[1] Manchester City Transport, *Manchester Rapid Transit Study*, Manchester, De Leuw, Cather & Partners in association with Hennessey, Chadwick, Oh Eocha & Partners, 1967.

design capacity of 10,000 persons per hour, about £5 million more than for the figure of eight system (table 11.3). The latter was nearly two and a half times as long but was costed as entirely in open cuttings, whereas the Manchester figure includes a contingency allowance of 15 per cent and provides for the track running underground for nearly half its length. Again, the station designs assumed here were much less elaborate than in the Manchester study, and land and property acquisition would be much cheaper in a new settlement than in Manchester. Since no contingency allowances were made here, the figures given in table 11.3 are under- rather than overestimates, but even so, the capital costs per head, approximately £200 to £260 excluding rolling stock, were about double those of the main road systems of the model settlements (chapter 8) and roads could only be partially replaced by railways.

The capacity of a rail system is very flexible; if required the system costed could carry three times the peak load assumed for design purposes. If the peak design capacity was raised from 10,000 to 30,000 passengers per hour, capital costs would only increase by 10 to 20 per cent,[1] and then capital costs per head of population would be reduced to about £80 or £100. However, this capacity would only be used if the settlement population was three quarters of a million rather than 250,000, and this would imply either a three-fold increase in the width of development on either side of the railway, so that some people would be 15, rather than 5, minutes walk from a station, or densities three times as great. The former would greatly reduce the convenience of the railway and the latter would greatly increase the costs of construction and maintenance of the settlement.

TRANSPORT SYSTEMS: CAPITAL COSTS
WITH AND WITHOUT RAILWAYS

No rail system in a settlement could eliminate the need for main roads; at best it would replace the use of roads for the journey to work and perhaps for some social and shopping journeys within the settlement. A main road system would still be needed for the movement of goods, for many services,[2] for some, perhaps most, shopping, recreational and social journeys within the settlement, and for all journeys out of the settlement. Moreover, if, as assumed, every household had at least one private car, there would be no saving on estate roads. A dual two-lane primary road system with roundabouts and a two-lane secondary road system with traffic lights at junctions would still be the minimum

[1] Manchester City Transport, *Manchester Rapid Transit Study*.
[2] E.g. furniture removal, maintenance, construction and ambulances, fire engines, etc.

requirements, with costs per head nearly £70 lower in a linear settlement than for main roads meeting the maximum demands of the
journey to work (that is assuming a random distribution of homes
and jobs). Thus, in a linear settlement for 250,000 persons the capital
costs of the transport system with a railway would be about £300
per head (£250 for the railway and £50 for the main roads), or
about £180 per head higher (150 per cent) than a main road system
alone.

While the railway in a figure of eight settlement would cost only
£195 per head (table 11.3), the main roads would be about 22 miles
longer than in a linear settlement, with many additional junctions, so
that these capital costs would be about £75 per head. Thus, to construct the combined transport system would still cost £150 per head
more (125 per cent) than the road system of a linear settlement.

The capital costs of a combined rail and road system in a star-shaped
settlement would compare with roads alone even less favourably than
in a linear settlement. The comparison in a cluster of settlements is a
little better, but the combined rail and road system would still cost about
twice as much as the road system required when distance is no deterrent
in the choice of jobs. The more extended the development, the less the
additional costs of a railway because, where homes and jobs are
distributed randomly, dispersion increases capital costs of roads more
than those of railways.

If the railway was accepted as convenient for the journey to work
and as close enough for driving to the station to be unnecessary, there
would be some saving on car parks, which might amount to about £20
per head. However, this would still leave rail systems as an expensive
addition to the capital costs of a settlement, especially as the figures
given are probably underestimates.

THE ECONOMICS OF RAILWAYS

In the Manchester study, buildings and structures were amortised over
60 years, signals and power supply over 30 years and rolling stock over
25 years, all at 6 per cent.[1] These assumptions were used to estimate
annual equivalent costs; running costs, except for administration and
overheads, were taken as proportional to the route mileage, that is
peak loads were assumed constant. Together these gave annual costs-
in-use which ranged from about £44 to £63 per worker (table 11.4).
Since the rail systems suitable for the different settlements varied mainly
in length, the costs-in-use differed in the same order as capital costs,
although the differences were less.

[1] Manchester City Transport, *Manchester Rapid Transit Study.*

Table 11.4. *Annual costs-in-use[a] of a railway in a partly
centralised settlement for 250,000 persons*

	Individual settlements			Cluster of 5 linear settlements
	Star	Linear	Figure 8	
	(£ millions)			
Annual equivalents[b]				
Land	0·09	0·08	0·06	0·07
Track, structures	3·31	3·01	2·24	2·51
Signals and power	0·70	0·62	0·49	0·50
Rolling stock	0·38	0·38	0·38	0·38
Total	4·48	4·09	3·17	3·46
Running costs				
Maintenance	1·10	0·92	0·72	0·73
Power	0·59	0·49	0·38	0·38
Labour	0·89	0·74	0·57	0·59
Administration and overheads	0·11	0·11	0·11	0·11
Total	2·69	2·26	1·78	1·81
Total costs-in-use	7·17	6·35	4·95	5·27
	(£)	(£)	(£)	(£)
Costs-in-use per worker[c]	*63·2*	*55·9*	*43·6*	*46·4*

SOURCE: NIESR estimates.

[a] At 1967 prices.
[b] Equivalents of capital costs in table 11.3.
[c] 113,500 workers, after an allowance for those living on the job.

To compare the annual costs of travelling to work by rail and by private car, it was necessary to include the value of travelling time (table 11.5). This was taken at half average earnings (20p an hour) and based on the time from leaving home to reaching the place of work.[1] Any such comparison also depends on the assumptions made about the use and ownership of cars. The total annual costs of the journey to work in a settlement with a railway exceeded those where cars had to be used, even when allowance was made for road costs, and when the running costs of the cars were charged (table 11.5). The rail system would, however, be cheaper if the car was purchased purely for the journey to work, since then annual standing charges of £170 (chapter 10) would have to be added to the running costs shown. In practice, most households would probably own a car whether it was used for the journey to work or not, so that standing charges should be excluded entirely; then costs by car would be half of rail costs or less. While the

[1] These figures cannot be directly compared with the costs given in table 10.1, because there the travelling time was charged at 70 per cent of average earnings, and vehicle costs were charged at 82p an hour, which includes standing charges *pro rata*. On the other hand, no charge was made for amortising the road or for its maintenance.

Table 11.5. *Annual costs of the journey to work
in settlements with and without railways*

£s per worker, 1967 prices

	Individual settlements			Cluster of 5 linear settlements
	Star	Linear	Figure 8	
Settlement with railway				
Costs-in-use of railway	63	56	44	46
Travelling time[a]	61	51	39	40
Costs-in-use of roads	3	3	5	3
Total	127	110	88	89
Settlement without railway				
Costs-in-use of roads	8	8	.	10
Costs of cars[b]				
(A) at full rates	70	78	.	72
(B) running costs only	35	39	.	36
Total: with (A)	78	86	.	82
with (B)	43	47	.	46

SOURCE: NIESR estimates.

[a] Assessed at 20p an hour on the assumptions:
  (i) that trains travelled at an average speed of 25 m.p.h.;
  (ii) that a change of trains involved 2 minutes' waiting;
  (iii) that walking from home to the station, and from the station to work each took
    5 minutes.
[b] Approximate figures, including travelling time at 20p an hour.

railway could also carry other types of traffic, it would do so less efficiently than a car, and the costs-in-use of those main roads needed still in a settlement with a railway made the comparison that much worse, as did the fact that, if anything, the rail costs were underestimated.

CHAPTER 12

FACTORS AFFECTING DEVELOPMENT COSTS

LAND PRICES AND DENSITY

Within the range of conditions considered in this book, total costs of developing a new settlement were most affected by the price of land, which could vary by a factor of ten with location and change total costs by over 6 per cent either way (table 9.16). On a rural site with land at £500 an acre, the cost per head of developing a settlement might be between £2,260 and £2,330, while on land ripe for development at £5,000 an acre, it might vary from £2,580 to £2,640. Of course, in the latter situation town expansion would be more likely than a new settlement.

Most buildings were in the residential, industrial and commercial areas, so that building density in these areas could have the greatest impact on the total costs of development. Traditional densities are about optimum, with costs rising below and, particularly, above this point. Density affects development costs in three ways: through the costs of building and estate development, through the amount of land used and through the costs of the main road system.

On virgin rural land a slight reduction in residential density, for example, from 37 to 30 persons per acre, might result in a small saving overall, but not unless the land was very cheap. On land at £2,000 an acre, increasing density to 50 persons per acre would add perhaps £40 per head to costs because more flats would probably have to be used, some of them in high blocks. At a given density the proportion of flats needed depends on the standards set; in theory houses only could be built at 50 persons per acre, but in practice this is unlikely over a whole settlement without a lower level of amenities than is generally acceptable. Some land in the residential area might be unsuitable for development and some local densities might be quite low, probably where the housing was to be owner-occupied. At £5,000 an acre, land costs per head would be about £30 higher at 30 than at 37 persons per acre; increasing density from 37 to 50 persons per acre would, at the same price, increase total costs of development only slightly, but if high flats were used to obtain very high densities the increase would be about 30 per cent. To save an acre of land might cost six to ten times its purchase price; moreover maintenance and management costs were also about 50 per cent higher for flatted blocks than for two storey houses.[1]

[1] Stone, *Housing, Town Development, Land and Costs.*

The cost per square foot of constructing factories also increases sharply if they are concrete-framed two-storey buildings rather than light-weight sheds. For deep buildings, costs rise less with the number of storeys than for narrow buildings such as housing, but an increase from two to seven storeys would add about 20 per cent to the costs.[1] Construction costs are not the only reason why most industrial buildings are usually single-storey: operating costs are often higher where production is on several floors; costs of internal transport and supervision are both likely to be affected; lighting costs are higher where natural light is only through side windows. Single-decked parking space is likely to be a more economic way of saving land in the industrial area, but even this, on land at £5,000 an acre, would increase costs by £14 per head of population.

In the commercial area, saving land might be secondary to the greater convenience of a more compact centre. The land required for the central core and parking area could be reduced by about a third by using either multi-storey parking or a shopping deck with two-level parking beneath. However, the land saved would not be worth more than 5 per cent of the cost of saving it, and on a virgin site costs would increase by over £50 per head of population. The best solution probably would be to build a centre initially with ground-level shopping and parking, which would be cheapest, easiest to plan, phase and develop, and extremely flexible; then the parking area could subsequently be decked or used for multi-storey development if the needs for commercial space or parking increased beyond expectation.

The residential areas usually take up about half the land in a settlement at basic densities, so that here savings in land could be greatest. Such savings could be used to reduce the size of the settlement and hence the length of the main roads. The effect of uniform changes in residential densities on the costs of main roads was quite small: about £2 per head for a decrease in density from 37 to 30 persons per acre, or for an increase from 37 to 50 persons per acre (chapter 8), which was much smaller than the effect of density changes on the costs of developing the residential areas. A reduction in the number of residential areas with increased densities could also be used to reduce road costs, but again not very much, and care would be needed to avoid the opposite effect from an increase in the average distance from homes to jobs (chapter 8).

[1] DSIR, *The Economics of Factory Buildings.*

BUILDING FORMS

At standards likely to be acceptable in this country, the proportions of land used for buildings and for the space around them remains much the same whatever building forms are used (see chapter 4 above). No substantial increase in density could therefore be achieved by making greater use of artificial internal environments, since the space about buildings would still be required for access, parking and other amenity areas. Nevertheless different building forms could radically change the urban form itself. Taller and larger buildings have to be further apart, but it would be technically possible to accommodate a large proportion (or even the whole) of the population of a town in a single building. If every room had to be lit and ventilated naturally the building could not be very deep, but artificial lighting and ventilation is practicable, though currently uneconomic in this country, and even in a deep building would not be needed in the peripheral rooms. However, the larger the complex of facilities under one roof, the greater the proportion of space needed within the building for circulation and storage, and this would be far more expensive than external space to provide and service. Internal transport would have to be electrically powered to overcome the problems of fire, pollution and noise. Thus the difficulties of housing a city in a single building are economic rather than technical.

Other imaginative suggestions made recently include running the roads on the roofs of the buildings, roofing the city over, using the city roof as a site for open space, and building the city underground. While these suggestions raise technical problems, they could all probably be solved on the basis of current knowledge, and the real problems are again economic. However the economic consequences are quite impossible to predict without first examining the technical problems in some detail.

Construction costs for road networks on the roofs of buildings would be considerable, including building frames strong enough to carry heavy live loads, bridges between the buildings and ramps at the boundaries of the development. At roof level the roads would be very exposed to wind and frost, and problems of noise and fumes would also have to be met – at extra cost.

Roofing over a city would have even greater consequences. There could be either a roof over the whole city on columns built to carry it, or roofing between the buildings, which would have to be strengthened to support it. If the whole city was covered, storm water would be a problem and, even if the roof were glazed (and any other solution is difficult to imagine), some natural light would be lost and lighting costs increased. The glass would need regular cleaning – an expensive operation – and in some climates frequent clearing of snow and ice. Solar gain and fumes would make efficient ventilation essential and reflected noise would also be a problem. Probably all power would have to be electric. On the other hand, the roofed-in city would be drier and warmer than a traditional city. In a cold wet climate there would be savings on heating, but in a warm climate ventilation costs would rise. Buildings would need less cladding and more activities could take place outside them – both factors which would lower building costs.

Most of these problems would also arise in an underground city, where additional costs for the provision and servicing of a permanent artificial environment would be only partly offset by savings on heating costs. There would also be costs for tanking the floor, roof and walls of the city.

Such cities would be far more integrated than conventional ones; they would be much less easy to phase and would probably have more resources under-employed in the early states of construction. They would be far less adaptable, or at least more expensive to change. People might eventually adapt to such conditions, although there must be doubts about the effects on physical and mental health, but there would inevitably be some loss of satisfaction, if only during the period of adaptation.

In the absence of details it was not possible to calculate the costs of these suggestions, but some idea of their scale could be obtained from the costs of comparable structures. Roofing over a city would probably cost at least £50,000 per acre. Motorways in bored tunnels cost 50 to 60 times as much as similar roads on the ground,[1] which suggested that space for an underground city might cost something over £4 million per acre, but perhaps only £1 million if built by the cut-and-cover method. Unless new engineering systems enabled such costs to be considerably reduced, they are not very likely to be met within the foreseeable future; but if they were, the integrated construction of a whole city would probably have to be a public enterprise.

Some of these town forms would save land – for example if roads were developed on the roofs of buildings, or if open space were provided there. Space for outdoor recreation could hardly be provided at con-ventional standards inside a roofed or enclosed city, but most of it could be provided outside the city (or on top of an underground one). The net saving in land would probably be small. Reclaiming land from the sea has been suggested not only for cities, but also for airports and ports; given favourable circumstances this would probably be the cheapest way of obtaining sites without using existing land. Costs of

[1] Goldstein, *Motorway Route Location Studies*.

reclamation could be as low as £5,000 per acre – less than a developer would generally have to pay for land for town development. From the point of view of the national economy, however, reclamation would be unlikely to be worthwhile as, in the final account, the land saved would be farmland with a capitalised value of only a few hundred pounds.

SIZE AND ECONOMIES OF SCALE

Economies of scale in developing a settlement can arise either from the provision of facilities or in construction: the space per person for some facility might fall if more people were served, or unit costs of constructing buildings and services might fall as their size increased. Economies in the facilities needed arise from indivisibility and from economies of scale. Some facilities cannot easily be provided below a certain size, for example fire-fighting equipment; the probability of any one building catching fire is low and so one set of appliances, the minimum provision, can handle likely calls from a large area. Similarly, there are minimum operative sizes for colleges of higher education and hospitals. For some facilities the requirements per head fall with the number of people served; a library, for example, needs a minimum number of volumes simply to provide a choice, but the number does not increase proportionately to readership. Economies in construction occur particularly in the case of containers and vessels: the envelopes of reservoirs, and of sewage and heating plants, increase in area far less than in proportion to capacity, so that unit construction costs, and often operating costs, fall with size. Construction and supply costs usually also fall with repetition, so that large-scale purchases of components may be made at substantially reduced prices.

The relationship between scale and unit cost varies with the scale itself; costs may fall at one point and rise at another. Generally the rate of change will fall as size increases. The smallest settlement examined in this book was for 50,000 persons and the smallest component area for 10,000; probably most economies of scale would be exhausted before these sizes were reached, but this depends on the facility.

The size of a settlement or its component areas has no effect on housing facilities required per head, but costs are affected by the way housing units are related. Economies in construction can usually be obtained by siting dwellings close together with a uniform layout and, of course, by greater use of terraces, but housing layout is not related to the scale of development. Again, economies with size and continuity of contracts would be likely to have ceased operating long before even the smallest settlement considered here; housing in villages might be more expensive to build than in small towns, but no appreciable savings would be likely on contracts already involving several hundred dwellings a year. Similarly, housing sites even in the smallest settlement were likely to be already too large to show further economies.

Neither form nor size of settlement affects the floor area required per employee in industry. Larger settlements are more likely to have larger industrial and commercial units, but costs per worker do not fall appreciably. Larger factories cost less to construct per square foot, but between buildings of 20,000 and 180,000 square feet the decrease would be only about an eighth.[1] The increase in productivity and the savings from repetition in the manufacture of building components would also soon be exhausted.[2]

Economies of scale would be more likely to occur with commercial and public buildings, probably in the form of savings on facilities rather than economies in construction. Turnover per square foot in shopping was found to be higher in those forms and sizes which lead to shopping concentration. Measurement was difficult, but the increase was more marked in settlements of predominant status, so that it might be caused more by shoppers from elsewhere than by the features of the settlement itself (see pages 161–2 below). Many social, communal and public facilities are indivisible and if provided in small settlements would be unnecessarily large. Hospitals and colleges of further education were therefore omitted from model settlements for 50,000 persons, which marginally increased the development costs per head for the larger models. This was, of course, not a diseconomy of size and would not increase national costs of education and hospitals. In some cases the size of the locality was important – for example, libraries could be provided more cheaply in districts than in neighbourhoods – but such economies were likely to be small, although there was no basis on which to measure them.

In very small schools the area per pupil for circulation and other auxiliary uses might be greater than in larger schools, but none of the schools considered in this study was small enough to be affected. Since schools are usually related to catchment areas of a standard size, the total need for schools would not generally be affected by the form or size of settlements.

No significant economies of scale were found for any of the public utility services over the range of sizes considered (chapter 9).

Main roads for model settlements had costs per head which increased with size though at a declining rate (chapter 8). Typical costs were about £80 per head for a settlement of 50,000 persons, £100 for one of 100,000 persons and £120 for one of 250,000 persons (table 8.2). Other things

[1] DSIR, *The Economics of Factory Buildings.*

[2] United Nations Economic Commission for Europe, *Cost, Repetition, Maintenance: related aspects of building prices*, Geneva, United Nations, 1963.

being equal, settlements for about half a million persons might have road costs of about £130 per head.[1] Of course, there might be economies of scale on road costs in very small settlements.

SHAPE, FORM AND ROAD NETWORKS

The shape and form of a settlement, as well as its size, would affect total construction costs through the costs of the main road system. One aspect of settlement shape has already been considered – height, which is intimately related to density and to building form. The effect considered here, of two-dimensional shape, was difficult to separate from that of a settlement form, because of their interactions with accessibility and the main road network.

Perhaps the simplest and most obvious form is the centralised or centre-orientated settlement, with all facilities other than housing in the centre. The other extreme is a settlement where all points are equally attractive, so that the pattern of journeys is random. Of course, a real settlement would be far more complex. The dwelling is still the origin of most journeys, but visits to other facilities vary considerably in frequency: places of work and education are visited daily, some shops and other services several times a day, some once or twice a week and some even more rarely. Moreover, facilities differ in linkage, in space required and in amenity, positive and negative. Places of work are usually grouped together because proximity has advantages; similarly shopping and service trades are grouped because several are usually visited in one trip. Some activities are better well away from the residential areas because they are noisy and create pollution, while others such as junior schools should be near the housing because young children cannot walk far and need to be accompanied by adults.

In practice, purely centre-orientated settlements rarely exist. Even in centralised towns there are still local centres containing shops and junior schools. In the older settlements the commercial facilities are usually in the centre, with a belt of industry around them and, outside that belt, the residential areas. Today, although still fairly evenly distributed in relation to the residential areas, industry is likely to be divided between a number of industrial areas, but there is little evidence to indicate their optimum size. Similarly the commercial centre need not be concentrated at a single point; small neighbourhood sub-centres meeting daily and weekly needs, or larger district sub-centres, are alternatives. The more the various service and employment areas are subdivided and spread among the residential areas the closer the settlement approximates to one with a random pattern of journeys.

[1] See also Smeed and Holroyd, *Some Factors affecting Congestion in Towns.*

Reynolds showed that theoretically journey lengths in a centre-orientated settlement were minimised when it was circular.[1] Fairthorne showed that this was equally true for a settlement with a random pattern of journeys.[2] Journey lengths are, however, not a direct measure of road construction costs, which rise more than proportionately to the volume of traffic, largely because of interchange problems. None of the model settlements studied was circular, but the results showed that rectangular settlements had less expensive main road systems than any other shape examined whatever the form or size (table 8.4); the average difference was about £15 per head. The smaller and more decentralised the settlement, also the less people were deterred from travelling by the length of journey, the greater was this advantage. Fully centralised settlements had main roads nearly a fifth more expensive to construct than decentralised ones, with partly centralised settlements generally somewhere between the two (table 8.5). There were also indications that road construction costs increased with the size of the component areas of a settlement (chart 8.2).

The propensity to make long journeys to work interacted strongly with the shape, form and density pattern of a settlement and the effect of these factors on the costs of developing the road system. If location and the length of the journey had no effect on the choice of a job, homes and work places would be distributed at random and travelling would be minimised by centralising employment. The more the length of the journey inhibited the choice of work the more decentralised employment areas reduced travelling and hence the roads required. The strength of this deterrent depended on the size of the settlement and the efficiency of its transport system.

Larger shopping centres have few advantages to set against the longer journey to reach them. With increasing standardisation their facilities tend to be duplicated; although they may have more shops, these will all sell much the same goods at much the same prices. However, for places of employment the situation is often very different. Even in the same trade, firms make different products by different methods, and have different staff relations and opportunities for promotion. A long journey to a particular job may be well worthwhile when the alternative of moving house is expensive, and often difficult because of the ties of other members of the household. A few large employment centres offering a wide range of jobs may, therefore, in the end, result in less travelling and hence lower road construction costs than a large number

[1] Reynolds, *Urban Layout and Transport Systems*.
[2] Q. Fairthorne, 'The distances between pairs of points in forms of simple geometric shape', *Proceedings of the Second Symposium on the Theory of Traffic Flow* (ed. Joyce Almond), Paris, OECD, 1965.

of small dispersed centres. How far workers are prepared to travel depends less on actual distance than on the time taken, which will be much shorter in new settlements with properly designed motorways than in existing towns. Distance may then be much less of a deterrent, though always some constraint. The deterrent effect of distance might be sufficient in a cluster of settlements to reduce the amount of travelling and thus the costs of road development. The conditions in which economies could be realised by creating a cluster of small settlements rather than one large one were explored in chapter 8. The more each separate settlement specialised in job opportunities and in services for the type of people to whom the jobs appealed the easier this would be. If distance was no deterrent to travelling, road costs per head for a cluster would, of course, be greater than the costs for individual settlements of the same size – the additional costs arising both from extra travelling by commuters and from extra roads required to connect the settlements. Road construction for a 50,000 person settlement forming part of a cluster could cost about 25 per cent more than for an individual settlement of that size (page 99), which was a measure of the costs of inter-settlement movement, in particular of commuting. Jamieson, Mackay and Latchford in their study of the main road requirements for adding settlements in the region of a large conurbation in the North West, showed that these costs could be very considerable.[1]

The costs of main road systems depend on three sets of factors: the first, which has already been considered, is the shape, form and density pattern of the settlement, particularly the distribution and densities of commercial centres and other employment areas in relation to the housing and to the propensity of the residents to make long journeys to work. The second is the extent to which the roads are used to capacity and the disproportionate rise in costs of interchanges as they grow in size and complexity. Road units (lanes) are indivisible, so that costs are minimised when each lane is used up to its optimum capacity. A main road network so fine that lane capacity is wasted is uneconomic. As traffic builds up and more lanes are required in each direction, interchanges become more and more complex, with increased weaving lengths and more flyovers to keep the different streams of traffic apart. Centralised and linear settlements were found to have more expensive road networks because of such concentrations.

The third factor in road costs, the extent to which traffic reduces amenity, is considered in the next section.

[1] G. B. Jamieson, W. K. Mackay and J. C. R. Latchford, 'Transportation and land use structures', *Urban Studies*, vol. 4, no. 3, November 1967.

TRAFFIC AND AMENITY

It is generally accepted that traffic, particularly in residential, shopping and recreational areas, reduces amenity by the noise, vibration, dirt, pollution, accident hazards, inconvenience to pedestrians and unsightliness which it creates. There is, however, a price to pay for preserving amenity which can be measured by decreased accessibility and additional road costs. The model settlements were designed to protect the environmental areas and they illustrated the prices which had to be paid (charts 5.2, 5.4 and 5.5). The main road networks and the different speed limits encouraged traffic to use the highest grade of road available. Traffic between neighbourhoods or districts and central or industrial areas was forced on to primary roads. Within such areas traffic had to stay on secondary roads until it reached the estate (access) road required. Through traffic in the environmental areas was prevented by the absence of through links.

These design principles added to the traffic on the main road system and hence to the costs of handling it. It could be argued that this price was too high. A throughway network of secondary roads would reduce the load on the primary roads and, if the environmental areas were made smaller and more regular in shape, the grid could be finer which would reduce distances. The price of this in terms of amenity might, however, be very high.

The noise along roads carrying heavy traffic, as well as near railways, some industrial plants and large airports, is quite unacceptable. Often the level reaches 90 decibels.[1] The costs of reducing the noise of traffic to an acceptable level are however very high. Some ways of doing this and their costs were given in chapter 9. One method which might be economic for buildings of several storeys, would be to roof in the traffic street. This would, of course, transfer costs from the private to the public sector.

Continuous terraces along the major streets would shield the areas lying behind from traffic noise. The rooms facing the shielded precincts would probably not need any special protection such as sealed glazing. The larger the areas developed in this way, the greater the proportion of floor area for which natural ventilation could be used and the lower the additional costs. However, this form of development is restricted in this country by the system of planning control, particularly that part intended to protect daylighting standards. The external walls of a building have to be far enough from the boundaries of the site for the light falling on the face of the building and its neighbours, to provide adequate lighting within the building in average conditions.[2] In practice

[1] Parker, 'Noise problems in buildings'.
[2] K. Watts, 'Functional control and town design', *Architects' Journal*, vol. 138, 23 October 1963.

internal daylight depends on many factors, particularly the way the building is glazed, the depth of rooms and their height from floor to ceiling. Many commercial buildings thus still do not have adequate daylight throughout and artificial lighting is necessary, increasing costs-in-use. However, the controls, particularly on expensive city sites, encourage free-standing slabs and towers, often on a podium, around which traffic and other external noise can circulate freely. Since noise is reduced little by height above the ground, it is much the same all over the building, and in noisy situations sealed glazing will be necessary for all windows, with mechanical ventilation or air conditioning in every room. Sealed windows are also likely to be needed for the higher storeys because of wind conditions intensified by the form of the building. Thus, partly because of changes in design fashion, planning controls intended to improve standards not only fail to achieve their object, but encourage a form of building and town development which uses far more resources and actually reduces standards.

If an all-purpose electrically propelled vehicle replaced the motor car, or some other equally satisfactory form of propulsion was developed, the planning difficulties resulting from the noise, dirt and pollution caused by traffic might disappear, or at least be largely reduced. The other detractions from amenity – accident hazards, inconvenience to pedestrians and unsightliness – would remain, although the first two could be reduced by building underpasses. However, these are too expensive, especially if escalators or other mechanical devices are included, to be used on any scale.

REGIONAL STATUS

The status of a settlement in its region was found to have an important effect on the activities within it and hence on its costs of construction. The major influence was on shopping and service facilities, and hence on the costs of the central areas. In a settlement with only subordinate regional status, the area of shopping might be 40 to 50 per cent less than in an average settlement (table 6.7), and of service trades and offices about 20 per cent less. Similarly a settlement with a predominant regional status would have substantially more shopping, service and office space (table 9.13).

Regional status also affects hospital, educational, cultural and recreational facilities and the number of jobs they create, so that, if industrial employment was unchanged, a higher status would increase the numbers commuting into the settlement to work, as well as those entering for shopping and other services. The increase in traffic would, of course, be influenced by the deterrent effect of long journeys to work.

6

If this was high, other types of employment, mainly in manufacturing, might change in scale to compensate for the variations in employment in service industry. The modal split and the peaking factor, as well as any spare capacity in the road system, would also affect the changes in costs, so that further models would be needed to measure the changes in any detail.

Roads in large settlements are, however, much more likely to be fully loaded than in small ones, and it is the large settlements which are most likely to attain a predominant regional status and vice versa. A predominant settlement with a population of 250,000 might, other things being equal, have a labour force about 10 per cent larger than a settlement of the same size of average status. A net commuter flow on this scale would require road capacity costing about 4 per cent extra. The reduction in costs for a small subordinate settlement would probably not be very significant.

The cost differences resulting from regional status were not, however, found to be associated with settlement form. Total national costs of development are unlikely to be affected very much, since it is the location of the marginal facilities which is changed and they must be provided somewhere.

POPULATION STRUCTURE AND STANDARDS

Migrants are generally younger than non-migrants, but those who move as a result of comprehensive redevelopment have a more normal age distribution (with more families containing teenage children) than people migrating mainly for jobs (see page 261 below). In overspill settlements therefore, the annual cohorts of migrants are likely to form new households sooner and to give rise to cycles with earlier peaks. However, the need to attract firms as well as migrants limits the extent to which a cross-section of households from redevelopment areas can be absorbed. The proportion would be high only if the settlement was a dormitory close to the exporting town. It was notable that, despite variations in the demographic structure of migrants, the differences between the age structures in existing and in new towns was small. Similarly, quite wide differences in migrant intakes had little effect on the demographic structure of the mature settlement. Thus, the characteristics of migrants would be likely to be more important for phasing than for a mature settlement and its development costs.

The activities of the population also affect the need for facilities, but since all the inhabitants need somewhere to live and most need places of work or education, total building would vary little with small changes in the pattern of activity. Changes in floor area standards were far more important and, as over two fifths of the costs were for housing, it was here that standards had the greatest effect. Current standards were assumed, so that, if these changed, costs could increase considerably. This has occurred over the last decade: costs of town development per person have nearly doubled, although building prices have increased by only about 35 per cent.

COMPARATIVE CONSTRUCTION COSTS

In the models studied main road construction costs, which were strongly influenced by the size of the settlement, ranged from about £60 to £150 a person, a variation equivalent to nearly 4 per cent of the total costs. The total ultimate cost differences arising from the main road system were many times greater, since running costs are five to ten times more important for the use of resources than capital costs. However, it was shown that size does not have much effect on other costs per head, nor does the size of component parts of the settlement.

The absence of economies of scale in the model settlements did not necessarily mean that there were no such economies; it might be simply that costs per head were fairly constant over the size range examined. Also, economies of scale in construction might be much more important, but these would depend on phasing.

The various aspects of settlement form also affected main road costs, but only density and building form had any appreciable effect on other costs of development over the range considered. Outside this range, shape would be unlikely to have much influence except on the costs of main roads. Concentration might have an effect but, in the absence of operational studies, no firm conclusions could be drawn. In the models, concentration of commercial functions made little difference to costs because the total facilities required were assumed to be unchanged by the distribution of the functions between town and neighbourhood centres, town and district centres, or in a single central area. Of course, if density and the consequential form of the buildings varied between different types of centre, the costs of central area development would be affected. For example, if town centres were decked, partly centralised settlements would be cheapest because they have smaller town centres than the other forms.

The costs examined in this book were essentially comparative. While the conditions were as far as possible those expected to apply in 20 to 25 years time at maturity of the settlements, the comparisons were not invalidated by the use of current prices and standards. Since, however, running as well as capital costs were involved, a consistent level of costing was needed, and this was obtained by using typical actual

6-2

volumes and costs. These operational data also made allowance for inevitable departures from the optimum: for example, densities actually achieved allowed for land not capable of development (not, of course, for the effect of large areas of agricultural or forest land within the urban fence), and road lengths measured from areas determined in this way allowed also for uneconomic layouts. Similarly, actual floor areas allowed for the inevitable incidental space, and actual price data in costs of buildings and site development for uneven sites and labour and management conditions. Thus the costs did, in fact, reflect the conditions likely to be met in developing a settlement; they would, of course, need adjustment for particularly awkward or particularly easy sites, and for non-average locations, but the data were insufficient to estimate these adjustments.

While the costs given for buildings and estate development should be of the correct order, they were likely to be too low where requirements were based directly on measurements from plans of the models, as for main roads and for electricity and gas services. These measurements were minimal and did not allow for non-urban land within the urban fence or for surface undulations, which would increase the length of roads, and of cables and pipes, but would not affect junctions and terminals. However, the difference for main roads was estimated at only about 1 per cent; the effect on gas and electricity services would be even less.

COMPARISONS WITH ACTUAL TOWNS

It is extremely difficult to estimate the costs of actual towns, even if they have been developed as new towns. Not only must annual expenditure figures be obtained from all the development agencies, but then it is necessary to trace what has been provided for the money and to allow for price and quality changes, before assessing what remains to be done in the light of changing needs. In fact, it again proved impossible to make reliable assessments for any of the towns for which data were collected, except in the case of one new town, Stevenage, where the estimates were sufficiently detailed and reliable to compare with the figures derived in this study. Published cost studies relate mainly to town expansion schemes which were not comparable with the estimates derived here. Only two other suitable studies were found: one on Hook,[1] and the 1957 study by the author on the comparative costs of housing people in new towns and existing cities.[2] The comparable costs inflated to 1967 price levels are shown below (table 12.1).

The differences in these figures arise partly from differences of

[1] London County Council, The Planning of a New Town.
[2] Stone, Housing, Town Development, Land and Costs.

Table 12.1. *Estimates of total construction costs
compared with costs of actual new towns*

£s per head, 1967 prices

	Author 1957[a]	Stevenage 1959[a]	Hook 1961[a]	This study 1967[a]
Residential	868	841	1091	1070[b]
Educational	72	105	89	98
Industrial	208	235	265	269[c]
Commerce and services	264	282	262	329[d]
Main roads	42	..	103	115
Sewerage	28	62	31	30
Water	20	23	30	25
Other utilities	88	90	88	103
Total	1590	1638[e]	1959	2039
Land (including fees)	7[f]	15	59	153[g]
TOTAL	1597	1653	2018	2192

SOURCES: Stone, *Housing, Town Development, Land and Costs*; London County Council, *The Planning of a New Town*; table 9.16.

[a] Dates of the original estimates.
[b] Costs of housing plus residential development.
[c] Total construction in industrial areas plus factories in central areas.
[d] All other building and development.
[e] Excluding main roads, for which no figures are available.
[f] At £100 an acre.
[g] At £2,500 an acre.

definition and in local needs, but mainly from variations in standards and solutions. It will be noted that total costs are lower the longer it is since the basic costing was carried out. The four sets of costs fall into two groups, with the figures for the 1950s in the first and those from the 1960s in the second.

Both sets in the first group related to Mark 1 new towns, to pre-Parker-Morris housing standards and to low car ownership rates. In the case of Stevenage, the absence of main road costs was offset by unusually high sewerage costs. The other differences between the two are partly accounted for by statistical errors arising from applying a single cost index to all the items, partly by rises in standards between 1957 and 1959, and partly by differences in concept.

The Hook study took place after the Cumbernauld proposals had been published and followed many of the Cumbernauld concepts. In particular it allowed for 100 per cent car ownership, for separation of pedestrian and vehicular traffic and for a multi-level central area. These concepts were reflected in the cost of the main roads and in the item 'commerce and services'. In fact the latter should be considered with the figures for industry, since the figures in this book reflect the changed employment structure expected by 1989. The high cost of the Hook residential area resulted from high densities rather than high housing standards; those standards are not as high as those anticipated at maturity of the model settlements.

The major differences between the two groups reflect the changes in standards and in concepts over the decade covering their basic costing. The large difference in costs of housing is mainly a result of applying Parker-Morris standards and of segregation of vehicular traffic. In industry, commerce and services, and in education, the differences are partly caused by building standards and partly by the changes in activity rates between the late 1950s and the 1980s. The cost of roads reflects the expected growth of traffic and improved road standards.

More recently, in January 1970, estimates have been published of the capital cost of construction per head of population for the urban areas which would accompany airports at Foulness, Nuthampstead, Cublington and Thurleigh.[1] These were given as £2,228, £2,170, £2,176 and £2,186 respectively, an average of £2,190. They would be at 1969 prices, and the difference between £2,190 and the estimate in this book of £2,039, about 7 per cent, could be accounted for by the change in price levels between 1967 and 1969.

[1] Department of Trade and Industry, *Commission on the Third London Airport: papers and proceedings*, vol. 8, part 1, *Stage III: Research and Investigation*, London, HMSO, 1970.

CHAPTER 13

COSTS-IN-USE OF SETTLEMENTS AND THEIR TRANSPORT SYSTEMS

RUNNING COSTS AND COSTS-IN-USE

So far in this book attention has focused on the needs and costs of developing settlements. This order of priorities was justified by the importance of capital costs in terms of both real resources required and finance; the latter has political implications because so much has to be raised through government agencies. In contrast, running costs, which together with the annual equivalents of the capital costs constitute the costs-in-use, are widely dispersed over all users of the settlement and so make less direct political impact. Nevertheless, settlement patterns have a profound effect on people's way of life, and hence on the costs they incur and the benefits they enjoy. This book is concerned with the broad aspects of size, shape and form of settlement, so that it was unnecessary to enquire into the effects on running costs of detailed differences, for example in the layout of buildings within the main settlement components, or in the design of the buildings themselves.

COSTS-IN-USE OF RESIDENTIAL AREAS

The residential areas considered in this book differed mainly in density, which ranged from 30 to 100 persons per acre. Household composition and standards of development were assumed to be fairly uniform. Even so, maintenance and management costs of dwellings depend on whether they are houses and bungalows or blocks of flats, and on the number of storeys in the latter.[1] Figures were available only for local authority housing, but these suggested that flatted blocks of five storeys or more have maintenance and management costs about two thirds higher than houses. At mid-1967 prices the annual costs per dwelling were £35 for houses, £40 for low flats (up to four storeys) and £58 for high flats.[2] These figures covered only minimum maintenance, together with communal lighting and general administration; if the occupiers wished to maintain a high standard of decoration and to keep fittings, fixtures and services up to contemporary standards, they would have had to spend considerably more. However, such additional expenditure

---

[1] Stone, *Housing, Town Development, Land and Costs*.
[2] Outside London and other large cities.

Table 13.1. *Annual costs-in-use of dwellings
per 10,000 persons by density*

£ thousands, 1967 prices

	Density per acre				
	30 persons, 41 rooms	37 persons, 51 rooms	50 persons, 68 rooms	75 persons, 102 rooms	100 persons, 137 rooms
Housing form[a]	100:0:0	80:20:0	60:30:10	20:50:30	0:25:75
Capital cost, annual equivalent[b]	678	693	750	857	1035
Maintenance, etc.					
Buildings	102	105	114	130	157
Estate roads	12	11	9	8	6
Public space	—	10	20	15	10
Total	792	819	893	1010	1208

SOURCE: NIESR estimates.

[a] Percentages of houses:low flats:high flats.
[b] Costs from tables 9.2 and 9.3 over 10 years assuming 7% interest.

would depend on the standards set and the layout of the dwellings rather than on density.

The density of development also affected the costs of maintaining and servicing the estate roads and landscaped areas.[1] Annual maintenance costs for estate roads, at mid-1967 prices, were about 30p per yard of frontage. Costs per dwelling of course declined with density. For houses laid out at a density of 30 persons per acre they would be just under £4 a year, which would drop to about £3 a year at 50 persons per acre and to just under £2 a year at 100 persons per acre. Equivalent costs per person housed were about £1·20, £0·90 and £0·60 respectively. The costs for flatted blocks would be a little lower.

Large paved areas cost annually between £70 to £140 an acre to maintain, and planted areas, mainly grass with some trees and shrubs, about £200 an acre.[1] Only where flatted blocks are used is the space about buildings a communal responsibility, and then it usually has to be maintained professionally and not by the occupiers. Labour costs per person housed for a typical combination of paved and planted areas (material costs would be similar whether the work was carried out by the householder or by professional labour) were about £2 a year per person for densities of 50 persons per acre and about £1 a year per person at 100 persons per acre.

[1] Stone, *Housing, Town Development, Land and Costs.*

Adding these various costs suggested that costs-in-use of housing, that is the annual equivalents of the capital costs together with the estate running costs, were about 50 per cent higher at densities of 100 than of 30 persons per acre (table 13.1). In the absence of differential subsidies, either rents would have to be increased in line, or the additional costs for higher densities met by the occupiers. Against the extra costs might be set any values attached to the occupiers' preference for higher density living.

The density and form of housing could also affect other operating costs associated with the dwellings themselves and with the running of the estate, such as heating, refuse handling, tradesmen's deliveries, removal expenses, and fire and ambulance services.

It was difficult to generalise about heating and fuel costs, since they depend so much on the type of heating and on standards. Clearly, more compact housing forms have smaller exposed surfaces, so that thermal losses would be less, for example, from terraced than from detached dwellings. Although more heat is lost through the roof than through a similar area of wall, the gains from building dwellings above each other are not large in practice, because roofs can be insulated effectively and cheaply. Where flats are entered through an internal lobby instead of directly from the open air, heat is saved, but taller buildings have a greater average exposure and so lose more heat. The disadvantages of heating flatted dwellings, particularly tall ones, are less now that solid fuel has largely given way to oil, gas and electricity. However, only electricity, and to a lesser extent gas hot air, really lend themselves to convenient individual flat heating schemes. Heating with other fuels is more efficient on a communal basis, but charging is more difficult, although it can be achieved indirectly by metering the power consumption of the electric pumps to give each household control over the heat consumed and its costs.

Refuse disposal also presents problems in blocks of flats. In dwellings on the ground, dustbins can be placed conveniently to the kitchen, but blocks of flats need either an area for single or collective bins, which may be some distance from individual flats, or else ducts which, while more convenient, are noisy and deal with only a part of the refuse. Ducts leading to collective bins would add only marginally to costs; water-borne refuse disposal is far more convenient and hygienic but would add about £100 to the construction costs of each dwelling.[1] Moreover, while the latter would show small savings on collection costs, it would be expensive to maintain and service, adding £8 a year or more to the costs-in-use of each flat; further, it could not handle the larger items of refuse.

[1] P. A. Stone, *Building Design Evaluation: costs-in-use*, Spon, 1967; Ministry of Housing and Local Government, *Homes for Today and Tomorrow*.

The costs of moving house increased with the number of storeys in the block, but, as average annual costs spread over the normal cycles of occupation, the differences from dwellings on the ground were small – perhaps 25p for low flats and about 50p for high flats.[1] Costs of other deliveries, trade and postal, as well as costs of fire and ambulance services, increased in the same way.

High blocks also cause inconvenience to the occupants of the dwellings. Lifts can save fatigue on stairs, but still cause delay and intensify the problems of supervising children and pets. Generally it would be financially impracticable to provide sufficient lifts for peak loads.

COSTS-IN-USE OF SERVICE CENTRES

The term services is used here to cover all services needed to support the style of life, as distinct from housing and employment, but excluding public utility services connected to each dwelling. Services can be broadly grouped into shopping, education, health and recreation.

Shopping and retail services are required with varying frequency. Perishable goods such as fresh food, newspapers and mail are needed daily, but the importance of daily purchase is declining as more and more food is sold in a less perishable state, and as the chilled storage capacity in homes increases. On the other hand, rising costs are reducing delivery services and increasing the weight and bulk of food which the housewife must carry herself. This applies also to other convenience goods.

The need for local shopping and service centres, and their spacing over a settlement depends on the availability of personal transport. Where the housewife has a car at her daily disposal, or if some form of door-to-door public transport is available at an acceptable price, distance to the service centre is not critical. In the absence of such transport, private or public, the convenience of local service centres within walking distance of the home is undeniable, especially where there are small children.

The smaller the service centre the fewer facilities it can offer and the higher the costs of providing each service. On the other hand, even though a more distant centre serving a larger number of households can offer a greater choice, the full effects of scale on costs, and hence on prices, may be lost if housewives without their own cars only shop when a car is available so that demand is highly peaked. Similar problems do not arise for durable goods, or for legal and financial services, which are required less frequently.

While health services are needed less often than shops, the convenience

[1] Stone, *Housing, Town Development, Land and Costs.*

of local lower-tier services is considerable, again especially where there are young children. At higher levels, for example hospitals, the advantages probably lie with scale. Similarly, for recreational facilities, some are required frequently, especially by children, others can be centralised.

There were some economies of scale in building shopping and other service facilities in large units, but there was no evidence that these savings would be substantial. On the other hand, large centres, being dependent on transport, required much larger parking areas and bus stations, and decking or multi-storey parking would often be needed for compactness. Thus capital costs tended to rise with the size of the centre. Central service areas on the ground cost about £2·8 million per 10,000 persons excluding land (table 9.12), but for a decked centre or one with multi-storey parking the cost might be as high as £4 million. This implies a rise in annual equivalent costs per 10,000 persons from about £200,000 to nearly £300,000.

The operating costs of service centres also increased with their size, particularly where they were decked. Bigger centres have more paved surfaces to maintain, clean and light, and decked centres have additional costs for the vertical movement of goods and people, for handling goods on the deck and for additional fire precautions. Shops in centres catering for as few as 10,000 persons can employ self-service and other modern retailing methods, and chains of stores enjoy the same advantages of bulk buying as large single stores, so that substantial economies of scale are unlikely in the operating costs of centres of the sizes considered here.

The costs of journeys to central areas for shopping and other services depend largely on the pattern followed by each housewife but, as an example, if she shops every day, in a square, centralised settlement for 100,000 persons, her average distance travelled per week would be about 21·5 miles. In a partly centralised settlement, this would fall to about 8 miles a week, even with a monthly visit to the town centre; in a decentralised settlement, a trip to the town centre would probably be needed each week, so that the total travelled would be about 14·5 miles. Journeys to local centres, either district or neighbourhood, would probably be on foot, but not journeys to the town centre. A private car (on the basis of running costs only) would cost about 26½p, 10p and 9p a week for these journeys; by public transport, costs would be about the same for the housewife herself but half as much again for each child she had to take with her (chapter 10). The above figures are for square settlements, districts and neighbourhoods; in more linear shapes the costs would be higher, rising in proportion to costs of the journey to work (chapter 10). For a centralised settlement the costs would increase with settlement size, again probably in the same proportion as for the journey to work, but in partly centralised and decentralised settlements they would be affected much less, if at all. Hence the larger the settlement and the more it departs from the square or circular shape, the stronger the economic grounds for local shopping centres.

The main differences in total costs-in-use were clearly between those of centralised and of decentralised settlements. As the size of settlement increased, the central area became more remote from the majority of households and travelling costs rose. Moreover, as the size of the centre increased it cost more to build and to operate. It is, however, important to appreciate the small differences involved. For a square, 100,000 person settlement, costs ranged only from about £5 to £15 a year per housewife. These figures would be higher if the settlement was linear or if the housewife had several children to take with her on shopping trips but, even if allowance was made for the housewife's time and inconvenience, still comparatively small except in large centralised settlements. Nevertheless there is clearly a case for providing convenient district or neighbourhood centres.

The arguments in favour of local schools are even stronger, since each child has to make the trip at least twice a day, and younger children must be accompanied. Where transport is needed, it involves additional vehicles and staff, whether provided by additional peak services on the public transport system or by special school buses. Schools should be as close as possible to homes as long as there are sufficient children to make the service viable, and for primary schools this is generally achieved by provision on a neighbourhood basis.

While the countryside is on average closer to homes in linear and in star-shaped settlements than in rectangular or circular ones, it is perhaps access to recreational centres rather than the countryside as such which most town dwellers want. Proximity to recreational centres, whether inside or outside the settlement, can be increased by a more compact settlement layout.

The conclusions were that, except in large settlements, layout did not greatly affect the costs and convenience of the inhabitants as users of services. The advantage lay with compact shapes and with the decentralisation of services to local centres so long as the services themselves remained viable.

RUNNING COSTS OF INDUSTRIAL AREAS

The operating costs of industry depend both on internal factors within the control of the management, such as the efficiency of the plant and the availability of capital, and on external factors which relate mainly to accessibility. The supply of capital is unlikely, in this country, to be affected by location, but markets, and also power, waste disposal, materials, services, labour and management, needed consideration.

In most cases power for industry means electricity, gas or oil. The first two are available universally in every new or expanded settlement; their costs of supply have already been taken into account in considering the costs of developing a settlement. The price of oil varies from one region to another, but it is not likely to be affected by the form of settlement. Similarly, water and waste disposal facilities such as sewerage and refuse disposal are available in all settlements, and their capital costs are not generally affected by the form of settlement, although there may be locations where, as a result of physical factors, some forms are more favourable than others. There will also, exceptionally, be industrial units which are such heavy users of water, or produce so much liquid waste, that their location is limited by proximity to watercourses, but even then the form of settlement will not usually be very important.

Where large, bulky and heavy materials are brought in for further processing, or where it is an advantage to retain the heat content of a material, distance from the supplier may be important, but not in most other cases. Within a settlement, loading and unloading costs are likely to be far higher than transport costs, so that the form of settlement will not have much effect on costs of materials.

The distance from the suppliers of machinery has little effect on costs, since it is purchased comparatively infrequently, but of far greater importance is a ready supply of replacements and tools, which might otherwise hold up production. Fitters and repair staff, an essential service for industry, need not be in close proximity but simply available somewhere in the region, and the same applies to many other services such as advertising and financial expertise. Time is more important than distance; it may take no longer to travel 30 miles to a small or medium-sized new settlement than 5 miles in a large city. Thus, once demand has created the supply, services spread over a region may be as accessible as they are in a conurbation.

The supply of labour needs to be more accessible than that of materials or services since daily journeys are involved. The worker needs a reasonable choice of employment within easy reach of his home and the employer requires a pool of labour large enough to meet changes in demand. Probably, except for very specialised workers and industrial units, an adequate pool of labour would be provided by an urban complex of about quarter of a million persons. Growing professionalism in management is reducing its specialisation in regard to products, so that managers can find a variety of opportunities and industry can find a large pool of managerial ability, even where there are few firms in any particular field. An urban complex for 250,000 should also be large enough to attract the managerial and professional staff required. Again, the form of the settlement is unlikely to be very important.

For marketing the product a well designed road network of adequate capacity is likely to be more important than distance within the industrial area or the form of the settlement. For a product marketed nationally or internationally many locations will be equally suitable.

Thus, for a large range of industry, new or expanded settlements are unlikely to result in higher production costs in the long run than existing cities or conurbations, and costs will be little affected by the form of the settlement. Costs may, however, be much higher in the short run as a result of moving the industrial unit or setting up a branch unit at a distance from the parent, or because, during the early phases of developing a settlement, it cannot offer services comparable to those of a mature urban complex.[1]

OPERATING COSTS OF PUBLIC UTILITIES AND OTHER SERVICES

Urban form and size did not have much effect on the capital costs of the various types of service installation. Economies of scale only arose in expanding from around the village size, and had been largely exhausted below the sizes considered in this book. The presumption was that running costs would follow a similar pattern.

Operating costs of services supplied by pipe or cable depend partly on terminal costs and partly on line costs, and both have costs of maintenance and servicing proportional to capital costs. The servicing of appliances and meter readings, for example, depend on accessibility; thus such costs would be least where the settlement was compact about each service centre. Costs rise as dispersion increases, but for public utilities servicing costs are a small part of total costs.

Consumer services provided by vehicle, for example refuse collection, ambulance and fire services, have costs related partly to services at the consumer, partly to services at the production terminal and partly to accessibility. In extremely dispersed settlements it might be economic to operate with a large number of small dispersed terminals, for example, branch libraries and branch local authority maintenance depots. However, such extreme dispersion was not covered by the models discussed in this book.

[1] W. F. Luttrell, *Factory Location and Industrial Movement*, London, National Institute of Economic and Social Research, 1962.

Road service costs, maintenance, lighting and cleaning depend, of course, on the length and surface area of roads. Such costs are broadly related to construction costs and to travelling costs, so that size and form of settlement affect them similarly, and the advantages lie with smaller and more compact settlements.

COSTS-IN-USE OF TRANSPORT

The form and size of a settlement thus affects both capital and running costs, together constituting the costs-in-use, mainly through accessibility. Society is becoming more mobile and less dependent on local facilities, so that the case for single, highly concentrated settlements is less and less pressing. The relation between homes and places of employment is less important than it was; people can more easily change their jobs without having to move house. However, accessibility has costs as well as benefits: the freer people are to live and work where they like, the more flexible the transport system must be, and the greater the capacity required. This would increase costs of construction and, if the facility was used, of travelling. At some point it becomes less expensive to accept limited accessibility and some degree of specialisation by settlement or locality, with the concomitant necessity of moving house when jobs or other needs change. Since many households move for reasons unconnected with accessibility, for example to obtain a dwelling of a higher standard or in a better neighbourhood, and such moves often become possible on changing employment, they are not necessarily a nuisance.

All the costs of constructing systems and of travelling are paid for by the consumer directly or indirectly. Other things being equal the consumer may prefer unlimited accessibility, but other things are not equal. The greater the accessibility the higher the costs, and there will be a limit to the degree of accessibility that consumers think worth purchasing. It is possible, however, that the degree to which public transport, buses or trains, is used instead of private cars has a major influence on these costs.

Roads for the journey to work

With the aid of the traffic model the costs of the journey to work were studied in detail for each size, shape and form of settlement, with a variety of traffic factors (chapter 10). For practical reasons vehicles and travelling time were costed at a single figure, but the effect of any other set of cost assumptions could be readily calculated. Taking full vehicle costs (standing charges as well as running costs), with travelling time valued at 10 per cent of average earnings (40p per hour in 1967), the door-to-door journey to work in individual settlements cost between £35 and about £90 per worker per year (table 10.1).

Travelling costs rose with the size of the settlement, but at a declining rate (chart 10.1). If journey length had a deterrent effect on travelling, the increase in costs with size was slightly smaller, but the results probably overstated the reduction that would be found in practice, because, in a new settlement specially designed for travelling to work by car, distance would have far less effect than in existing settlements of the same size. Travelling costs per head were lowest in rectangular settlements, which were the most compact shape tested (table 10.3), and this advantage was greater the larger the settlement. Centralisation of employment would be more likely to be worthwhile in smaller settlements, but generally had little effect on costs of travelling to work (table 10.4). Of all the sub-regional forms tested, a rectangular decentralised individual settlement showed up most favourably (table 10.7). Where journey length was a deterrent to travelling, clusters always had lower travelling costs than individual settlements,[1] with greater advantage the larger the settlement. Of course, the concomitant of cheaper travelling in such clusters was a reduced choice of employment, but up to a point this might not represent any real loss of economic freedom, so long as each type of worker had alternative outlets if one or two trades suffered a recession.

The economics of buses

The capacity of a public transport system is determined by the maximum load, usually of the journey to work. Costs of constructing and operating the system would be lowest per passenger-mile when it was evenly loaded, that is when the demands of the journey to work were as little as possible above those over the rest of the day. The main road system also requires sufficient capacity for the peak flow of the journey to work, but this requirement falls with a greater use of public transport, because buses carry more people than cars in relation to the road space used. By examining the costs-in-use of transport as a whole, cars and buses, and their road and parking costs, the optimum division between public and private transport could be found. However, the road capacity then needed for the journey to work might be lower than for some other peak flow. Moreover, there might be no spare capacity for anyone wishing to change their method of travel. Flexibility and freedom of choice are not compatible with the most economic system.

A two-lane single carriageway is the minimum practical road size, and this would often be adequate even when cars predominated, which restricted the possible savings from greater use of buses. If buses were

---

[1] Where journey length was no deterrent, the converse was not always true.

used for 63 per cent of journeys to work instead of about 10 per cent, capital costs of main roads would fall by between £20 and £50 per head (table 11.1). These savings would increase with the size of settlement, but decline if journey length had a deterrent effect on travelling. About £20 per head would also be saved on car parks.

Instead of operating on the normal road system, buses could be provided with bus links to make the service more direct, or they could run on specially designed bus-only roads (chapter 11). Bus links would only cost £1 to £2 per head of population, but a system of bus-only roads would be expensive, especially its crossings with the ordinary road system. In settlements for 50,000 persons it would cost between £34 and £45 per person (table 11.2) – about the same as the savings would be on the ordinary road system from the increased use of buses for the journey to work. The convenience of other journeys might, however, be reduced by thus restricting the capacity of the main roads.

The relation between travelling costs of buses and of cars on various assumptions was shown in chart 11.1. If the family car was used for the journey to work so that running costs only affected the comparison, at market prices costs by car would be lower than those by bus even if practically no value was attached to travelling time; in terms of resources (factor costs), the journey by car would be cheaper even if travelling time by bus was worth about 5p less than by car. If a car was bought especially for the journey to work, because for example the wife needed the family car, full costs would be appropriate, and cars and buses would not break even unless travelling time was charged at about 50p an hour or, in resource costs, at about 20p an hour.

These costs assumed that the buses would have a two-man crew (chapters 10 and 11). However, recent experience in London suggests that buses with a one-man crew, even if a little smaller, may be more economic, although more standing passengers, longer stopping times and a single fare (or at least fewer different fares) could discourage passengers.

Journey costs can sometimes be decreased up to two and a half times by using the largest rather than the smallest buses.[1] Of course, this would involve a less frequent service and a longer journey time. In Milton Keynes, buses carrying 14 persons could be six times as frequent as those carrying 83, the average journey time of the smaller bus being little more than two thirds that of the larger bus. Additional operating costs per head for the smaller buses should be set against the savings on travelling time however it is valued.

Total costs-in-use of cars for the journey to work include track costs, even though these are not normally borne directly by the traveller.

[1] Ministry of Housing and Local Government, *New Towns Act 1965. Reports of the Development Corporations to March 31, 1970.*

Track costs could be charged either by making all vehicles pay for the use of the track, or by paying a subsidy to buses equal to the saving on road construction and servicing costs from a modal split biased against cars. This saving was not more than 2p per person per day (chapter 11) which, even if applied only to the journey to work, would be about half the subsidy buses get already from the incidence of taxation (chapter 10). Real costs of buses and cars were about equal when 50 per cent of workers travelled by bus.

Any cost advantages in the use of buses rather than cars for the journey to work were marginal, so that although a bus service is essential for some people, there would be little point in putting pressure on others to travel to work by bus when they would rather use the family car. There might be savings on construction of the road system in a new settlement if it was designed for a large proportion of workers to travel by bus, but congestion on the roads at other peak times, for example the weekly shopping expedition, might result, and the road system would lack flexibility. Once a new settlement has reached a certain stage, it is similar to an existing town, where additional roads and parking space can only be provided at considerable expense by clearing existing development and building multi-storey car parks. A road system designed to handle a large proportion of cars is far more flexible and, since the advantages of buses are so doubtful, the case for providing sufficient capacity to handle the maximum proportion of cars is strong.

The economics of railways

Some form of tracked transport would be an alternative to buses in a new settlement. This too would have to compete with private cars in convenience and cost. If a railway is to be no more inconvenient than buses, no walk to or from a station should be over quarter of a mile. Systems which would meet this criterion in linear and star settlements for 250,000 persons and in a settlement cluster were illustrated in chart 11.2. This also showed the ideal settlement shape for a railway – a figure of eight – but then the development would enclose a large area of land within the loops, and there would be a long and complicated system of primary roads.

The most complete study of tracked systems available was that for Manchester,[1] from which data for the ordinary duorail (which was found to be cheapest) were applied to the systems in chart 11.2. Capital costs varied from £195 to £277 per person (table 11.3); the system of the star-shaped settlement being most expensive, and that for the figure of eight the cheapest. Thus the costs of the railway, even excluding rolling stock at just under £20 per person, were about double those of the main roads, which it could only partially replace.

[1] Manchester City Transport, *Manchester Rapid Transit Study.*

Table 13.2. *Capital costs of transport systems in settlements[a]*
with and without railways

£s per head, 1967 prices

	Individual settlements			Cluster of 5 linear settlements
	Star	Linear	Figure 8	
Combined				
Railway[b]	280	250	195	210
Roads[c]	50	50	75	70
Total	330	300	270	280
Roads only[d]	120	120	n.a.	140
Percentage difference	*175*	*150*	n.a.	*100*

SOURCE: NIESR estimates.

[a] Partly centralised for 250,000 persons.
[b] Rounded from table 11.3.
[c] Approximate figures, see chapter 11.
[d] Rounded from tables 8.2 and 8.9.

If most people used the railway for the journey to work, and some for shopping, social and recreational journeys, the primary road system might be reduced to dual two-lane roads with roundabouts and the secondary road system to two-lane roads with traffic lights. The capital costs of transport systems in the various settlements with and without railways are compared in table 13.2. These figures show combined systems at their best, by assuming that journey length is no deterrent to travelling. With a deterrent roads would be cheaper, but there would be no corresponding savings on the costs of the railway. Of course, acceptance of the railway for the journey to work would also mean savings on car parks, but at only about £20 per person this had little effect on the comparison.

In comparing total annual costs of the journey to work on combined rail and road systems with roads only, certain assumptions had to be made. If workers were not deterred by the length of the journey, and if the family car was used, at factor cost a combined rail and road system would be two to three times as expensive as a system of roads only (table 11.5). Even if the car was purchased especially, at factor cost roads alone would be cheaper, though not by much in the settlement cluster. At market prices a combined rail and road system would be just cheaper than roads if cars were used for the journey to work, though not if buses were used; but even in settlements for as many as 250,000 persons, railways would be likely to be uneconomic generally.

CHAPTER 14

NEW AND EXPANDED SETTLEMENTS

NEW AND EXISTING DEVELOPMENT

Most locations suitable for a large settlement already contain sub-stantial development. The larger the scale the more likely this is, and the more problems there are in incorporating the existing structure into the new settlement. The structure of both the new settlement and the existing one may have to be modified in ways that detract from the benefits they provide. Often the development of the new settlement as far as possible independently of the old is the most economic solution, minimising the extent to which existing development needs to be demolished.

Sometimes, however, there are advantages in deliberately choosing the area of an existing town for a new development. Country towns whose importance has declined often have both urban facilities and skilled labour which are under-employed. Grafting on new develop-ment will restore the town's viability and, at the same time, its spare capacity offers facilities to migrants which could not otherwise be provided for some years and which would, in any case, have both real and financial costs. The town expansion programmes of the 1950s, many of them organised in partnership with the London County Council or other conurbation authorities under the Town Development Act, 1952, were attractive to the receiving authorities in offering both increased viability, and grants from government and others to finance infra-structure improvements. Frequently, however, the ultimate size planned and the relative isolation of the towns made them unattractive to industry; hence some of the current interest in larger new settlements.

A fusion of old and new is worth considering provided there is no loss in values in relation to costs as compared with developing each settle-ment in isolation. This would be so provided the gains from the fusion over using the optimum form of the new settlement and the evolving form of the existing settlement were not offset by the losses resulting from destroying facilities in the existing settlement. Since both settle-ments are evolving, the fusion would be a dynamic process. At one extreme, a possible solution would be to plan the new settlement to fit and make the best use of the existing development – the absolute opti-mum of form being sacrificed to this end; at the other extreme, the

Chart 14.1. *Expansion of existing settlements*

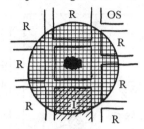

A. Centre of a
new settlement

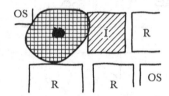

B. District

KEY

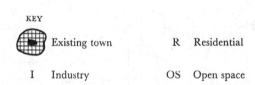

Existing town   R   Residential

I   Industry   OS   Open space

boundaries of the proposed new settlement could be shifted to avoid the need for any change in its optimum pattern due to fusing with the existing settlement.

The discussion of alternative urban forms implies, of course, that the growth of existing towns is not accepted as inevitable, and that development should be controlled with some optimum size and form of settlement in view. This is, of course, not a static concept: it does not mean that, once a master plan has been prepared, all development must conform with it for the foreseeable future, only that, other things being equal, the settlement should develop as nearly as possible in an optimum pattern that is constantly evolving with changes in needs and technical possibilities. The master plan of yesterday has no certain relevance to the optimum pattern for tomorrow, which can be determined only by the needs actually arising, the ways then open to meet them and the development already on the ground.[1] Thus the differences between

---

[1] This statement does not argue that planning for the future is unnecessary or unfruitful, for clearly an optimum pattern cannot be established without considering future requirements, but, because requirements change, any plan must be subject to review.

Chart 14.2. *Patterns of sub-regional development*

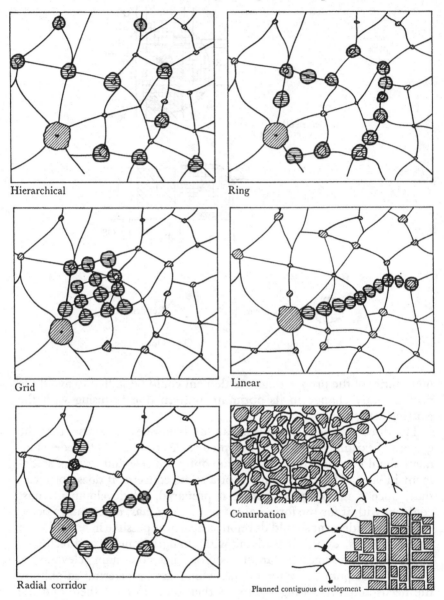

Hierarchical

Ring

Grid

Linear

Radial corridor

Conurbation

Planned contiguous development

expanding an existing settlement and a stage in the development of a new settlement is one of scale, not of kind.

Past costs have no relevance to the optimum solution, which depends entirely on future costs and values, and which is the one where the discounted excess of values over costs is greatest.[1] This excess will be affected by the size and form of both the existing town and the new settlement.

There are three broad degrees of relationship between a new settlement and a large existing town:

(a) The new settlement can be built around the existing town, the centre of which can become the centre of the new settlement (chart 14.1A).

or (b) The existing town can become a district of the new settlement (chart 14.1B).

or (c) The new settlement can develop separately from the existing town, related only within the sub-region, perhaps in one of the patterns illustrated in chart 14.2.

The first solution (a) is generally known as town expansion – the new settlement developing through additions to the existing town, whose component parts and transport network are expanded to balance the growth. Such development can change the form as well as the size of the existing town, but the freedom to do this will be limited by resources and financial considerations, and hence by the existing development and the nature of the site. Departures in the new development from the absolute optimum may be justified economically by the potential of the existing town: for example, a partly centralised form might minimise the expansion of the central area. The second solution (b) involves less interaction between the existing town and the new settlement. The existing town would be able to retain more of its original form, but its growth and future development would be restricted and its potential might not be so well employed. The third solution (c) leaves the existing town to develop in its own way, subject to some restraint on growth. Its spare capacity would probably only be used sub-regionally, for example, through movements for work and for specialised services.

The value of the existing town to the developing settlement would be greatest in the early stages of construction and, after a point, would decline, as facilities needed replacement or resiting in a more convenient form and place. A full evaluation of the economics of developing about an existing town can, therefore, only be made in terms of a phasing study. Since facilities available in the early years are so much more valuable than later on, a comparison limited to the capital costs at the maturity of the settlement would inevitably be biased against development about an existing town.

[1] Stone, *Building Design Evaluation*.

THE CONTRIBUTION OF EXISTING DEVELOPMENT

An existing town contributes to a new development facilities which migrants and their families require. The amounts available depend on the volume, quality and life of facilities not required by the population expected in the future, and are reduced by shortening the lives of existing facilities in the process of fitting the existing town into the new urban form.

There would probably not be any appreciable amount of surplus housing of an acceptable quality in the existing town. If there were any empty factories they would probably be unsuitable, at least without alteration, for the industry likely to be attracted to the new settlement; similarly, suitable buildings for offices and other service industry are unlikely to be available. Again, there is normally a shortage of educational, health and social facilities at a standard now considered appropriate. The main road system might at present have some spare capacity, but this is likely to be absorbed in future with increased car ownership. Public utility networks are not generally built with spare capacity, but are supplemented as need arises, and water and sewage works are usually in a similar situation, although they may be able to accommodate additional population in the short run.

There remain shops and other service buildings, municipal offices and services, and such communal buildings as cinemas and churches. Shops in subordinate towns have a lower turnover per square foot than in average towns, but usually this cannot be raised very far without considerable alterations and refitting at least internally, which might cost half as much as a new shop. Often other buildings in this class can meet the needs of an increased population and, in fact, such services enjoy a considerable prosperity in the early stages of development. However, these facilities would not account for more than about 5 per cent of the costs per head of developing a new settlement (chapter 9).[1] The commercial and public buildings in many of the towns likely to be considered as a base for redevelopment are 50 to 60 years old. Even with some modernisation they would probably be replaced over the next 20 to 25 years, that is by the maturity of the new settlement, and would thus show no savings on capital costs in the long run, although some of the capital expenditure might be delayed and interest saved.

Some assessment of the problem could be made by developing a simple model of a likely situation. This assumed that an existing town of 50,000 persons was to be incorporated into a new settlement for

---

[1] This discussion relates to expansions on a considerable scale. Many towns are able to absorb marginal increases in population without carrying out major new development, except perhaps of residential facilities. This might be described as 'infilling'.

250,000 persons over a period of 20 years, and that, by modernising the commercial centre of the existing town at a cost of £400,000, expenditure of £2 million could be deferred for 20 years. At a discount rate of 6 per cent the net saving would be about £1 million,[1] but this was less than 0·5 per cent of the capital cost, as developing an independent settlement for the additional 200,000 persons would cost about £20 million a year for 20 years, the discounted value of which would be about £249 million.

There would also be some savings on running costs and some general benefits. The existing centre would provide the early migrants with services of a quality they could not otherwise enjoy for some years, and so perhaps would reduce journeys to other centres. The capitalised saving in travelling costs might be as great as on construction costs. Moreover, the nucleus of development provided by the existing town would probably attract migrants and industry, and would establish habits of using shops and other services locally rather than in some adjacent town. Patterns of shopping elsewhere are often difficult to change even when local facilities become adequate; moreover, by encouraging the growth of facilities in other towns, they make it more difficult to establish viable centres in the new settlement.

Some existing towns have good rail facilities, which would help growth by providing links with important industrial and commercial centres. Branch lines might be used as a system of internal transport, although the results in chapter 11 were not very encouraging; even when basic facilities were already available, a railway would tend to restrict development and increase costs.

THE DISADVANTAGES OF EXISTING DEVELOPMENT

The economic disadvantages in relating a new settlement closely to an existing town are also considerable. They arise both because the existing town affects the form of the new settlement, and because the overall plan and phasing needs of the new settlement affect development of the existing town. These two effects are, of course, interrelated; the larger the existing town and the more closely it is integrated into the new settlement, the greater they are likely to be.

Any departure from the optimum form of settlement reduces values and raises costs. Clearly, a substantial area of development will distort the communications network, and upset its loading by unbalancing the settlement components. Moreover, the network is likely to pass through the built up area of the existing town. Some idea of the scale of costs could be obtained by using the simplified model discussed in the pre-

---

[1] The higher the discount rate the less the current net saving.

Table 14.1. *Additional capital costs of developing a settlement around an existing town*[a]

£ millions, 1967 prices

	Development of existing town			
	Separate (sub-regionally related)	As district of new settlement	As town centre of new settlement	
			Partly centralised	Decentralised
Increased price of undeveloped land	6	39	39	39
Developed land for:				
Main roads	2	7	7	7
Town centre	—	—	9	20
Construction of:				
Main roads	2	5	5	5
Town centre	—	—	1	3
Total	10	51	61	74

SOURCE: NIESR estimates.

[a] Additional costs for an ultimate settlement for 250,000 persons built around an existing town for 50,000. The total cost of new development for 200,000 on a virgin site would be – land about £6 million and construction about £400 million.

vious section. It would not be unreasonable to suppose that distortions to the optimum road network might add about 10 per cent to costs, and that the part of the network within the existing town, say 20 per cent, might be 50 per cent more expensive to construct than on a virgin site.[1] The road construction costs might therefore be increased by about 20 per cent, or about £5 million (table 14.1). This was small in relation to total construction costs of the settlement, only just over 1 per cent, but more important would be the effect on the costs of land for the road reservations. In the existing town about half the land required for roads might be developed land costing £50,000 to £100,000 an acre and hence adding perhaps £7 million to costs. There might, of course, be some savings when redeveloping the existing town from the presence of these roads, but there might also be additional expenditure in rounding off and modifying areas through which the roads had passed.

In general land is more valuable close to a sizeable town than in a rural area, so that the price of land for a new settlement built around an existing town of 50,000 persons would be at the upper end of the range, which extended, in 1967, from about £500 to £5,000 an acre. The addi-

[1] Stone, *Urban Development in Britain*, vol. i.

tional cost of land for the settlement might therefore be between £10 and £50 million. However, unless the roads and services were exceptionally well developed over the whole area and the demand for land was very high, the price would decline as the development was extended and more remote land was purchased. If the price fell by £1,000 an acre for each additional 50,000 persons, the extra cost of land for 200,000 persons would be about £39 million (table 14.1). The timing of land purchase might be important, since the growth of the settlement would itself encourage land values to rise, and it might be less costly to purchase land before the development began. Higher market prices would be unavoidable if it was decided, after the initial decision to expand, to enlarge the development yet further.

In most existing towns the centre is both the town centre and the site of other central area facilities for the older parts of the town around the centre. If, for example, the town centre provided full facilities for about half the population, with neighbourhood centres for the other half, and this pattern was preserved for the existing town, but the new parts of the settlement (for 200,000 persons) were treated as districts, an extra 80 acres of land would be needed for the town centre of the new settlement (this would be about 220 acres if the new parts were treated as neighbourhoods). This land would probably be partly residential and partly industrial and might cost about £75,000 an acre, so that for a partly centralised settlement the additional cost would be about £6 million and for a decentralised settlement about £16·5 million. Over the 20 years to maturity of the new settlement it would be necessary to redevelop more of the existing centre than if the town had continued to exist independently. If two thirds of the original centre of 100 acres were redeveloped instead of one third, the increased area required would be about 33 acres, which at £100,000 an acre would add about £3·3 million to costs. Total additional costs of land for expanding and redeveloping the town centre would therefore be £9 million and £20 million for a partly centralised and decentralised settlement respectively (table 14.1).

Redeveloping a site costs about 50 per cent more than development on virgin land.[1] The foundations of the buildings also cost more on disturbed land. Moreover, as a consequence of the difficulties of acquiring land when needed and of operating in areas in use, redevelopment is generally slower and less efficient than new development. Construction costs of the town centre might therefore be increased by about £10,000 per acre, that is £1·1 million and £2·5 million in the two forms of settlement considered (table 14.1).

Thus, in the circumstances assumed, total costs would increase

[1] Stone, *Urban Development in Britain*, vol. 1.

by between £10 million and £74 million, that is between 2 and 16 per cent, depending on the solution adopted (table 14.1). It would be cheapest to treat the existing town as separate, related only within the sub-region, but then few advantages would accrue from it during the new development. The next cheapest solution would be for the existing town to be treated as a district of the new settlement and left comparatively free to develop separately; this would give most of the advantages of starting from a viable development. The most expensive solutions, involving redevelopment of the existing town centre and the area around it, would not have many additional advantages.

THE COSTS OF TOWN EXPANSION

A new settlement built in the area of scattered small settlements would be less expensive than one incorporating a large existing town. Smaller settlements would usually be more easily absorbed without distorting the road network or requiring much redevelopment themselves. Moreover, land prices would probably be lower than in the neighbourhood of a large town. Advantages over development on a virgin site would, however, be few. The larger the new development in relation to the size of that existing already, the lower the costs per additional person

Table 14.2. *Effect of ultimate size on additional capital costs[a]*
of town expansion[b]

| | Ultimate settlement for: | | | |
	100,000 persons	150,000 persons	200,000 persons	250,000 persons
	(£ millions)			
Increased price of undeveloped land	14	25	33	39
Developed land for:				
Main roads	7	7	7	7
Town centre	7	11	16	20
Construction of:				
Main roads	5	5	5	5
Town centre	1	1	2	3
Total	34	49	63	74
	(£)	(£)	(£)	(£)
Per additional person	*680*	*490*	*420*	*370*

SOURCE: NIESR estimates.

[a] At 1967 prices.
[b] Existing town of 50,000 population developed as town centre of decentralised settlement.

Table 14.3. *Actual and theoretical costs of town expansion*

£s per head, 1967 prices

| | Population expanded by | | | Greenfield development |
	50%	100%	200%	
Basingstoke	..	..	2800	.
Peterborough[a]	4000	3100	..	.
Worcester[a]	4000	3000	..	.
Theoretical[b]	..	3100	2800	2400

SOURCE: NIESR estimates.

[a] Ministry of Housing and Local Government, *Peterborough: an expansion study 1963* by Henry W. Wells and *Worcester Expansion Study, June 1963* by J. H. D. Madin and Partners, London, 1963.

[b] Greenfield costs from table 9.16 plus additional costs per head from table 9.2, all rounded to the nearest hundred.

housed. The influence of the existing town on land values would fall with distance. On the other hand, the larger the ultimate settlement, the more the existing town would be disturbed if its centre was redeveloped to serve the new settlement and the less satisfactory this would be; although, of course, the larger the population of the new settlement, the more widely redevelopment costs could be spread and the lower would be costs per head. The figures would vary considerably with actual conditions, particularly the price of land, but the estimates for different scales of development were probably not unrealistic (table 14.2). Since costs were little more than doubled when the additional population increased four times, additional costs per person were nearly halved over the range considered.

The figures available for actual town expansion schemes, although only broadly comparable, supported these theoretical results. Generally, costs per head of additional population are substantially greater for expanded towns than for greenfield settlements, but fall with increasing intake (table 14.3). Part of the costs of expansion can be attributed to improvements in facilities for the existing population. In the figures for Worcester this element could be removed completely, and costs per head for the additional population were then reduced to about £2,700 for 100 per cent expansion and £3,400 for 50 per cent expansion.[1]

FINANCIAL AND RESOURCE COSTS

The financial costs of developing a settlement are not, of course, the same as the capital costs. The capital is required not all at once but

[1] Ministry of Housing and Local Government, *Worcester Expansion Study*.

spread over the period of development, perhaps 20 years. If the areas were acquired only when they were ripe for redevelopment, the financial costs of acquiring land and development might be substantially lower than the capital costs.[1] It might be worthwhile to phase and plan the form of development with this in view.

Costs of incorporating existing development could be as high as half as much again over the costs of greenfield development. If costs of redeveloping existing facilities for the present population were included, the increase could be as much as three quarters. It is doubtful whether the development could often create facilities capable of earning additional revenue of this order. Town expansion may be a convenient way of obtaining the finance to redevelop an existing town, but it is unlikely to be economic to incur the additional costs for this purpose. If existing towns cannot afford to redevelop their infra-structure, it suggests a need for new financial arrangements, with perhaps larger contributions from the Exchequer.

Of course, not all the capital required represents real resources. Much of the additional land would be agricultural land, of which the product is small in relation to the price for its transfer. The difference between the price of agricultural land with and without planning consent often reflects real resources only to a small extent; most of the difference is a windfall gain or transfer payment from one part of the community to another.[2] A large part of the additional costs of land used for town expansion rather than developing a new settlement in a greenfield situation is of this kind. On the other hand, most of the cost of developed sites acquired for redevelopment represents the remaining value of the buildings and works on them, and hence the value of real resources used in the process of replacing the original development.

[1] Although there might also be an increase in 'hope value' to offset against the savings.
[2] A distinction needs to be made, of course, between the financial cost of land to the Development Corporation and to the government agencies. Taxation could reduce the net receipts from land sales to the original owners by a substantial amount, at present about 40 per cent. This money would be received by the central government.

CHAPTER 15

FINANCING DEVELOPMENT

DEVELOPMENT AGENCIES

The responsibility for developing a new town is divided between a number of organisations of which the Development Corporation is the most important, and in this book it was assumed that this pattern would continue. Others playing an important part are local authorities, commercial and industrial developers, and the public utility organisations.

Capital accounts could be compiled for each developer and for a whole settlement. For revenue accounts it was necessary to know a developer's total financial operation, and as local authorities balance their revenue from rates, and public utilities' revenue depends on regionally determined charges as well as local activities, no meaningful revenue accounts could be prepared for them. However, Development Corporations and commercial developers rely largely upon market determined rents for their revenue and cannot generally subsidise with earnings from outside the settlement. Although it was not possible to separate completely commercial development for investment and for the developer's use, revenue accounts were compiled for the Development Corporation and for commercial development for investment.

Each agency was considered in turn: accounts were prepared initially for one set of settlement characteristics – a partly centralised settlement with a population of 100,000, housing at medium density, land at £2,000 per acre and road costs at £120 a head. Subsequently, the effects of varying these characteristics were examined. Finally, all the accounts were brought together to produce a total picture for the settlement.

COSTS OF 'GENERAL DEVELOPMENT'

The first account required was for the costs of 'general development' undertaken by the Development Corporation, covering all facilities which benefit the whole settlement and not just a particular part of it. Main road costs, losses on land transferred or sold at nominal prices to other agencies, and site development on this land, plus fees, administrative expenses and interest resulting from these sales and works, were included. Main sewerage and public utilities were regarded as self-financing for this purpose and considered later.

The land used for general development amounted to 135·4 acres per 10,000 population. Of this, 19·4 acres sold to the public utilities was for sewerage and water works in the industrial areas, 79 acres was open space in various areas, and 37 acres was for main roads and would be transferred free to the local authority. The most complex part of the calculations was allocating road costs between the three contributors: the Development Corporation, the local highway authority (usually the County Council) and the Ministry of Transport. Only costs of classified roads are shared; other roads are paid for by the Corporation. As the distinction between primary and secondary distributors used in the traffic model coincided in no way with the classification (actual classification depends very much on geographical situation), a crude estimate had to be used. It appeared that main roads would have cost the Development Corporation about 60 per cent of their total cost, the balance being paid by the County Council and the Ministry of Transport.[1]

Fees, administrative expenses and interest were taken as 10 per cent of the sum of land, site development and construction costs in all cases, and it was assumed that the Development Corporation would also receive 40 per cent of these costs as grants. Fees on land sold by the Development Corporation would be small and would fall mainly on the purchaser, so no allowance was made. When the area of land imputed to general development was deducted from the total of 557 acres required for 10,000 persons (table 5.1) and the expenditure spread over the balance of 421·6 acres, this gave general development expenditure per acre of £2,925.

PUBLIC AUTHORITY HOUSING

It was assumed that half the dwellings in the settlement (1,463 per 10,000 population) would be provided by the Development Corporation for rent and the other half would be provided by commercial developers for sale. The medium density housing considered here implied private housing at 10 dwellings per acre and public housing at 11·8 dwellings per acre. The total area of 270 acres of residential land per 10,000 persons (table 5.1) was divided into 146·3 acres for private

---

[1] In most cases classified roads would be required to meet the needs and obligations of both the Development Corporation as the developer, and the County Council or highway authority. Accordingly the cost of construction is normally apportioned on an agreed basis between the Corporation and the County Council, whose share of the cost would generally qualify for an Exchequer grant payable under the Highways Act, 1959, by the Ministry of Transport. The rates of grant in 1967 were 75 per cent for Class I roads, 60 per cent for Class II roads and 50 per cent for Class III roads. The actual distribution of costs was thus dependent in part upon the precise classification of the roads and in part upon the results of negotiations between authorities.

housing and 123·7 acres for public housing.[1] To the latter was added 10 acres of open space, which was assumed to be provided in the housing area by the Development Corporation.[2]

Within the public housing account it was necessary to distinguish the expenditure that would be eligible for a subsidy. In addition to the rate fund grant of £12 per annum per dwelling for 10 years, housing subsidies operated in 1967 so that the effective rate of interest the authority had to pay on housing finance was approximately 4 per cent. The subsidy was not calculated upon the actual rates at which particular authorities borrowed, but upon an average rate, selected as representative of the borrowing experience of housing authorities at that time. Here it was assumed that the rate selected was 6 per cent and, as housing loans would be paid back over 60 years in equal instalments of principal and interest, the subsidy was in effect the difference between 60-year annuities at 6 and at 4 per cent. The subsidy was paid only on the costs of dwellings, and those dwellings had to satisfy certain cost conditions. Dwellings which cost not more than a yardstick (assumed here to be identical with prices for the basic Parker-Morris standards) were subsidised, but not dwellings costing more than 10 per cent over the yardstick.[3]

All flats were assumed to be in the public sector, so that, at medium density, 40 per cent of public dwellings would be flats (see chapter 9). Further, about 15 per cent of these flats, 88 of them, were taken as built at 25 per cent over Parker-Morris standards and so ineligible for subsidy. The cost of 9,960 square feet of corner shopping was added to the unsubsidised housing costs.

Land and general development costs were calculated on 133·7 acres (including the open space). The site development cost for the density used (11·8 dwellings per acre) was interpolated as £312 per dwelling, and development of open space was added at £650 per acre. Lacking any better guide, land and site development costs were divided into subsidised and non-subsidised in the same proportion as building costs. General development costs would not be subsidised. Fees, administrative expenses and interest were calculated in the usual way. This gave total costs for public authority housing of £6,325,900 per 10,000 population.

[1] The area for public housing also included a small element of shopping.

[2] The assumptions that all public authority housing and all the open space would be provided by the Development Corporation are reasonably close to reality for accounting purposes. Usually, of course, local authorities provide a small proportion of the public housing.

[3] Dwellings costing up to 10 per cent over the yardstick received a subsidy based on the yardstick cost.

LAND SALES[1]

The price at which the Corporation can sell land for residential development varies with both the size of the settlement and the density of development allowed. In the case considered, 146·3 acres for development at 10 dwellings per acre, total receipts would have been £1,360,600 for 10,000 persons. The Corporation's only expenses would be the land's original cost at £2,000 per acre, fees, administrative expenses and interest on this cost, and the appropriate share of general development expenditure. Receipts would be nearly double the expenses, giving a surplus of over £600,000.

Although the sale of non-residential land is not encouraged, certain development agencies, such as public utilities, local authorities and some charitable bodies are allowed to buy freehold land for developments for which they are responsible. Other public agencies are allowed to purchase land they need for buildings for their own use. All the extra-curtilage site development for the latter is carried out by the Corporation and financed from the price received.[2] The surplus from this type of sale was calculated at £248,600 per 10,000 population. The prices taken were rather arbitrary and the expenses were not always charged in full, so that this surplus cannot be regarded as a commercial return, as can the surplus on the sale of housing land.

NON-RESIDENTIAL DEVELOPMENT BY THE CORPORATION

There remained the land in the industrial and central areas developed by the Corporation and rented either as bare sites or with buildings at a rack rent. For convenience, site development of this land was first costed at the basic overall figure of £4,000 per acre; additions were made for those sites requiring more expensive development – the central core at a total of £13,000 per acre and land for industry at a total of £6,000 per acre. The cost of intra-curtilage works was added for open space, gardens and car parks.

It was assumed that the Development Corporation would build for rack renting half of all industrial and commercial buildings in the settlement. Half of the construction cost of industrial buildings per 10,000 population would be £1,052,000 (table 9.6). Building costs for shops in chapter 9 included shop-fitting which would not be carried out by the developer. After subtracting this, general development expenditure and fees, administrative expenses and interest were calcu-

[1] The prices assumed for residential and non-residential land are given in appendix tables B.1 and B.2 (see p. 271 below).

[2] The extra-curtilage development in the case of the educational area and the hospital area was included in the development costs of adjacent areas.

lated as before, making the total capital cost to the Corporation of developing the industrial and central areas £2,958,400.

It was assumed that half the net area would be let at ground rents and the Corporation would build on the other half. This did not, of course, necessarily follow from the earlier assumption that half the cost of building was incurred by the Corporation. In the industrial area 14 acres of land and 243,400 square feet of industrial and commercial building were therefore assumed to be let to give a total annual revenue of £115,300.[1] In the district centre, the provision of shops, offices and service industry would be shared between the Corporation and private developers, but other buildings, such as public houses and hotels, would almost always be built by private enterprise. An estimate of £5,000 was added for ground rents on these sites, to give a total revenue of £107,100. The town centre calculation was similar, again with miscellaneous ground rents on sites for a cinema, hotel, bowling alley and dance hall, which would amount to about £10,000. Revenue from the town centre would be about £36,700 on this basis, making total rents of £259,100 per annum on all non-residential development by the Corporation.

THE FINANCE OF THE DEVELOPMENT CORPORATION

The separate accounts could be consolidated into a capital account for the Development Corporation. Public authority housing was kept separate because it was only required to break even after the receipt of subsidies. Other development was expected to meet more stringent financial tests, which will be considered below. General development expenditure being an accounting figure only, used to allocate costs between different areas, the gross amount was necessary in sectional accounts, but it could be included net in the consolidated account. Total capital expenditure excluding public housing would, on the assumptions made, be £4,035,400 per 10,000 population, against which capital receipts of about £1,936,400 could be offset.

Returns from public authority housing

The total expenditure eligible for subsidy was calculated at £4,985,000. At 6 per cent an annual payment is 0·06188 times the principal and at 4 per cent 0·04420 times; the annual subsidy would therefore be £88,100 plus, for 10 years only, a rate fund grant of £16,500 per annum on the 1,375 subsidised dwellings. To estimate the rent revenue, the distribution of public authority housing by size was taken to be the same as for all dwellings (table 9.1). The public sector revenue net of

[1] Based on the net annual rents shown in appendix table B.3.

maintenance and management costs would be £300,000 a year,[1] which, with the estimated revenue from corner-shops, would amount in total to £307,500.

Voids were allowed for in the management charges, so it was sufficient to check whether net rents and subsidies covered the interest and capital repayments. The total cost of public authority housing, including general development, was about £6,326,000 per 10,000 population (page 193). Strictly, the capital used for corner-shops should be deducted, but for simplicity this cost (less than £75,000) was included. With interest at 6 per cent, the annual repayments of interest and principal would be £391,500.

The housing account would have an annual surplus of £20,600 for the first 10 years (about £14 per dwelling), and £4,100 (under £3 per dwelling) thereafter. These figures indicate how finely balanced the account would be; any small extra cost or a rent rebate would throw it into deficit. In accounting terms, at current rents substantial surpluses might be achieved through inflation; real returns would, however, be marginal.

Of the settlement characteristics which have so far been kept constant only three affected the housing account – housing density, road costs and land costs. Three levels of density were considered – 41, 57 and 68 habitable rooms per acre. A change in density would affect the area of the whole settlement, as well as the housing area, and hence the general development costs. During the first 10 years revenue would exceed capital costs for any of these densities, but once the rate fund grant ceased, only at medium density would the development remain in surplus in real terms. The advantage of medium over low density lay in the higher rents charged for flats than for houses. In comparing medium with high density, the extra cost of high flats outweighed the increased rents and the high flats subsidy. Land prices considered were £500, £2,000 and £5,000 per acre.[2] Changes in these prices affected the cost of housing directly and through the cost of general development. Road costs, which fell mainly within the range £80 to £150 per head, affected general development costs. For all but the most expensive roads, the public housing account would be in surplus if the land cost not more than £2,000 per acre (chart 15.1). Conversely, not even the cheapest roads could give a surplus with land costing £2,750 per acre or more. As the road costs rose the amount which could be found out of revenue for purchasing land naturally fell (chart 15.2).

---

[1] Based on the net annual rents shown in appendix table B.4.

[2] An expensive sites subsidy was payable in 1967 at an annual rate of £34 per £1,000 for 60 years on the amount by which the site cost exceeded £4,000 per acre. This was changed, however, by the 1972 Housing Finance Act.

Chart 15.1. *The public housing account with different road costs and land prices*

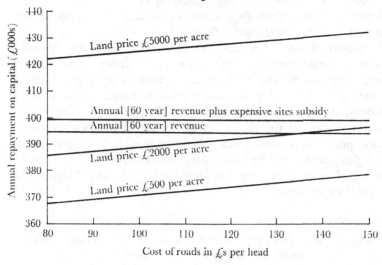

SOURCE: NIESR estimates.

Chart 15.2. *Road costs and land prices for which the public housing account would break even*

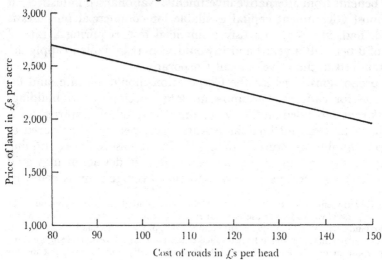

SOURCE: NIESR estimates.

Land for public authority housing would be cheaper than for private housing – £2,000 basic plus £2,925 for general development, against over £10,000 at the public housing density of 11·8 dwellings per acre. The difference of more than £5,000 was equivalent to an annual subsidy of about £25 per dwelling for 60 years.

The inclusion of the Corporation's land and general development costs in the public housing account was rather confusing. It was clearer to separate completely the Corporation's functions in providing a social housing service and as a developer. A separate public housing account debited with the cost of land purchased from the Corporation as a developer showed the true costs of the social housing service as £7,028,600 per 10,000 population. This gave a slightly larger annual surplus of £22,900 for the first 10 years, because the subsidies rose by £45,700, which was more than the increase in the annual equivalent of the capital expenditure.

Returns from other activities

In providing sites for sale or lease and non-residential buildings for lease, the Corporation would be engaged in a commercial enterprise. Government capital is scarce and the Corporation competes for its requirements with other government enterprises. While a satisfactory financial return might not have been essential, it would probably be sufficient, prima facie, to justify an investment. If the financial return was unsatisfactory it would be necessary to appeal to non-financial arguments; social benefits would have to be assessed and compared with similar benefits from alternative investments. Nationalised industries, in which most government capital available for commercial purposes is invested, had, in 1967, to satisfy a financial test, requiring a rate of return of 8 per cent a year,[1] and it would seem reasonable to apply the same standard to the Development Corporation.

The proportions in which the Corporation should allocate land for sale, as sites for leasing at a ground rent, or for developing with buildings at a rack rent depended on the availability of capital, the returns which could be obtained, and how far private developers were prepared to develop a suitable structure at the right time to ensure the continuing viability of the settlement. It was assumed that development would follow current government policy, and that average returns could be

---

[1] 'The Government will expect projects which are submitted to it for approval to be expressed in present values by the use of a test rate of discount. . . . It is essential that the nationalised industries should use consistent methods of appraisal and should adopt the same test discount rate. The Government have decided that 8 per cent is a reasonable figure to use for this purpose in present circumstances. The test rate of discount . . . does not include allowance for the risks of individual investments.' Treasury, *Nationalised Industries: a review of economic and financial objectives*, Cmnd 3437, London, HMSO, 1967.

estimated with sufficient accuracy by comparing expenditure on completion with prices and rents for mature development. The 8 per cent criterion appeared to be satisfied by most of the different types of activity.

The return on land sales of between 11 and 12 per cent was dominated by that from private housing (11·2 per cent). Other returns on land sales were not easily interpreted because prices could not easily be determined from available market information; educational, hospital and some other sites did not bear all the expenses of their development. In the industrial and central areas receipts were depressed by the sale of land at £10,000 per acre to the local authorities and at £2,500 to charitable bodies, but as comparatively little land was involved the shortfall was not very important. The overall surplus from land sales would, of course, be greatly increased and the overall return much improved if land for public housing was included at its market price.

While the returns in real terms on site development in the central area were comparatively high (12–13 per cent), those in the industrial area were very low, under 5 per cent or only about half the acceptable minimum. Development costs could not be determined precisely, but any overestimates for the industrial area were unlikely to be large enough to affect the returns by more than about 1 per cent. Open space in the industrial area, initially about a quarter of the land, reduced the return. If this land was to be retained permanently for industrial playing fields, it might have been more consistent to remove it from the account for industrial site development. This would have increased this return to about 5 per cent, although other returns would have been depressed by the increase in general development expenditure per acre. On the other hand, the land might eventually be required for industrial sites, when the area capable of earning a revenue would be increased and with it the return on industrial land. Even so, unless industrial ground rents were increased about three-fold, the returns would still be below the level required. It would be politic to keep rents low in the early stages of development, but there would be little reason to do so at maturity of the settlement when all the industry required should have been established. Industrial sites would be unlikely to be so cheap elsewhere, certainly not without subsidies, and it might be that industrial ground rents were set too low. Again, of course, the effect of inflation might be large enough to mask such low real returns and to give the impression that returns were satisfactory.

The return on industrial buildings was also below 8 per cent. The return on central area buildings was better (about 11 per cent), though less than that from site development in the central areas. Buildings were costed at average prices and it could be that the rack rents would apply only to the cheaper types; more elaborate buildings might be

constructed mainly by the users. Buildings would be unlikely to
continue to earn current real levels of rent for 60 years, the period
over which they were depreciated, without considerable modification.
Moreover, they would be more likely than sites to be unoccupied at
times. Some allowance for these contingencies was made in the net
rack rents, but even so it was doubtful whether the return from central
area buildings was high enough, and the return from industrial buildings was definitely too low.

The results showed that, at the prices used, it would be more profitable
for the Corporation to sell industrial sites than to let them at a ground
rent. With limited capital, returns could be increased by concentrating
on buildings in the central areas. This would be restricted, of course,
by the need to attract sufficient business to the settlement. So far it has
been assumed, at least implicitly, that after the initial development described the Corporation could leave the remainder of industrial and commercial building to private developers. The return on all activities
(between 9 and 10 per cent) showed that the Corporation would then
be financially viable, even if not as profitable as it might be. But if
private enterprise failed to develop particular facilities, the Corporation
would have to do so, and this would probably be the least profitable
development, so that returns overall would be lower than indicated.
Moreover, unless additional capital was available, the Corporation
would have to reduce investment in the more profitable facilities and
thus returns would be further depressed.

Effects of varying the settlement factors

Changes in the net residential density for private housing affected the
area to be developed and sold, and the price realised per acre. The
return on the capital invested increased substantially with density, from
72 per cent at 8 dwellings per acre to 82 per cent at 10 dwellings per
acre and 104 per cent at 13 dwellings per acre. The returns on residential land sales would not have been greatly affected by any likely
changes in the costs of the main roads, but possible changes in the price
of land would have had a considerable effect. A change of £1 per head
of population in road costs would only have changed the general
development cost per acre marginally, so that even with a rise of £20 to
£30 a head, a substantial increase in this item, developed costs would
only have risen by a few hundred pounds per acre. On the other hand,
the basic price of land affected costs both directly and through general
development costs, so that even a moderate increase of £1,000 an acre
would have raised developed costs per acre by over £1,400. At 10
dwellings per acre, the surplus would become a deficit if the land cost
£5,000 per acre.

Variations in the cost of the main roads, or in the cost of land, did not affect the returns from non-residential buildings, since both construction costs and the differences between rack and ground rents would have been unchanged. However, the cost of land in particular affected returns from ground rents: if it was £3,000 instead of £2,000 an acre, the cost of providing industrial sites would increase by about 12 per cent and the rate of return would fall by about an eighth; returns on central area sites would also be substantially reduced, by nearly 10 per cent.

The degree of centralisation of a settlement affected expenditure on site development in the central areas, although not by very much. It also affected rents in the central area, but not elsewhere; the more development in the town centre, the greater the revenue. Ground rents were substantially higher in a fully centralised settlement, but the rents used may have overestimated the effect of centrality, because as the centre grows average rents fall, due both to the increasing average distance from the focal point of the centre and to the increasing number of marginally central businesses. This effect would probably be insignificant in the town centres of decentralised and partly centralised settlements, but might lower considerably the revenue from the centre of a fully centralised settlement.

Differences in settlement size had a marked effect on land prices and ground rents, and some effect on rack rents. Returns from all activities therefore increased with the size of the settlement. Variations in the road costs with changes in residential density, centralisation, or size of settlement would have a significant effect only in extreme cases.

Effects of inflation

As mentioned already, prices and rents as well as the costs of development were considered at the levels prevailing in 1967. Prices and rents might change because the supply of properties fell in relation to demand, or because profits from the businesses carried on there increased, so that the rents worth paying rose. However, as all prices and rents were estimated for a mature settlement, increases from these causes did not affect the situations examined in this book. On the other hand, prices and rents also rise as the value of money falls and it would be unrealistic not to have assumed that this fall would continue. Since a developer normally sells on completion of development, inflationary increases in land prices are not important to him, but rents are usually fixed for some years at a time, based on expected free market rents over that period. If rents rose with inflation but the cost of servicing the loan (the annual equivalent of the capital cost) was fixed, the net return in money values would increase faster than the rate of inflation, even though growth of the real return was slower than with no inflation. The greater the increases in rents the faster the real net return would grow, unless lenders anticipated inflation in fixing the rate of interest, when this inflationary gain might well be lost. Given the growing recognition that inflation is likely to continue, the central government will probably be able to borrow in the long run only at a rate which reflects the falling value of money. Thus, even if the Development Corporation borrowed from the central government at a fixed rate of interest, and showed a book return increased by inflation, such an increase would not necessarily be enjoyed by the central government. The conclusion was therefore that inflation was unlikely to raise real rates of return much above the levels based on 1967 costs and revenue.

COMMERCIAL DEVELOPERS' FINANCE

Commercial enterprises would develop both private housing and non-residential buildings. The housing would be mainly for sale, although a small amount might be rented and some plots might be sold for the purchasers to build their own homes. No information was available on the selling prices of dwellings or of plots for dwellings, but it was understood that a surplus on total construction expenditure of about 15 per cent would be expected. Costs would be affected by the price of land, which rose both with the size of the settlement and with density.

Non-residential buildings would be constructed by commercial developers partly for letting at a rack rent and partly for their own use. Given the earlier assumptions of the proportions of such buildings constructed by the Development Corporation, it was simple to estimate the balancing investment by commercial developers. The financial returns to these developers could not be estimated in any useful way without considerably more information on the use of the buildings, the development undertaken by users themselves, and the costs and rents applicable. The net return calculated on the difference between rack and ground rents as a percentage of building costs would probably be about the same as for the Development Corporation, between 9 and 10 per cent. However, this average had little meaning; it depended on the share of each type of development left to the commercial developers, and, for example, would fall as their share of industrial development rose. Industrial buildings and perhaps other types with a low return would probably be developed by the users, who would be less concerned with rates of return. Moreover, the Development Corporation would probably be left to develop the least profitable buildings.

LOCAL AUTHORITY FINANCE

The term 'local authority' is used here to cover all local government bodies; no attempt was made to separate the accounts for different authorities.

Sewerage was the most complicated financial problem. No arrangement was laid down by the Ministry, but there were two possible solutions; either the local authority provided for the new town, or the Development Corporation took on sewerage powers itself under section 34 of the New Towns Act, 1965. Among existing new towns, the latter was, in 1967, by far the most common, but in either case the cost would be shared between the Corporation and the local authority. Even if the local authority could provide sewerage for the new town, it would be under no obligation to do so in advance of development, and it could not compel the developer to reimburse the cost. A compromise would therefore be necessary, with the developer contributing towards capital costs and also, where capacity was at first excessive, towards loan charges. When the Development Corporation took on sewerage powers, the local authority was required (section 34(4) of the 1965 Act) to contribute, usually towards both annual loan charges and cost; the local authority took over full operational and financial responsibility as soon as it could, for a transfer price expected to be not greater than the capital cost less depreciation. Thus, in the long run, the authority met the capital cost, but the Development Corporation broadly covered the costs incurred by development ahead of need. The capitalised value of such payments probably increased general development expenditure by 3 or 4 per cent, about £75 per acre.

Gross capital expenditure on all services by the local authority was about £270 per head, which was equivalent to less than £20 a year per head (less than £60 per dwelling). This amount could not be related directly to the rates, since the full annual cost also included running costs, and central government grants had to be deducted.

Changes in road costs, but not in any other factors of form, affected this account. After allowing for the grant from the Ministry of Transport, about one tenth of the road costs would be borne by the local authority, but this was under 5 per cent of the authority's total expenditure, so changes in these costs made little difference.

PUBLIC UTILITY FINANCE

The total capital expenditure by public utilities was calculated at about £160 per head. Since the Water Resources Act, 1965, this utility has been self-financing, so that there was no reason to include it in the local authority accounts. None of the public utilities was affected by variations in the factors of size and form.

THE COMBINED CAPITAL ACCOUNT

Adding the accounts of the separate agencies taking part in developing the settlement gave a total capital cost which agreed broadly with the total resource costs of about £2,400 per head in chapter 9. There were slight differences arising from applying a lower average land cost and the allowances for fees and interest item by item. Land purchases and sales by the Development Corporation were combined, so that the total land cost did not include transfer payments between the agencies; similarly grants received and paid out were included net to eliminate double counting. No allowance was made for capital grants except for roads and charities because of their uncertainty. Receipts from housing sold freehold were estimated at cost including the land, plus profits of 15 per cent on the costs of site development and building.

Charitable bodies, who would be responsible for churches, youth clubs and community centres, would buy land from the Development Corporation at the concessionary rate of £2,500 per acre. They would also receive small grants of about £2,000 per youth club from the local authority. Their total costs were about £19 per head and were not affected by urban form.

The major central government expenditure was on construction of a hospital. This would amount to about £60 per head and would only be incurred in a settlement for 250,000 people. The central government also makes capital grants to local authorities, of which that for roads, about half the total, was taken into account. The most important annual payments by the central governments were housing subsidies which, if capitalised at 6 per cent, would have amounted to about £1,700,000 per 10,000 population, or about £170 per head. The central government is also responsible for providing the capital required by the Development Corporation, and most of that for the local authorities and the public utilities.

The total capital cost of the settlement on this basis was estimated at about £24 million per 10,000 population, of which some £400,000 would be met by the road fund contribution. After the sale of land and buildings, the developing agencies would be left with a capital burden of nearly £15 million per 10,000 population. Central and local government agencies would need to find about £13·5 million of this, mostly through central government borrowing.

FINANCING TOWN EXPANSION

Adding development to an existing town rather than building a new settlement on a virgin site would increase costs of roads, of land and of central area development. On the other hand, the present value of the total investment could be reduced by postponing expenditure, temporary use being made of existing facilities. The present value of the total revenue might increase, because higher rents could be charged from the beginning for some facilities, particularly shops. These effects were discussed and quantified in chapter 14.

For a partly centralised settlement for 250,000 persons developed from a town for 50,000 persons the average price of land would be £4,000 to £5,000 per acre, and road construction would be increased by about 20 per cent, so that general development expenditure would rise to over £4,000 an acre; the public authority housing account would then be in deficit even during the first 10 years and more so thereafter.

The surplus on the sale of land for private housing would be considerably smaller in an expanded town. The creation of a large settlement from a small base town would have least effect, since land prices and rents increase with the size of the settlement, but the additional costs of expansion would rise less than proportionately to increases in size (chapter 14). Even in a settlement for 250,000 persons, the surplus obtainable on a greenfield site would be reduced by about 55 per cent. Returns on other land sales would also fall.

The returns to the Development Corporation on non-residential development would also be lower in an expanded town because of increased capital costs. The rates of return on site development would be only just above the 8 per cent criterion. The returns on construction of buildings would still be between 9 and 10 per cent.

Costs of developing the town centre would be raised, not only by higher general development and land costs, but also by the extra cost of building on land previously developed. The more important the existing town's centre is to be in the expanded town, the greater the additional capital costs. The returns would be even lower if the town was expanded into a decentralised settlement but, of course, not so low if the existing town was to be a district of the new settlement.

Even the most favourable way of expanding a town would be more expensive and would offer less attractive returns to the Development Corporation than development on a virgin site. Some benefits showed up when phasing was considered: for example, there would be a capital saving of about £1 million from postponing some shopping development, and shops would immediately earn the rents payable in a town of the size to which it was to be expanded. In any case rents rise with increasing population, and discounting the alternative revenue flows over a 20-year period of even growth showed that an expanded town would give a higher present value for shopping than a completely new settlement, but the difference was very small, only about 5 per cent. The costs and returns to the other developers would also be affected in comparable ways.

CHAPTER 16

PHASING AND ADAPTABILITY OF SETTLEMENTS

STATIC AND DYNAMIC CONCEPTS

It was convenient in considering urban form and development to study in the main the position at maturity of the settlement. The use of this static concept is less valid now than it was earlier in the new town programme, because when that programme was first developed the expectation was of a rapidly increasing national population, a rapidly rising labour force and national economic growth. These conditions implied the need for rapid additional urban development and the availability of a large volume of footloose industry which could be encouraged to set up in new areas.

Today the national population is expected to increase only slowly, and the need for more settlements and for settlement expansion arises less from population growth than from the additional land required for development and redevelopment at considerably lower densities than in present towns. Because it is desired strictly to limit the physical growth of existing metropolitan areas and conurbations, new development is needed in virgin areas or in areas adjacent to small free-standing towns. At the same time the comparative scarcity of new footloose industry increases the difficulties of developing new settlements.

However, conditions can change very rapidly. The factors determining population growth are little understood.[1] The current downward trend in fertility rates could equally well be reversed, with consequential changes in the supply of labour and demand for homes in the decades ahead. Similarly, economic changes might result in rapid economic growth and the creation of new firms, which would increase the supply of footloose industry.

Thus, over the development period of new and expanded towns, the scale of development required and its form could change. Settlements are unlikely to be completed either on the scale or in the form in which they were first conceived, and the rates of development are likely to be varied from time to time. Consequently it is necessary to consider the efficiency of settlement sizes and forms, not just in regard to the construction and operation of the mature settlement, but also from the point of view of phasing and adaptability.

[1] Stone, *Urban Development in Britain*, vol. i.

THE EFFICIENT USE OF CAPITAL RESOURCES

Capital resources are being used inefficiently while they are tied up in facilities which cannot be fully utilised. With less 'lumpy' investment this is not a problem (dwellings and unit shops can be occupied one by one as they are completed), but the larger and more complex the development the greater the delay in using all its facilities. Roads and services can be extended in step with the building of new houses and shop parades, but with blocks of flats, the superstructure, foundations and services, including lifts, must be completed before any flat can be occupied. Similarly for decked shopping centres – the deck with its services must be finished before the shops can be occupied.

Generally, the larger the building the longer resources will be frozen and the more capital will be tied up unremuneratively. The losses thus occasioned, both in real and in financial terms, may in many cases outweigh the economies of scale obtained from larger buildings.

How far there is a choice in the size of a building depends on its type and function. Where a building consists of a number of units operated independently, such as dwellings or unit shops, there is functionally a free choice. However, where a building is a single functional unit, such as a factory, a school or a library, size depends on the function and may be determined by industrial or commercial factors, or by the population to be served. Thus the size of the local sector of a settlement, or of the settlement itself, may determine sizes and forms of facilities, and hence their overall economies.

Generally, the smaller the settlement the smaller the functional areas within it – residential, commercial and industrial – although these sizes also depend on settlement form. Neighbourhood shopping and service areas will be smaller than those for districts, and central shopping and service areas will, other things being equal, be largest in centralised settlements and smallest in decentralised ones. In practice, larger areas are generally developed at greater densities with, on average, larger buildings. Higher densities, whether occasioned by size or otherwise, usually involve higher and larger building complexes, and hence relatively inefficient use of capital resources.

Smaller areas usually provide greater flexibility of development. With a number of small residential areas, capital can be brought more rapidly into productive use by completing one area at a time. For some facilities, however, this causes difficulties, particularly where demand is strongly age-related as, for example, for schools. In the past, households moving into a new area of a settlement have tended to be of much the same age, have had young children and have rapidly completed their families. As a result the needs for schools and other facilities for young people have risen to a maximum over a fairly short period and then declined, leaving the facilities under-used. (This feature of the new towns may, however, be less extreme in future.) To avoid this problem, either each area must be built up slowly, several areas being developed concurrently, or temporary buildings must be used – a further alternative would be 'busing' children from one area to another.

Developing several residential areas at a time involves duplication of the facilities accompanying the housing at each centre, unless the inhabitants are to be forced to travel to other areas for the services they need. While the local shopping will generally consist of small unit shops, which can be assembled in small blocks, a number of shops, or a sizeable department store will be needed to supply the full range of services required. Thus in the early stages of development there is likely to be some duplication of buildings. Until there are sufficient inhabitants to provide trade adequate in volume to make the shops and services viable, their rents would have to be low enough to subsidise the businesses and might even need to be negative. Similar difficulties would arise in the case of public services such as libraries, clinics and recreational centres. It is unlikely therefore that, other things being equal, the inhabitants would be served as well while a number of residential areas were being developed as when there was only one.

Temporary buildings, for schools and other buildings for which demands change with the age distribution of the inhabitants, have their own advantages and disadvantages. Such buildings are generally no cheaper than permanent buildings and can be more expensive. Costs also arise for dismantling, transporting, reassembling, and repairing and redecorating the buildings in their new location. It might be that the use of flexible permanent buildings, which could be adapted to meet changing needs as the age structure of the population changed, would be just as (or more) economical.

At some stage in the development of the residential areas, busing and other forms of travel from one area to another will be necessary to obtain a full range of local services. This can lead to both inconvenience and the use of additional resources for transport. It would generally not be economically feasible to provide fully convenient bus services from one residential area to another.

Probably the most convenient and economic solution is to develop residential areas one by one, and to aim at a balanced cross-section of population. This would also have social advantages. The best solution in any given situation can be found by comparing the balance between the discounted costs and the benefits of the alternatives.

Similar problems arise in meeting non-residential needs. Again, less capital is likely to be tied up non-productively if only one of each type of area is developed at a time. There would not usually be advantages in developing factories in any particular location pattern; given reasonable accessibility and as long as there was room for expansion on each site, industrial estates could be completed and filled one at a time. Sometimes offices will be developed on the industrial estates, but more often in conjunction with commercial centres. Although some offices would be in the neighbourhood or district centres, most would usually be in the central area. While the offices could be started before the commercial area of the settlement centres, they might have limited drawing power until the services were provided. In the past, offices in new settlements have not generally been developed until the settlement was well established, because the early inhabitants were usually industrial workers and there was no pool of office labour until their children reached working age. If future settlements are developed with migrants from a more balanced cross-section of the population as is currently proposed, offices will be needed earlier.

The problems of providing town services are greater than those of neighbourhood and district services, because larger populations are required to support facilities such as specialist shops, higher forms of education, hospitals and town recreational services. If they are provided early, heavily subsidised or perhaps negative rents will be needed, and there will be losses, not only from under-utilised capital, but also from uneconomic running expenses. However, in the absence of such services, additional costs and inconvenience for journeys to other settlements will arise, as will the dangers of establishing behaviour patterns difficult to change once local facilities are available, and of stimulating investment in other settlements which may not be viable if the behaviour pattern does change. Development around an existing settlement which can meet demand in the early days of growth helps to solve these problems. The existing settlement also provides additional customers, so bringing forward the time when new facilities will be viable. However, phasing will be easier and less capital will be tied up unproductively where the additional units of facilities are small and flexible.

Expenditure on the terminal works of most public utility services tends to be 'lumpy'. Usually, however, it is technically possible to provide a number of small facilities instead of one or two very large ones. While the smaller facilities are more expensive per unit of service, the economies of scale are generally fairly soon exhausted and the savings in costs from combining two or three medium-sized facilities are small (chapter 9). Moreover, there may be offsetting savings from shorter mains connections.

One of the 'lumpiest' facilities is the main road system. Clearly there must be road links between the new settlement and others, their capacity increasing with the growth of the settlement and of vehicle ownership. There must also be links between the residential and other areas within the settlement. The more areas are developed at the same time, the more links will have to be constructed in the early stages. Since a road cannot generally have less than a lane in each direction, its capacity may be excessive for some time, although it may be possible, of course, to use existing roads. Other things being equal, main road construction can be delayed longer if development is concentrated in the fewest possible adjacent areas.

The cost of main road development and its phasing will also depend on the planned final form of the settlement and the type of road system. The least 'lumpy' system would be a grid of two-lane roads with level junctions, which could be extended without alteration as development proceeded provided that the total size of the settlement was not too large. A final grid of dual four-lane roads with level junctions could be developed from the two-lane road system by building parallel two-lane roads to provide two carriageways as the need arose, or less cheaply by widening the existing roads. (It is necessary to consider not only the costs of constructing, servicing and extending road systems, but also the costs of time lost and of the inconvenience to road users during reconstruction.) Costs of the extension of roads start to rise when the interchanges need to be at grade, which involves sterilising large areas of land and often the reconstruction of existing roads when the interchanges are built.

Ring road systems and, even more, linear road systems in linear settlements, are much more expensive to extend in terms of discounted costs than the simpler systems discussed earlier. Beyond a certain point, ring routes function inefficiently until the ring is complete, even though this provides considerable excess capacity. Linear road systems for large linear settlements require either considerable capital tied up in a road system with substantial unused capacity until the settlement is complete, or repeated reconstruction of the system if it is expanded as capacity is required.

Similarly railways are 'lumpy' investments. For most settlements, one up and one down track will be all that is ever required. While the system may be extended as the settlement is built, each part of it will generally need to be built to full standards from the beginning.

It is clear that a nuclear settlement will require least unproductive capital resources, since capacity in all facilities can most easily be developed in step with need and the smaller each unit the easier this would be. Thus, from this point of view, decentralisation would be an advantage – decentralisation not only into clusters of settlements rather than one large settlement, but also of each settlement within the cluster.

THE FLEXIBILITY OF SETTLEMENT FORMS

While it is desirable to determine the most economic form and size of settlement, it can by no means be assumed that the settlement will be developed to maturity and beyond according to the chosen strategy. Conditions change, particularly population expectations and economic viability, life-styles do not always follow expectations and new technology produces unexpected results. The Mark 1 new towns were built in the expectation of moderate increases in national population and purchasing power, and without anticipation of a high rate of car ownership; some of them in fact were built with extensive systems of cycle tracks.

The planned population of a settlement may either exceed or be exceeded by the population achieved at maturity, as a consequence of changes in national population levels, the national economy or the viability of the settlement itself. If national or regional population increases much faster than expected and it is desired to limit the growth of existing cities and conurbations, it may be considered easier to develop new and expanded centres to larger sizes than to create further ones. Alternatively, if population increases more slowly than expected and the economy lacks buoyancy (or if the settlement lacks viability), it may be impossible to obtain the population or for employment to reach the planned size. Moreover, there is likely to be some growth after the date set for maturity of the settlement.

Probably only rarely will a new or expanded settlement be completed at its planned size. It is, therefore, important that the settlement should be flexible enough, or its form sufficiently adaptable, to accommodate considerable changes in planned size, without reducing the efficiency with which it can be developed and operated. Most basic cells in a settlement are complete in themselves; an increase or decrease in population simply changes the number of such cells – for example, the number of residential areas, industrial areas, recreational areas and neighbourhood or district centres. Of course, such changes in population might be met by changing the density of development of areas or parts of areas not at that time developed, but this would change the facilities of the settlement away from the levels planned as providing the best compromise, and hence usually reduce the amenities. The major difficulty would be with cells or facility systems which served the whole settlement – for example, central areas, public utilities such as sewerage and water, the transport network, hospitals and colleges of higher education.

Some of the Mark 1 new towns have already run into difficulties in expanding their town centres when their population target has been raised, because the centre has been surrounded by residential areas,

with no space for expansion. The problem might be solved by developing future settlements with an area of open space, either around the
town centre or at each end of it. This would provide space for expansion,
but would tend to reduce the convenience of the town centre as planned,
especially for the inner residential areas which, as in Cumbernauld,
might have fewer facilities within their local centres, or no local commercial centres. Such a form might be unsatisfactory also for a settlement of larger area: the expansion of a small settlement centre would
result in a set of facilities on a small scale, which could be extended only
by duplication at that scale or by larger scale facilities at the periphery
of the central areas; neither solution would be very convenient. If, on
the other hand, the planned size was reduced, too much land would be
left, and there would be the inconveniences of a loosely fitting and perhaps lop-sided central area. Moreover, some of the facilities in it would
be out of scale and perhaps never viable.

Clearly the tighter and more centralised the settlement, the greater
the difficulties changes in planned size would cause. In a very loose
form of settlement the central area might have its status changed simply
by changing the relationships and centres of areas still to be built, and
by replanning the undeveloped space adjacent to the centre. This
might change the form of the settlement as well as of the centre and
result in some hybrid form. The scale of change necessary would, of
course, depend on phasing. The faster the development the more
facilities created before the change in size was decided upon and the
more difficult change would be. On the other hand, if development was
very slow and the changes much delayed, some facilities might be ripe
for redevelopment when that was desirable.

Changes in the form and size of the central area would clearly be
most difficult in a circular or square settlement and rather easier in a
linear, cruciform or necklace shape, where the development was narrow
enough to provide undeveloped land for sideways expansion, and where
a narrowing of development would not increase the inconvenience of
operating the settlement. Again, difficulties would tend to be greater
where the density and form of development required a decked settlement centre, since it would be less easy to develop even more densely
and less adaptable if less space was required than had been planned.

Such public utilities as sewerage and water supply are not always
developed as single facilities, but where the topography of the site or
phasing made it necessary to do so additional separate facilities would
be needed if the planned settlement size was increased, and there would
be surplus capacity if the size was reduced. Where several facilities
were planned it might be possible to re-plan one or more of those not
already built.

The transport network would also be very vulnerable to changes in size. Increases in planned size would generally increase traffic more than proportionately. For a limited increase it might be possible to accommodate the additional traffic within the spare potential of the road system, but if additional links were needed, they might be difficult to provide without clearing existing property and damaging the planned structure of the settlement and its amenities. Often, moreover, an increase in size would create a demand for considerable additional capacity, at least on some links, and it would be necessary to add lanes and provide junctions at grade (which would be likely to involve considerable costs and damage to amenities), or to restrict the use of private cars and provide public transport. Again the vulnerability of the system would depend on its form. The more concentrated the form, the more difficult it would be to adapt it to size changes in either direction. A linear primary road system would be the most vulnerable, a radial system would increase in vulnerability the tighter the inter-change system, while a fine grid would be least vulnerable. A rail system would have the greatest spare capacity, but additional links might be difficult to fit into a comprehensive system.

Up to a point, single facilities such as hospitals and colleges of higher education would be the easiest to adapt to changes in scale, but ineffici-ency might result. Alternatively, some people might be catered for in simi-lar institutions elsewhere, or people might be absorbed from other areas.

Size is not the only characteristic which might be changed: equally population structure, or employment structure and social class, or life-styles and technology might be altered.

Generally, population structure, employment structure and social class change only gradually. They affect life-styles only slowly, in ways that could be accommodated in future development, although a few existing facilities might need adaptation as well. However, changes in life-styles associated with greater and growing affluence might be much more dramatic and would tend to influence the whole population. They would probably have an important effect on housing standards, shopping, recreational facilities and transport.

With the increasing ownership of material goods, fittings, furniture, and personal possessions such as clothes, electrical appliances, cars and recreation equipment, the home would need more space: inside, particularly in the kitchen, and for more bathrooms and storage; outside, for garaging, for the storage of boats, caravans and other equipment, perhaps in some cases for swimming pools. Moreover, with a wider range of indoor recreation and entertainments, more rooms and more spacious rooms would be needed to house the family at leisure. At the same time, with more to spend on housing, standards of finish and equipment would rise. While this wish to up-grade might result partly in improvements and extensions to existing housing, it might also encourage a general move to bigger and better dwellings. (This already occurs in the new towns – residents moving after a time from lower to higher standard dwellings.) If growing affluence raised standards substantially, it might lead to pressure for a higher quality of new housing and leave blocks of low standard dwellings obsolete unless they could be converted and up-graded.

Affluence might also lead to a demand for higher class shopping and more recreational space – for example, golf courses and facilities for water sports, restaurants and clubs. Shopping and other central area facilities, and the areas of recreational space would then have to be reconstructed.

Growing affluence generally leads to more movement, particularly by private cars, which would increasingly be used for the journey to work. The amount of traffic might then exceed the capacity of the road system. If adequate reservations had been provided, it would be physically possible to increase road capacity without demolishing existing development, but it would still tend to be more expensive than if sufficient capacity had been provided originally. In the absence of adequate reservations, extensive redevelopment would be necessary, perhaps including roads on aqueducts or in tunnels. The situation would be similar to that of an existing town trying to deal with a substantial growth of traffic, and it might be less expensive to restrict the use of private cars and provide more public transport, probably buses.

The effects of technological change are more difficult to analyse because of the problem of predicting what changes might occur affecting the built environment. It is notable that, over the last century, only the development of the internal combustion engine has caused serious problems for urban form and its adaptability. Even in this case the problems have resulted less from a change in motive power than from the growth of affluence which, coupled with increasingly efficient production, has led to near universal ownership of cars.

Again, the more highly centralised, compact and rigid the settlement, the more difficult it would be to adapt it to the various types of change discussed above. Smaller settlements are likely to be easier to adapt than large ones; low-density, decentralised, cluster settlements would be the easiest.

THE DURATION AND PHASING OF DEVELOPMENT

Generally the faster the development the less capital is tied up in it unproductively; even the 'lumpier' investments will be utilised more fully the more rapidly population is built up. There will, of course, be

some patterns of phasing which give better results than others, and these
patterns vary with the form and size of the settlement.

Broadly it will be those forms of settlement which involve the 'lumpiest' investments which show the best results when population is built
up rapidly, although the pace must, of course, be related to the development of facilities to obtain the best results. Such forms are highly
compact and centralised and require large individual facilities (such as
decked town centres, large, tall blocks of flats, large schools, recreational centres, libraries and other buildings), large-capacity integrated
road systems, bus-only roads and tracked transport, and single water,
sewerage and drainage systems. Conversely, the looser the settlement
form, the easier it is to develop separate parts such as neighbourhoods
and districts, industrial areas and separate sections of the road and
public utility systems. For a cluster, settlements could be developed one
at a time and the road system extended in step.

The faster the population of a settlement is built up the more important the phasing of development becomes and the more it is liable to be
influenced by changes in the buoyancy of the national economy, in the
national population growth and in political opinion. A rapid build-up
also means that the development will be more homogeneous in planning
and architectural style, but, because it is influenced by current expectations, it will be less likely to meet changes in age structure, especially
when there are large unbalanced blocks of population. Population
increases, if faster in the future, are likely to create a demand for settlement growth to continue beyond the planned size, with resulting
difficulties.

It is necessary to phase the various types of development so that they
are closely integrated – to ensure, on the one hand, that the facilities
needed by the population are available when required and, on the
other, that facilities are fully utilised and viable as soon as they are
complete. For example, housing must be provided in step with the
creation of employment, especially if the new or expanded settlement is
some distance from other sources of labour or housing. The occupants of
the housing need adequate public utilities, and transport and communication services, as does industry; also, they need educational, shopping,
health, recreational and other services. Public services will be expensive
to provide per head of population, and commercial services will not be
viable, unless the number of people matches the organisational units in
which the services are operated. If services or jobs are inadequate it will
be difficult to attract migrants.

To secure a balanced development it is necessary to attract population and firms providing the basic employment, and to ensure that the
public services will be provided and that commercial firms will set up

for the provision of other services. The migrants will have their attachments to the areas from which they came and will need finance for moving – some even if rented accommodation is to be provided. Firms providing basic employment will have their own financial, management and marketing problems. They may have to secure markets for their additional output, additional supplies of materials, new machinery, plant and transport, servicing for their plant, industrial development certificates and office development permissions from the central government, additional managerial staff; they will need some guarantee that suitable labour will migrate to the settlement and will need adequate financial resources. Firms providing services, and public utility and other service organisations will have parallel problems. Their ability to solve them will depend more on their internal economies and organisation than on the demands of the developing settlement. All these many requirements should be integrated by the Corporation or the local authority developing the settlement; they will need considerable managerial expertise and will increase in difficulty the greater the speed of development.

The developing agencies are all affected by the buoyancy of the national economy, which influences the demand for additional output and the willingness of firms to build new plants, expand production and create new jobs; also, generally, by their ability to obtain finance and the cost of this in relation to the expectation of profits. In buoyant circumstances the central government is usually readier to grant the various type of development certificates and to lend or allow development authorities to raise capital; although, against these advantages, development will probably be relatively expensive, contracts more difficult to let and completion to secure in the planned time. In times of economic stagnation the positions will be reversed. Hence development programmes will be liable to distortion as the economic situation changes, making it difficult to ensure that they are phased to produce optimum results.

The rate of national population growth changes for reasons which are still imperfectly understood. The major factors are birth rates and the balance of external migration. While birth rates were very low in the early 1940s, they increased rapidly after the end of the second world war, dropped again in the mid-1950s and then increased steadily up to the mid-1960s.[1] In the early 1960s, marriage rates were high at all ages, particularly the younger ones, and fertility rates were comparatively high for all ages and durations of marriage. In the early 1950s more people were leaving the country to live abroad than immigrating to the country; this position was reversed in the late 1950s and early

[1] Stone, *Urban Development in Britain*, vol. 1.

1960s.[1] For the decade up to the mid-1960s population expectations were rapidly rising; since then they have been falling equally rapidly. Thus the Mark 1 new towns, in the main the group around London, were planned for a moderately rising national population. When in the mid-1960s an even more rapid population increase was expected, the Mark 3 new towns and many large town expansion schemes were planned (for example, the growth areas in the South East),[2] but today in the early 1970s national population is expected to expand comparatively slowly and there is some doubt as to where their inhabitants will be found. Such shifts in expected and actual rates of population increase create difficulties in planning and achieving phasing programmes.

Political climate is affected by changes in national economic conditions and in national population, and by other factors. For some time it has been government policy to take work to the worker rather than the other way round. This policy is based to some extent on the unsubstantiated belief that, because urban facilities and infra-structure exist where the workers live, it is more economic to create additional employment in those areas than to build additional infra-structure in areas of buoyant economy with a need for more labour.[3] In fact, many of the areas with high unemployment have an obsolete infra-structure. They are excessively dense conurbations with comparatively few amenities, and it may be necessary to redevelop and improve much of the area before industry can be attracted. To some extent this is beginning to be recognised, as indicated by the special grants for such improvements. Moreover, with the reduced rate of population increase, particularly the lack of increase in the population of working age, and the general decline in the number of jobs, there is a danger that additional jobs can only be created in the more depressed areas at the risk of reducing the economic viability of the more prosperous areas from which employment is being shifted. With a view to persuading industry to move out of such areas, industrial development certificates are difficult to obtain in places like London and Birmingham, not only for new developments and extension, but even for the redevelopment of existing industrial sites. Thus, not only firms wishing to set up and expand in such areas, but also those wishing to modernise and rationalise their equipment, are forced out. Since new towns and expanding towns take second place to Development Areas in the issue of industrial development certificates, a great deal of industry needs to move from the

[1] Stone, *Urban Development in Britain*, vol. 1.
[2] Department of Economic Affairs, *A Strategy for the South East*, London, HMSO, 1967.
[3] A. E. Holmans, 'Restriction of industrial expansion in South East England: a reappraisal', *Oxford Economic Papers*, vol. 16, no. 2, July 1964; C. D. Foster, 'Public finance aspects of national settlement patterns', *Urban Studies*, vol. 9, no. 1, February 1972.

relatively prosperous areas before much employment is provided in new and expanding settlements. There is thus a danger that new employment in such settlements may be in much shorter supply in the future, making it more difficult to plan and phase their development.

Ideas about the planning and layout of developments and the design of buildings tend to change over time. At any time they depend partly on expectations about life-styles and the needs they create, partly on technological requirements and expectations and the available building technology, but also to a large extent on design fashions, which are often irrelevant and unsuitable to the needs of the building users. The more rapidly a settlement is developed, the more likely it is that it will all be in the same design idiom (bringing monotony) and, if it is irrelevant to future needs, difficult to adapt, so that it all becomes obsolete over a short period. Then adaptation to meet new needs and subsequent redevelopment will be that much larger a problem.

A rapid build-up of population also creates difficulties over future rates of population increase. As shown in appendix A,[1] the shorter the period to maturity the greater the future rate of population growth. The second generation tends to have a limited age range, so that its demand for age-related facilities and services peaks rapidly and declines equally rapidly. As it grows up it creates a large supply of labour, which may be too well educated to accept unskilled work, but has little experience, so that suitable job opportunities may be difficult to provide without a balance of other labour. Again, a third generation may be produced over a short period with its attendant problems, although the peaking should, of course, be reduced with each generation. The peaking difficulties can be largely avoided both by spreading the build-up of population over a long period, and also by planning for as balanced an intake as possible, with young families, who are the natural migrants, balanced by households with mature families and some elderly people. The Mark 1 new towns avoided serious peaking after the early years and secured populations not too dissimilar from the national demographic structure.

---

[1] See p. 268 and table A.11.

CHAPTER 17

URBAN FORM, OPERATING COSTS AND VALUES

THE EFFECTS OF URBAN FORM

So far much of the discussion in this book has been in terms of the capital costs of development. Operating costs were considered in detail for transport systems, where they are even more important than development costs in relation to road designs and different transport forms; when time costs are added to vehicle operation costs, it gives a measure of accessibility and hence of value. Some discussion in chapter 13 considered operating costs of buildings and developments in relation to building form. Now, costs and values need to be considered together.

Urban form and location are likely to affect operation costs and values differently according to the type of organisation or person concerned. It is convenient to divide these into four groups: existing land users; industrial and commercial firms; public and semi-public organisations; and persons – residents, visitors and commuters to the settlement.

Firms and organisations of all types, or private persons, can, as existing users of land, be forced to change their location or their operation when the land is taken for settlement development and expansion, but farmers are the most likely to be affected.

Agricultural, industrial and commercial firms are all broadly concerned with market operations and, except for shopping and retail services, are likely to be only marginally affected by the form of the settlement and where they are located in it or in relation to it. The influence on their revenue and expenditure is at second-hand, though the effects of form and location on employees and management and, in the case of retail services, on customers. The advantages and disadvantages of particular locations and forms will tend to be offset through purchase prices for sites and ground rents.

Direct revenue of public and semi-public services is not generally expected to cover the total expenditure; water and power are exceptions. The balance, in some cases a large share of the expenses, is derived from taxation and grants. The operation of the services is, however, considerably affected by urban form and location. Services are usually expected to be uniform over the settlement, so that its size and form affect the cost of their provision, even though a uniform standard of service is, in fact, seldom possible. Thus the effect of urban form and location on standards of services is reflected in the benefits to residents and other users. It is with these users that the problem really lies, since each person is a user in many senses. Some of the results affect his resources, whilst others affect values.

URBAN FORM AND EXISTING LAND USERS

Form, size and location of settlements affect existing land users in varying degrees. The market values of the effects of planning alternatives on direct users are, of course, reflected in the financial costs of acquisition, but these by no means cover total differences in the resources used, or the whole change in values, which may be indirect and need tracing through to effects on firms and on persons.

Where development takes place under the Town and Country Planning Act, 1959, land is acquired at broadly its value in current use (see chapter 9). The valuations will include an allowance for reasonable expectation of changes in use, other than changes which would come about only if a planned settlement were developed there. Thus agricultural land will be valued in that use, plus some allowance for 'hope value' on the basis that no new or expanded settlement was likely. In small rural villages in thinly populated areas the 'hope value' would be very small, while for agricultural land on the periphery of a growing town it might be quite large. Similarly, the value of land already in urban use will depend on growth prospects: in a town of declining economic activity and residential demand, value in its present use would generally be at a maximum, but in an area of natural growth, values might be expected to rise from future use of the land either for a higher value purpose or at a greater density.

Generally the landowner will be reasonably compensated for any financial losses he sustains. While occupiers would be compensated for loss of business and disturbance, this might be insufficient for them to re-establish themselves elsewhere; for example, neither farmers, nor industrial and commercial firms might find premises available at a low enough price to make their business viable. Similarly the owner–occupiers of housing might not be able to find dwellings they could afford, and though generally they would be offered public housing, this might not be acceptable.

Under present legislation neither owners and occupiers whose land and premises were not acquired, nor members of the public, would be compensated for loss of business or of amenity.[1] Of course, they might not suffer loss; the development of new or expanded settlements might bring additional business, additional facilities and new amenities to

---

[1] The government have now (October 1972) proposed legislation providing compensation where people are adversely affected by development.

some people, though to others, besides diverting business, it might bring noise and pollution, and would take away from many the amenities of the open countryside.

URBAN FORM AND BUSINESSES

The effect of urban form and location on businesses can be considered entirely in terms of their revenue and expenditure. There are six main channels through which expenditure and revenue are likely to be affected: (1) costs of goods and services bought; (2) costs of labour; (3) costs of organisation; (4) costs of transporting goods to the markets; (5) the size of the market; and (6) costs of the premises and of operation within them.

Costs of goods and services bought may vary either because location affects the distance travelled or the frequency of delivery and availability, or because form affects the time taken per unit distance travelled. The costs of transporting goods depend partly on loading and unloading times, which are not usually affected by distance but may be reduced by new and properly designed facilities in a new development. They also depend on journey time, which may be increased if the source of supply remains where it is while the business moves to a new settlement further away. On the other hand, if both move to a new settlement, not only will distance be reduced but the average speed of travel will be increased. A slightly more rapid journey may result in significant cost savings if journeys per vehicle per day are thereby increased. Generally, however, the costs of transport are not a large element in total costs of goods bought, but frequency of supply and its effect on stockholding may be more important.

Perhaps, however, the effect of location on services may be greater than the effect on the costs of materials. For industries which normally concentrate in a particular area because local linkages are important, particularly with their services and markets, movement out of that area may add directly and indirectly to costs. The linkage effect is not, however, confined to industries which concentrate, but may affect services to other industries. If machine parts and repair services, special materials, advisory services and so on are not readily available, production time is wasted. The supply of such services depends on the concentration of customers in an area; firms in individual towns in rural areas may be badly served, whilst firms in an urbanised region may be well served even though the individual settlements are widely spread. In fact, firms in new settlements developed in an urbanised region may be better served because of better communications, particularly road networks, than firms in a conurbation or metropolitan region. Probably the actual size of industrial or commercial areas is of little importance.

The costs of labour will be reflected in wage rates, productivity, time keeping, sickness and labour turnover. Wage rates may vary because the cost of living differs between settlements, or because of differences in journey lengths and in the balance of supply and demand, even though organised labour tries to establish national rates. The cost of living might be higher in new settlements in the early stages of development, but because they are smaller, with more convenient layouts and better designed communications, journeys to work should generally be cheaper, particularly than in older conurbations. The supply of labour may be more limited in new settlements, particularly small ones, but the labour market too will be restricted. Demand and supply is, however, for particular skills and needs to be considered in terms of occupations and training. Productivity, time keeping and sickness are affected only marginally by detailed settlement layout, but the last two should both be improved by getting away from the older conurbations and larger cities, with their pollution, obsolete development and longer journeys to work. Labour turnover may be less in new settlements, partly because of greater satisfaction with living conditions generally and partly because of less opportunity to change employer.

The costs of organisation are likely to be affected partly through the recruitment of management staff, partly through internal organisation and partly through communications. Management staff will be affected to some extent by similar forces to those considered above as affecting labour. Additional difficulties may arise in recruiting management staff from the relative isolation of some new settlements, making contacts for the exchange of information and for continued education more difficult; the smaller units and poorer chances of internal promotion may also be a deterrent. Internal organisation could be affected by the form of settlement if, for example, sites did not allow sufficient space for expansion, so that a manufacturer had to operate in a number of small works widely distributed over the settlement, or if there were many small centres, so that large retailers had to operate several small unit shops rather than one or two large self-service stores. Efficiency of operation is affected by speed of communication both within and without the firm, and by accessibility. Such attributes are likely to be determined more by location than by factors associated with urban form.

The costs of transporting goods to the markets also depend more on location than on urban form. Loading and unloading costs are constant whatever the distance, but again there are likely to be economies in the packing process in working from a new, purpose-designed building. The time taken to travel out from a new settlement, with its purpose-designed road system, is likely to be far less than from an old town or conurbation. Good proximity to markets may also result in overall time savings. Time saved on transport to markets may again have a more than proportionate effect, because more journeys may be achieved by each vehicle in a day. However, such costs are not usually of major significance.

The size of the market depends most of all on the nature of the business, and generally for manufacturing firms is not affected by either the size or the locality of the settlement. For services, particularly retail services, the volume of turnover per establishment varies with the size of settlement, the concentration of settlements in the region, and the settlement's regional and sub-regional status. It is also affected by the size, layout and status of the centre within the settlement. Generally, the greater the concentration of settlements within the region, the larger the settlement, the more centralised it is and the higher the status of the settlement and centre the larger the market will be.

Costs of the premises and of operations within them depend partly on the form of the premises, their layout and standards, and partly on the size and form of the settlement. Generally, the larger the settlement, the nearer development is to its focal centre and the higher the densities of development the greater the land costs. The topography of the site, the density of development, and in some cases the form of development, may also affect building costs. High density also affects the costs of servicing the buildings, and creates a congested environment, with excessive noise and low levels of light and privacy, so that satisfactory working conditions are more expensive to maintain. Moreover, internal transport and communications, and supervision tend to be cheaper when operating on one floor than on several. Again, retail sales are greater on the ground floor than on floors above or below.

URBAN FORM AND PUBLIC SERVICES

As mentioned earlier, while the prices of public services other than transport are generally uniform in so far as they are charged directly, standards and total costs vary considerably with the form and size of settlement. The effects of size, and particularly of form, depend on the type of service, seven of which can usefully be distinguished: (1) roads; (2) piped and wired services; (3) services to dwellings and their occupants; (4) education, and social and recreational services; (5) protection services; (6) legal and administrative services; and (7) public transport.

Road requirements depend on the size and form of settlement, as well as on the ownership of vehicles and the propensity to make journeys, which is related to settlement form and size as well as to the number of vehicles. The relationships between main roads, journey costs and size and form of settlement were dealt with in chapters 8 and 10. The length of estate roads and the costs of their construction and servicing have also been considered (chapters 9 and 13).[1] The standard of roads provided tends to be uniform amongst newly planned settlements.

Piped and wired services include electricity, gas, sewerage, telephones and water. Economies of scale are generally exhausted before settlements of the size discussed in this book are reached. Clearly the costs of provision and operating costs rise as density falls, but there is no evidence that other aspects of urban form have important cost consequences, although the topography of the settlement site can affect the way the service is developed and its costs. Standards of performance of recent installations are generally uniform for all settlements, whatever their size and form. While the system of charging varies from one service to another, generally the charges bear little relation to the costs incurred for the individual consumer.

Services to dwellings and their occupants include the maintenance and servicing of the dwellings, refuse collection, and public and commercial deliveries and collections. The costs of such services vary mainly with the density and form of development of dwellings. The costs of maintaining and servicing dwellings are usually met by the occupants; the other costs are included in rates or in the costs of goods and services provided, and are not generally related to density or form of settlement, which equally do not affect the quality of services.

Educational, social and recreational services include schools, libraries, churches, health centres, clubs, cultural centres and various types of open space. Given standards of service require both given standards at each centre and sufficient centres to maintain accessibility. The volume of buildings and works and the operating resources necessary to achieve equal standards at both levels are affected by the size and form of settlement and by the transport available. However, the relation between these factors and the services varies both within and between the services.

Primary schools are usually provided within a quarter of a mile of the home, so that the greater the residential density the greater the choice of school. At extremely low densities, where settlements are small and scattered, schools will tend to be further away and perhaps so small that full standards cannot be provided with the same resources. Although secondary schools are further from some houses and can take a variety of forms, the same generalisations apply, but at greater distances. For older children at higher levels of education, units large

---

[1] Also in Stone, *Urban Development in Britain*, vol. i.

enough to provide a full service are more dispersed and accessibility falls more as density declines.

Similarly there are minimum units for services such as libraries and health centres. The optimum size generally serves larger populations than schools at the lower levels of education. Thus accessibility is more of a problem, especially by public transport. Hence again, services provided for the same capital and operating costs will be of a higher standard and more accessible the greater the density of the development, the more compact and, up to a point, the larger, the settlement. However, the larger the optimum unit and the optimum population for the service the more it is the town density of development which matters rather than the density of the residential areas. The higher residential densities are the more they must rise to achieve a given proportionate increase in town densities,[1] and raising residential densities substantially increases both capital and operating costs per person housed,[2] and usually reduces housing amenities. Of course, private cars make accessibility much less of a problem.

Several types of recreational space are required – local, district, metropolitan and country parks – each with a different level of accessibility.[3] Standards depend on their size and distance from the home. It does not follow, however, that more space is needed for recreation when densities of development are lower and the settlements are smaller and more widespread, because both these factors tend to reduce the need for public open space. Again, of course, private cars increase accessibility at any given distance. Accessibility may be reduced if the road network is external to the residential areas, as in Cumbernauld.

Protection services such as police and fire are again affected by the size and form of the settlement. The resources required for policing at a given standard increase with the proportion of passages, pedestrian underpasses, bridges and decks concealed from direct public observation, particularly if they are ill lit, and with shops and other premises located away from well used and easily patrolled roads. Flatted blocks, particularly if high and extensive, also increase the resources required for policing, which rise with density and enclosure of developments rather than with the physical size of the settlement.

Fire services of a given standard also require more resources the greater the density of development and the more properties there are away from vehicular roads. Costs also rise with the height of development, and the use of inflammable building materials and enclosed spaces. Up to a point resources may be saved by centrality and compactness.

---

[1] Stone, *Housing, Town Development, Land and Costs*.
[2] Stone, *Urban Development in Britain*, vol. i.
[3] Greater London Council, *Report of Studies*, London, 1969.

The effect of size depends on the relation between size of settlement and the optimum size of fire service units.

Legal and administrative services tend to be more centralised than most other public services, and hence less affected by urban form. Up to a point the costs of these services at a given standard decline as the size of settlement rises, but most of such economies of scale would be exhausted before the range of settlement sizes considered in this book.

Public transport costs have already been considered earlier, and the way they are affected by size and form of settlement has been described in chapters 11 and 13.

URBAN FORM AND PERSONS

Individual people, as the ultimate consumers, are affected in many ways and through many aspects of their lives by the form and size of a settlement, and by their location in it. The ways in which urban form affects the costs of services, or the standards at which they are provided, have already been discussed above. The remaining effects to be considered are on the amenities provided by the various types of environmental area and on the accessibility of the various locations residents wish to reach from their homes.

Amenities of environmental areas

The costs and amenities to persons which result from differences in urban form, settlement size and location will vary both with the stage reached in the development of the settlement, including possible redevelopment occasioned by unexpected changes in planned size and form, and with changes in technology, life-styles, the socio-economic population structure and price relatives. It will only be possible to point out the major effects of change, and generally the position is best considered at the planned maturity of the settlement.

The dwelling and its immediate environment consists of a housing area with up to about 5,000 inhabitants. As visualised in this book it would have access but no distributor roads, and hence no through traffic. It would contain only dwellings, garages, utility buildings and local open space for use by the inhabitants, perhaps with a few cornershops. Most of the housing areas would be purely residential, but there might be a few small ones integrated with commercial areas in major or minor centres. In this book housing areas have been defined in terms of a density, which could usually be achieved with various forms of housing. The actual form and its layout would generally not interact with the rest of the settlement except through density and hence the area required, although the use of tall buildings might affect the aesthetics of the townscape, and detailed layout and building form might marginally influence the volume of accidents, or privacy and other amenities.

As density increases from extremely low to moderate levels, both development and running costs, and hence costs-in-use, decline, but with continued increases in density costs rise – markedly at the points where houses are replaced by flatted blocks and where the number of storeys involves the use of framed buildings with lifts (chapter 9). Houses with gardens are usually thought to provide greater amenity than dwellings off the ground. Other things being equal, taller blocks and smaller private gardens enable more public space to be provided, which may give a greater sense of spaciousness, but possibly at a loss of privacy and certainly of private space about buildings.

Costs-in-use of housing areas can generally be estimated without great difficulty. Some assessment of value could be made by asking the inhabitants about perceived values, and possibly how they would spend resources differently.

The residential locality is a neighbourhood or district, which could house from 10,000 to 25,000 persons, exceptionally even more, and would generally contain most of the day-to-day facilities required by the residents, including some shopping, primary education, and social and health services. The road system would usually exclude through traffic, except possibly buses. The localities would be directly linked, both with each other and with other centres, by distributor roads. Generally, in larger residential localities a greater variety of services can be provided, but on average they are further from the homes. If vehicles and pedestrians are to be completely separated, either the road network must be developed outward towards a ring road and the pedestrian ways inwards to the service heart of the area, or there must be considerable expenditure on underpasses and bridges. In a centralised settlement the problem would be greater, since the housing areas would be grouped about a single service centre.

The various forms of development have different costs-in-use and, as mentioned above, form affects the operating costs of the services. Form and size of residential locality also affect the amenities of the localities and the way the inhabitants use them through possible differences in appearance, noise, privacy, accidents, the convenience of the services and the range of choice. The values attributed to such differences would depend on factors such as the socio-economic class of the inhabitants, their age and life-styles, and on the forms and convenience of transport available. Again, evaluation would involve questioning users about their perceived values and how they would spend the resources differently.

The major and minor centres of the settlement require consideration in themselves, with the attributes of their forms as distinct from their relationship with the housing areas they serve. Smaller centres can be more compact with less distance to be covered in using their various facilities; vehicles can approach closer for both delivery and collection of goods, but the services are generally less comprehensive. Smaller centres have lower costs-in-use for the provision of equivalent accessibility within them, but probably also lower perceived values.

The employment areas are those which provide basic employment, that is goods and services mainly for export from the area. Generally manufacturing firms occupy the industrial areas, while large commercial offices are in the settlement centres, although some of them, and offices attached to factories together with warehouses, may be in the industrial areas. Workers generally prefer to work in a centre because of convenient access to shopping and other services and, in the case of offices, greater proximity to professional colleagues. If suitable employment is provided in the major centres, car-parking and services such as catering can have dual uses, by workers during the day and for social functions at night. Again, a more regular demand for public transport implies better and more convenient access for visitors to the centres and others travelling to them at irregular hours. Costs-in-use of the facilities would probably not be much affected, but the perceived values would vary, perhaps being higher for facilities in the centres.

The educational, social and recreational areas contain such services outside the residential areas, for example, secondary and higher education, cultural and other major social centres, and major recreational centres – stadia, swimming baths and golf courses. Some of them would be close to or part of the central areas, while others, particularly those requiring a large amount of land, would usually be at the periphery of the settlement. Again, the costs-in-use of the facilities would probably not be affected, but perceived values would depend on the choice of services provided close to the home.

The out of town facilities would be those available in other settlements, regional recreational centres and natural facilities such as rivers, lakes and the coast. The only additional resources involved would be roads and perhaps other methods of transport. Perceived values would vary with the scale, quality and convenience of the facilities.

Location and accessibility

Accessibility implies more than just transport costs; it includes the time taken by the journey and its comfort and convenience. Accessibility will normally be measured from the home, and will depend first on whether a private vehicle is available, or whether public transport or walking is the mode of travel. The availability of a private vehicle depends on

the socio-economic class and the ability to drive, and comfort and
convenience depends on the type of vehicle (car, motor-cycle or
bicycle) and how many vehicles there are per family. Convenience also
depends on where the vehicle is parked in relation to the home. The
comfort and convenience of public transport depends on distance to the
boarding point, and on such factors as protection from the weather, the
frequency of the service and the need to change vehicles or modes of
transport. For journeys on foot, again distances, protection from weather
and the attributes of the path (for example, steps, ramps and gradients)
are important.

Accessibility can also be defined as a measure of the opportunities
within the settlement and the surrounding area to fulfil given needs.
Account must be taken both of the number of places available and of
how many people wish to make use of them. For example, the opportunities to obtain an education within a given area around the home
would be measured by the number of school places available for a given
age group divided by the number of children in that age group in the
area. As the area considered accessible is increased, the numbers of
both places and persons requiring the opportunity generally rise, but
not necessarily in the same proportion, so that the opportunity ratio
probably changes. As the area increases so do average distances or,
perhaps more important, journey times, and beyond a certain point
some people will not be willing to make the journey. Each person has
his own scale of distance–time preferences for each facility. The proportion of people prepared to travel to a given type and quality of
facility tends to decline with distance and time, being greater for some
facilities than others and varying with the cost, convenience and
comfort of the journey. The probability that journeys of any particular
length–time are undertaken depends on factors such as the cost, inconvenience and discomfort of the journey, and the relative perceived
values of the facilities and amenities at different places around the
home. Some recreational journeys may themselves be counted as an
amenity and have a positive rather than a negative distance–time value.

The cost of travelling includes both resource and time costs. Since
accessibility is examined here in terms of personal movement, time
costs do not involve market resources unless it is argued, in the case of
the journey to work, that the period of employment should be measured
from leaving home in the morning to returning home at night. The
evaluation of this travelling time by the person involved then takes
account of his perceived discomfort and inconvenience, and the other
satisfactions and dissatisfactions of making the journey. Travelling
costs themselves can be based on the costs-in-use of private and public
vehicles as explained earlier (chapter 10).

Again, in considering accessibility it is only possible to generalise and to consider the major effects of change. The position must be considered both at maturity of the settlement and during development.

Places of employment include the central area and the other centres, the industrial areas, areas providing special services, to a small extent even residential areas and places of employment outside the settlement. The employment to which access is required is that appropriate to the skills and experience of the resident–worker. Jobs offer both varying satisfactions and different levels of earnings. Generally, the greater the earnings and satisfaction the further and the longer workers will be prepared to travel; convenience, comfort and expense will also affect their decisions. The interactions between settlement form and size and journeys to work have already been discussed in chapters 10 and 13.

Places of education include nursery, primary and secondary schools and colleges of higher education. Nursery education must generally be very accessible to the mother, being close to either the home or her place of work. Primary education must usually be close to the home, possibly with footpath connections, unless transport is provided by the education authority. Choice of schools to some extent involves lower accessibility. At the secondary and especially the higher stages of education, units need to be larger and to provide a greater range of choice. Whether this choice is acceptable depends on the values of different characteristics set against the costs and inconvenience of longer and perhaps more awkward journeys.

The communal services include social, health and other services. Some of these, for example, the local health services, doctors and dentists, and social services, are provided locally, while others, such as the hospital, will be on their own site, normally in one of the outer neighbourhoods or districts. Accessibility depends on the particular type of service and on the form, density and size of the settlement. Up to a point local health and social services can be dispersed for convenience of the users. However, in smaller centres the choice and range of service is limited and duplication is more likely, so that the quality of service will be lower and costs higher. On the other hand, larger centres will, on average, be less accessible; average accessibility also falls with density. Neighbourhood centres will generally be within walking distance, but with district centres distances will be too great for many of the residents to visit them on foot. Hence, unless a car is available, accessibility depends on the frequency and routing of public transport.

A hospital needs to be fairly large if it is to provide a full range of services, and only the larger settlements, or the central settlement in a cluster, are likely to possess one. Only a few people will live close enough to attend or visit it on foot. Accessibility will depend on the availability of a private car or public transport, and may be lower in small settlements than large ones.

However, individuals will not generally need the communal services, such as hospitals, very often; hence their accessibility is far less important than that of employment, education and retail services.

Shopping and other retail services will be provided mainly in neighbourhood, district or town centres. Smaller shopping and retail centres are more accessible, but their range of services is narrower and more frequent visits to higher level centres are needed. Accessibility on foot is improved the smaller the population served and the greater the density of development. Convenience is also affected by the topography of the area and the protection provided from the weather. Given sufficiently high densities and not too large a settlement, reasonable walking access can be provided to a single settlement centre. However, in larger settlements it is less convenient to make frequent purchases or to carry home large volumes of shopping on foot, so that single centre shopping may become largely motorised, with one large weekly shopping trip. The decision depends on the balance between the values assigned to a wide choice of goods and service establishments (and its encouragement of competitive pricing), and the inconvenience and cost of longer journeys to the centre.

Recreational areas include play-spaces, grass and landscaped areas in the housing areas, the local, district and town parks, specialised sports areas such as playing fields, golf courses, stadia and swimming baths, and rural parks and other rural recreational areas. Recreational areas within the housing areas and the local parks create no particular accessibility problems. Generally, the plan would provide pedestrian access without crossing distributor, roads or in some cases any roads. District parks would probably involve more travel, although less than the town facilities (some of which might be at the periphery of the settlement) and the out of town recreational areas. The more distant facilities would be visited less frequently, the distance–time of the journey depending on the form, size and density of the settlement. Some journeys, especially to outer facilities, might be judged to have a utility of themselves and not be counted as a cost.

Social visits tend to be unrelated to the structure of the settlement or its location, although probably frequency of particular visits depends on the distance–time for the journey. Hence social visiting may be more convenient on average where there are concentrations of housing by socio-economic class. Accessibility will be increased where the road system minimises the distance–time of journeys, and where a convenient and regular system of public transport is provided.

CHAPTER 18

THE ECONOMICS OF GROWING AND DECLINING SETTLEMENTS

THE SCALE OF URBAN DEVELOPMENT IN GREAT BRITAIN

Estimating the likely scale of urban development in Great Britain in the next three or four decades is very difficult because the future level of population is so uncertain. In 1964 the Registrars General projected a population for Great Britain four decades hence of about 72 million people. At that time, recent changes in the demographic trends indicated that the population might increase to as much as 85 million over that period, or only to 65 million.[1] Current demographic trends suggest that the lower figure is now more likely, implying that there will be only about half as many additional people as was expected less than 10 years ago. Because current densities of development are substantially less than those of the areas to be redeveloped, additional land will be needed to accommodate many of those currently housed. Probably over the next three or four decades new development will be required for about 15 million people.

The type of location where these people should be housed needs consideration. The main alternatives are at the periphery of existing free-standing settlements or in new settlements. The first choice can be subdivided into the growth of existing settlements of all sizes and the planned transformation of the smaller existing settlements into expanded single settlements, clusters, or more extended city regions of half to one million people.[2] Concentration on new towns, town expansions and the development of city regions might imply that many larger towns and cities lose, on redevelopment, the population they could not accommodate at contemporary and expected future space standards within their present urban fence. This could represent a substantial loss for some large towns and cities. In fact many large urban areas have already lost considerable numbers of people; for example, the population of London has declined by about a tenth in two decades, and only one of the nine conurbations did not lose population during the years 1961–71.[3] With the decreased projections of future population, there is a risk that the fulfilment of the present programme of town

[1] Stone, *Urban Development in Britain*, vol. 1.
[2] E.g. as is implied in Department of Economic Affairs, *A Strategy for the South East*.
[3] Office of Population Censuses and Surveys, *Census 1971. Great Britain, Advance Analysis*, London, HMSO, 1972, table 3.

development will draw away the population and economic activities of existing metropolitan settlements to a degree which might be dangerous for them.

THE GROWTH AND DECLINE OF SETTLEMENTS

Settlements are rarely static in size, but grow or decline in physical area, in population, or in both. As space standards increase, settlements can grow in area while the population declines, or population can decline so fast that, despite an increase in space standards, the area required also declines. This would produce an area of physical and functional obsolescence which in time might become derelict. In such a situation, if economic activity declined it would exacerbate the effects of population decrease; the extent of the resulting difficulties would depend on the respective rates of decline.

Inevitably a population decrease would cause a relative decline in the service sector of the settlement. There would also be some decline in basic industries unless labour productivity rose sufficiently, or the labour loss was made good by commuting from other settlements. Thus, even if no frictions or disequilibria arose, which is most unlikely, a declining population would probably result in declining economic activity, with output and perhaps household and corporate incomes also falling. In consequence there would be less private redevelopment of the infra-structure and a smaller tax base to provide public funds for redevelopment, so that urban facilities and amenities would probably deteriorate. It would be especially difficult to maintain a balance if the settlement population and economic activity were falling rapidly; then disequilibria could arise in a number of ways, depending on how the migration from the existing settlement took place.

In large existing cities there is little virgin land and most new development must take place in redevelopment areas. Comparable land in existing centres is more expensive than in other areas; costs of building in redevelopment areas are higher than on virgin land.[1] Thus private developers have an incentive to leave the old cities, particularly their centres, and to develop on virgin land in and around small towns and in rural areas. Households also are attracted to such developments, where living costs are lower and values higher. They tend initially to settle within commuting distance of the cities and jobs from which they have migrated; even if husbands and some single people commute, working wives' labour will generally be lost to the cities. (Those leaving will usually be the younger, more enterprising and more affluent households.) However, as population and a labour force build up in settle-

[1] Stone, *Urban Development in Britain*, vol. I.

ments outside the city, entrepreneurs have an additional incentive to set up factories, offices and other enterprises there, and the parent city will lose some of the labour commuting to it for employment.

The tendency for firms to migrate from the old cities is increased if government controls create a disincentive or prohibition against firms setting up, expanding or even modernising in them. Such disincentives are operated in this country by the central government, particularly where the old cities are not in Development Areas, for example negatively by means of industrial development certificates and 'office development permissions', and positively by grants towards development in selected areas, employment subsidies (now being phased out) and additional tax incentives. The system of industrial development certificates is particularly restrictive against cities not in Development Areas, since they apply not only to firms new to an area, but also to firms already operating there who wish to modernise their premises. The payment of subsidies to develop elsewhere is an added inducement to expand or even migrate outside the city.

When activities leave a city, the forces tying those remaining weaken, so that there is a danger of setting up a force towards migration which, at least in the short and perhaps the medium term, is self-perpetuating and cumulative. It tends to be the activities with the greatest growth potential and the firms with the greatest relative finance and managerial efficiency which wish to expand or reorganise themselves. Thus cities from which economic activities are migrating are likely to be left with industries with least growth potential and firms with least enterprise, efficiency and capital.

Moreover, large-scale migration is unlikely without frictional unemployment. Firms which move out take with them the managerial and skilled workers, and leave behind the more easily replaced semi-skilled and unskilled labour. Such workers find it particularly difficult to migrate on their own account, since they tend to be poorly paid and unable to purchase housing for themselves. Without employment in the new and expanding settlements, they have the lowest priority for public housing. However, without skills and generally with minimal educational standards, they have difficulty in finding new jobs in the cities, except perhaps in the poorest paid and declining service industry, much of which offers only female employment. Thus employment may fall as well as the level of wages.

Such movements reinforce the effects of migration of higher-income households and the more efficient and growth-orientated firms in reducing household and corporate income levels as well as the number of incomes. There would be reduced incentives for private redevelopment, a smaller tax base for financing public redevelopment, a growth of derelict areas and a fall in the standards of the built environment. Moreover, the costs of maintaining public services would not decline as fast as population, so that costs *per capita* would often rise, even though the tax base was falling. The position in growth areas would be the reverse: development costs per facility would be lower than in the city, household and corporate incomes and the tax base would rise both in total and *per capita*; in consequence social welfare would rise.

THE CLOSING OF SETTLEMENTS

Some settlements lose their original function without finding a new one. They may have been created on the basis of local supplies of raw material, power, or servicing needs, or for other reasons which have lost their validity, so that the settlement stagnates and declines. In some cases it can be revived by bringing in new activities and stimulating economic growth to provide the resources for improving and modernising the urban fabric. The Town Development Act, 1952, provided a mechanism for combining the interests, experience and resources of cities which wished to export population and activities with those which wished to receive them. Many partnerships on this basis have been formed and, as indicated already, this limited type of settlement expansion is often the most economic.

Not all existing settlements can, however, be revived in this way. Some, for example old mining settlements, are no longer viable. Their built environment is worn out and much of it is derelict. The younger and more enterprising citizens have left or will leave, so that the older, less skilled and less enterprising remain, and it is unlikely that any fresh private capital will be invested. As the population declines the costs per head of providing public services rise and the costs per head of improving the built environment to current standards become more and more prohibitive. In such cases a point must inevitably be reached where the welfare standards of those remaining cease to be tolerable. Some mechanism is needed for closing such settlements before welfare standards fall too far and costs become unreasonable.

NATIONAL POLICY FOR SETTLEMENT CREATION
AND EXPANSION

It could be argued that the transfer of affluence from declining cities to the creation and expansion of new settlements and city regions might bring national advantages, even though the central government would also need to make fiscal adjustments to secure balanced welfare objectives. There is no doubt that both resource and financial costs of development are lower on virgin land in and around small urban settlements and in rural areas than in existing cities. The national gains are not, however, as great as differences in the unit costs of facilities would indicate. Many facilities which have to be provided in the new areas either already exist in the cities with an unexhausted life, or must be provided there for the population which remains. Long-run savings might be made in the cities if obsolete facilities were not replaced but merely cleared, so that eventually large areas reverted to agriculture or forestry, or became open space. Clearly such a policy would involve leaving areas to become semi-derelict with declining standards. At the limit of acceptable standards, public authorities would have to use compulsory purchase to enforce the relocation of people and economic activities. However, the greater the scale and speed of such clearance the greater the destruction of facilities with further useful life, so that even if the policy were practicable it would not necessarily save resources. Nor is it easy so to organise migration from the cities that the population and its demographic composition in each area balances with the useful facilities available there.

Further, against the savings which could be made in the costs of providing and operating the built environment must be set the balance of gains and losses from the movement of population and economic activities from cities to new settlements. Insufficient work has been done to determine where this balance lies. Current policy for population location can only be based on hunch.

Even if the rundown of cities and the transfer of population and economic activities does prove to increase national welfare, the need to sustain the welfare of the cities remains. Three policy options appear to exist. First, the rate of rundown of cities might be controlled so that no adverse welfare trends occurred – a difficult if not unfeasible policy given limited knowledge, the crudity of the implements of control and the number of planning authorities which would be involved. Secondly, regional authorities could be created, large enough to encompass both the city and the area over which its population and activities were being dispersed. Authorities on this scale would create many problems which cannot be discussed in this book, but they would need to be single bodies large enough to plan migration with a better social and economic balance than is possible with separate authorities. With responsibility for the viability of the declining city as well as of the developing settlements, they would be able to use the rising tax base of the latter to subsidise the former. Whether, in practice, the intra-regional balancing would be any better than it is in the smaller regions of today remains doubtful. A third and perhaps simpler method would be for the national government to change its basis of grant distribution in favour of the deprived city areas and to take over the co-ordination of migration at the regional level.

Thus the problem of settlement development is not just to choose the most economic size and form, taking into account costs and performance throughout the construction period as well as at maturity, but also to consider the total consequences of implementing such development, including those for the cities from which population and economic activities are removed. Since conditions, including the scale of migration, are subject to change, a flexible and adaptable form of development, which is likely to provide good value for money whatever the size and phasing of settlement construction, is essential. In order to achieve the best results a much greater understanding than is currently available of settlement operation and perceived values, and of the consequences of reducing the population and economic activities of existing cities, is required. A full examination of the consequences of the currently proposed scale of development in new and expanded settlements and the creation of city regions is most necessary.

CHAPTER 19

CONCLUSIONS

SETTLEMENT POPULATION AND THE NEED FOR FACILITIES

The need for urban facilities arises from population and its activities. The demographic structure of population depends on the structure of a generation earlier, and on the birth and death rates experienced by that generation. Studies of the demographic structure of the population of towns in Great Britain indicated that local variations in population structure in the past had had little effect in the long run on current population structures. No significant variations could be found with town size or other factors. It appeared reasonable to assume that there would be no significant differences between the structures of the base population of new settlements. The age and sex structure of migrants were found to differ to some extent from that of non-migrants. There were also differences between the various types of migrants, but generally not large enough to produce substantial effects on the structure of the population of a mature settlement. On the other hand, scale and speed of development had an important influence on the growth rate after the end of migration. Of course, if national birth and death rates were to change to a marked degree from those now expected, the demographic structure of all populations might be significantly altered.

The capital costs of developing a settlement would depend on the facilities required in the mature settlement and hence on the activities of the population at that time. It was, therefore, necessary to consider not only the demographic structure of the population at maturity, but the levels of activity then expected. For example, rates of household formation, domestic space standards and the proportions of older children in full-time education were all expected to rise, and the age of retirement to fall. Consequently fewer young people would be in employment, and fewer young wives and old people, but the activity rates of other women were expected to rise. The projected growth of industries varied widely: employment in several manufacturing industries was expected to decline absolutely, while some service industries were expected to grow considerably. Overall, the proportion of workers in service industries was expected to grow to about 60 per cent by 1989. Sales per head were expected to rise in retail trade, and so were sales per square foot; the floor area per head appeared likely to be 25 per cent less for convenience goods, but 50 per cent more for

durable goods. The pattern of demand for other services and the efficiency with which floor space would be used were also likely to change,
as was the space needed for social services. For example, the hospital
beds needed for general purposes and mental illness would decrease,
while those for maternity and mental subnormality would increase. The
expected rise in the ownership of cars and other vehicles would increase
the need for roads and parking, also vehicle sales and servicing.

CONSTRUCTION AND LAND PRICES

There was no basis on which future cost and price levels could be
projected and no point in adding an arbitrary percentage to current
prices. Everything was, therefore, priced at mid-1967 levels.

Development costs were estimated by averaging the prices of actual
buildings and works. By using this approach it was possible to reflect in
the costs the effects of actual site, erection and contracting conditions,
and of building standards. Generally departures from traditional forms
of construction increased the costs: for example, costs rose with the
number of storeys and with the amount of decking. Up to a point, costs
per head of estate roads and estate services fell as the number of building units they served was increased, but total costs tended to rise in
relation to the density of development.

The cost of undeveloped land depended largely on the type of planning consent which could be obtained for it and on its location in
relation to local centres of development. Land in an area ripe for
development was worth about ten times as much as land in a completely
rural area – £5,000 as against £500 an acre. Developed land was
generally much more costly than undeveloped land, the cost depending
on use and location, and on the value of the property standing on it.
Usually, developed land would cost £50,000 to £100,000 an acre.

The price of land sold for private development with housing depended
on the size of the settlement and on density. Rents of public authority
housing, however, appeared to reflect rather the costs of provision and
the level of subsidies. Both ground and rack rents of industrial and
social premises were affected by the position and size of the centre in the
settlement where they were located. The type of planning consent and
the standard of premises were also important.

SETTLEMENT SIZE AND COSTS OF DEVELOPMENT

Size affected the scale and type of facilities in a settlement, and the
unit costs of their provision. Naturally the larger the settlement the
greater the costs; the interest lay mainly in departures from propor-

tionality. Generally, the types of facilities required were similar in settlements within the size range investigated in this book, 50,000 to 250,000 persons. Some facilities, for example general hospitals, colleges of higher education and some types of shopping and other service facilities, were not required in sufficient volume to justify their provision in every settlement. They were therefore provided on a regional or sub-regional basis, and usually sited in the largest and most central settlement. While this marginally increased the capital costs of constructing such settlements, the increase was not a consequence of size and did not change the national costs of settlement provision, which were typically around £2,400 per head of population.

Basic land prices varied with the type of planning consent which could have been obtained in the absence of official planned settlement development rather than with actual settlement size. However, the larger the settlement to be developed, the more likely it was that land in the vicinity of existing settlements and developed land within them would be needed, so the higher land costs would probably be. One of the principal reasons for the markedly greater costs of town expansion was the greater cost of acquiring land already ripe for development. Even in greenfield developments, cost per person for land could vary from £30 to £300; in town expansions it could be some hundreds of pounds more again.

It did not appear that building costs were much affected by the size of settlement. In a few cases the size of building increased less than proportionately to the size of settlement and some economies in construction were possible, but these were in fact unlikely to be realised, since any saving would probably be used to improve standards and appearance; this is usually considered necessary for buildings of comparative importance.

Development costs of individual sites were independent of the size of the settlement, but those of estates, public utility services and the main road network could be affected. Only for roads, however, was there a very appreciable effect over the range of settlement sizes considered in this book. Estate development costs were only likely to be affected either if the settlement contained a very large number of small estates, or if it was so small that estates large enough for economic construction were impossible. The *per capita* costs of public utility services did not change appreciably for settlements of 50,000 to 250,000 persons; they might be substantially higher for village development, although it was doubtful if the increases would be very great in relation to the total costs of developing a settlement.

The effect of settlement size on the construction costs of the main road network was much more important. Construction costs *per capita* were found to rise from about £80 to £100 between main road networks for a 50,000 person and a 100,000 person settlement, and from about £100 to £120 between a 100,000 person and a 250,000 person settlement, that is by 25 and 20 per cent respectively. Probably the rate of rise would continue to fall with increases in size, and costs *per capita* for a settlement of 500,000 might be about £130. It would be unwise to speculate too far, since the scale of road provision for large cities might change the observed trend with size. While these cost differences were substantial in relation to main road costs, they were fairly small in relation to total construction costs *per capita*. The main road construction costs were based on roads designed for traffic on the journey to work. It was not possible to test exhaustively their capacity for other types of movement, but it appeared generally to be sufficient. The figures given above were based on the assumption that workers would not be deterred by the length of the journey to work (reasonable for settlements where journey time would not exceed 20 minutes). If the length of the journey substantially deterred the inhabitants from taking jobs far from home, the reductions in travelling would not generally be enough to reduce road costs by more than about 10 per cent; the weaker this deterrent, the more the rise in *per capita* construction costs would tend to accelerate as the size of the settlement increased.

The effect of settlement size on the costs of travelling to work was found to be more important than on road construction costs. If the cost of the journey to work was measured in terms of total vehicle cost and time at about two thirds of average earnings, annual travelling costs *per capita* increased from about £40 to £50 between settlement sizes of 50,000 and 100,000 persons, and from £50 to £80 between settlement sizes of 100,000 and 250,000 persons. Travelling costs would be reduced by about 60 per cent if they were based on the running costs of vehicles and time was valued at about a third of average earnings. Naturally travelling costs *per capita* would be reduced if workers were deterred by the length of the journey; the larger the settlement the greater would be the reduction, which was found, for the sizes of settlement considered, to be between 10 and 20 per cent according to the degree of deterrence. Since, however, travelling costs are recurrent throughout the life of the settlement, their importance relative to construction costs is several times their annual amount. Travelling costs at the higher rate are about ten times as important as construction costs; even if they were based on running costs and reduced time costs, they would still be four to five times as important.

Thus the effect of increasing settlement size from 50,000 to 100,000 persons would be to raise the combined capitalised costs of the main road network and the journey to work by between £100 and £200 a person. Increasing settlement size from 50,000 to 250,000 persons would raise these costs by between £500 and £900.

SUB-REGIONAL FORM AND COSTS

Sub-regional form, the way in which individual settlements are related to form major areas, affects construction costs mainly through the cost of the main road networks. The more a major area is divided into sub-settlements and the further the member settlements of such clusters are pushed apart, the longer the journeys to work and the greater the effect of the deterrent of length of journey on the amount of travelling, and hence on costs of road construction and travelling.

It was found that, where the length of the journey to work had no deterrent effect, cluster forms for 250,000 persons had main road networks with *per capita* costs £20 to £40 (up to a third) more expensive than individual settlements with the same population. Under the same conditions, however, there would be only small differences in the costs of travelling, which averaged around £75 a year *per capita*. Of the forms of cluster settlements, the linear line and the linear block (one strand) were most expensive under these conditions.

Naturally, the greater the deterrent effect of the length of the journey to work, the greater the reduction in the amount of travelling in dispersed clusters as compared with more compact individual settlements of the same size. Where there was a strong deterrent effect, the construction costs of the main road networks for settlements of 250,000 population appeared much the same in clusters as in individual settlements, although some forms of individual settlement considered still had lower road construction costs than the equivalent cluster. Proportionate reductions in travelling costs resulting from the deterrent effect were greater than in construction costs. Where there was a strong deterrent, travelling costs were halved in cluster settlements but only reduced moderately, by 10 to 20 per cent, in individual settlements of the same population. Thus a cluster of five 50,000 person settlements might save travelling costs per head of about £20 to £25 a year as compared with one settlement for 250,000 persons. This would be equivalent to a capital saving of between £400 and £500 *per capita*. Where there was a fairly strong deterrent effect, there would probably be some savings in construction costs as well as in travelling costs in larger urban developments for over 250,000 persons from using clusters of small settlements rather than one large one. The form of cluster was probably less important than the form of the individual settlements within it, although for developments of 250,000 persons, where workers were deterred by the length of journey to a considerable degree, a linear line had marginally less expensive travelling costs than the other forms examined; its construction costs were also reasonably low. For a really large development a linearly related set of settlements based on crosses might show the best results.

The savings from dispersing population into related settlements instead of creating one large settlement depended on workers exercising a preference for working near their homes. Unless the distribution of workplaces gave workers an adequate choice of jobs within their own settlement, choice and accessibility of jobs would have been sacrificed to reduce road construction and travelling costs. Thus it would be an advantage for each settlement in a cluster to specialise in a range of employment which matched the skills of its inhabitants and to provide services appropriate to their tastes.

OTHER SETTLEMENT CHARACTERISTICS AND COSTS

The shape of the settlement did not, of course, affect costs of the individual units of a facility, but only of the networks connecting them. The information obtained from the public utility undertakings did not indicate any significant relationship between settlement shape and their costs *per capita*. The main influence of shape appeared to be on the costs of the main road networks, which in star and linear settlements was about a sixth (£14 to £17 *per capita*) more than in rectangular settlements. The effect of shape on travelling costs was as great: star-shaped settlements were about an eighth more expensive than rectangular ones, and linear about a quarter more expensive (£5 to £10 *per capita* a year). The advantages of the compact rectangular shape over the others in road construction costs declined with increasing size of settlement, although its advantages in travelling costs increased with settlement size. In capitalised costs per head, the rectangular shape appeared to be £50 to £200 cheaper for road construction and travelling costs than the others.

The degree of centralisation affected development costs, again mainly through the main road network. Whereas the traditional, compact, rectangular settlement had the lowest costs, the traditional, centralised settlement was the least favourable of those examined. Construction costs of the main road network for a partly centralised settlement were not much greater than for a decentralised one; those of a centralised settlement were about 20 per cent greater. There was some indication that small self-contained localities for about 10,000 persons might compare favourably with other sizes in terms of *per capita* costs for road networks. Probably these costs would increase steeply at first as the size of the locality rose; they might be £20 (25 per cent) more for a 50,000 person locality than for one of 10,000 persons. Again, the greater proportion of the workers who lived and worked in the locality, the lower road construction costs would be. The overall effect of centralisation on travelling costs appeared small. Different results were obtained with different shapes of settlement – results depending perhaps as much on the particular plans compared as on the shape itself. Centralisation of facilities reduced travelling if people were not deterred by the length of journey, but increased it if they were sensitive enough in this respect to locate themselves so as to minimise travelling. Again, until travelling habits are more fully understood it will be difficult to determine the form that is likely to be optimum from the point of view of costs. The effect of centralisation on the costs of shopping and obtaining other services was not large, but the additional costs in fully centralised settlements were greater in proportion.

Density interacted with the costs of most of the facilities in a settlement. It affected both the costs of building and estate development, and the costs of the town networks.

Housing, even when provided at moderate densities, accounted for nearly 50 per cent of the costs of developing a settlement. Housing construction costs appeared to be at a minimum at densities of somewhere around 30 persons per acre, depending on the size of household and the type of housing. Costs tended to rise as densities were reduced, with more detached dwellings, spaced further apart; halving densities would raise the costs of building and site development by about 20 per cent. Increasing densities by a half would increase costs by about 10 per cent, and costs would rise faster as further increases in density necessitated the use of high flats and multi-level car space. Development costs would depend on the provision of space about buildings and its treatment. Total costs of high density development could be half to two thirds greater than for medium density. To save land in this way could cost as much as £50,000 an acre.

The operating costs of dwellings also varied with density. Maintenance and management costs of high-rise blocks were about 50 per cent greater than for low-rise housing. All types of services to the dwellings (for example, refuse collection, deliveries of goods and ambulance services) tended to cost more in high-rise than in low-rise housing. Further, high-rise housing is probably less accessible to its occupants.

Industrial and commercial development were each only about a fifth of the cost of residential development, and hence changes in their density would neither save as much land nor affect costs as much. The most economic way of achieving higher densities in the industrial area would be by putting a single car deck over ground-level parking, although to save land in this way would still be expensive at £40,000 to £50,000 an acre. Saving of any appreciable amount of land in the commercial centres would necessitate either a decked centre or multi-storey car parks. This would be twice as expensive as the other methods discussed for saving land.

No appreciable amount of land could be saved on other facilities by changing the form of building development. About 80 per cent of the land in a settlement actually covered by buildings was used for housing, industrial and commercial buildings. Open space and other recreational land could be reduced, but only with some loss of amenity.

The greater the density of development, the shorter the main road and public utility networks. It was found, however, that even quite substantial changes in density only changed road construction costs and journey to work costs by a few pounds *per capita*. Since the total cost of public utility networks was similar to main road costs, savings there from an increase in density would not be any greater than on the main roads.

BUILDING FORM AND COSTS

The conventional form of building, normally limited (unless it is single-storey) to a width capable of being naturally lit, is by no means the only possible form. Already buildings with an artificial environment are accepted for some uses. Generally, however, such buildings were found to be more expensive both to construct and to operate. The greater the complex of spaces under one roof the more circulation and storage space needed within the building, the greater the costs and the less the flexibility. Thus housing a city in a single building would be quite uneconomic at the current levels of relative costs. Other imaginative ideas, such as putting the roads on the roofs of buildings, roofing over a city, using a city roof for open space and building a city underground, appear equally unattractive from an economic point of view.

On the other hand, some forms of building layout have clear economic advantages in particular circumstances. In towns, the problem of traffic noise is growing. Even along a fully utilised two-lane road the noise level is greater than is acceptable in most circumstances. Insulation requires double glazing with some form of forced ventilation, which adds to both construction and operating costs, increasing them by a factor of a quarter to a third. The amount of space affected by traffic noise depends on the layout of the buildings. The contemporary tower on a podium is the least satisfactory, since traffic noise travels right round the building and affects all the rooms. The most satisfactory are buildings in unbroken formation along the traffic roads, with enclosed courts behind which are free of traffic noise. If the main rooms face on to the courts they can be ventilated naturally. Much of the space along the street fronts can be used for access, ancillary and other space for which noise is unimportant. Of course, if electrically propelled vehicles became universal, planning against traffic noise would be largely unnecessary.

ROADS, TRANSPORT AND COSTS

It was not possible to separate the effects of settlement shape from the form of the main road network, but the greater economy of the rectangular–box network over star–radial networks and linear shapes and networks has already been noted. Within the linear form, two-strand networks were found to be cheaper both in construction and travelling costs than one or three strands. It is possible, however, that the savings from a two-strand network resulted more from a more nearly rectangular shape than from the road system.

The load of traffic on the road network could be considerably reduced by the use of public transport instead of private cars, particularly for the journey to work. However, in view of the expected level of car ownership, probably not more than 50 per cent of the journeys to work would be made by public transport, however convenient it was made. Buses appeared to be the only form of mass transport likely to be economic and convenient in the range of settlements under considera-tion. If, in a new settlement, the proportion of journeys to work made by car could be reduced from about four fifths to a quarter, the *per capita* cost of the main road network would be £20 to £50 lower, increasing with the size of the settlement. Savings of about £20 *per capita* could also be obtained by reducing parking facilities. These savings would be used up if bus-only roads were provided.

However, unless a car was bought especially for the journey to work, it would probably be cheaper to use a car than to go by bus unless fares were subsidised. Bus fares are, in effect, already subsidised in relation to journeys by car by the incidence of taxation, particularly on fuel. Nevertheless, in most new settlements the annual savings on the construction costs of roads and parking, even with some allowance for savings on maintenance and from accidents, would not provide a large enough subsidy to ensure that the buses were more economic than private cars.

The position in existing settlements, especially where they are large, might be very different. The economic advantages of mass transport would be greater than in new settlements because of the high cost of building additional roads in existing settlements. The position might be similar during the early stages of town expansion, and in new towns developed before the extent of car ownership was realised, or to be expanded beyond the size for which they were designed.

Even in settlements as large as a quarter of a million people, rail systems would be far more costly to build and operate than road networks with buses or cars. Railways would be quite uneconomic, except possibly for large centralised conurbations with radial travel patterns.

TOWN EXPANSION AND COSTS

It was not possible to develop detailed models for town expansion in the same way as for greenfield development. Estimates suggested that, except perhaps where little more than infilling and rounding-off of an existing town was involved, town expansion might be a fifth to two fifths more expensive than greenfield development. The additional costs result to a large extent from the higher price of land in the vicinity of an existing town. Of course, 40 per cent of this additional cost would return to government agencies, either through taxation or through the activities of the Land Commission.[1] The high costs of developed land with standing buildings in good condition would also be important, as would the additional construction costs arising from departures from the optimum form and from developing on land previously developed. Costs *per capita* of population intake would fall as the size of the new settlement rose in relation to that of the existing settlement.

Expanding a settlement would be the most expensive way of incorporating existing development into a new urban complex. More economic would be to leave the existing settlement as a district of the new settlement; the less the existing settlement needed to be redeveloped to fit into the new complex and incorporate it, and the less the optimum form of the new settlement needed modification the lower costs would be. The most economic solution might be to treat the new and existing settlements as separate but related members of the same cluster.

SETTLEMENT FORM AND FINANCIAL RETURNS

The major responsibility for developing a settlement under the New Town Acts lies with the Development Corporations. The capital required depends on the proportions of the facilities the Corporation develops itself or retains as an investment. About a sixth out of the total development cost of some £2,400 *per capita* fell on local authorities and public utility undertakings. If the activities of public and private developers were about equally divided in the remainder of the field, each would provide initially something over a third of the capital.

[1] Subsequently reduced to 30 per cent in the case of individual owners when the Land Commission and separate treatment of capital gains on land sales was ended. In the case of companies such gains are subject to corporation tax.

However, commercial developers would be expected to sell the housing which accounts for about three quarters of their costs, so that the final capital position would be very different. Over a third of the capital required for a settlement would be provided by private owners of housing, and a similar amount by the Development Corporation, a sixth by local authorities and public utilities together, and the balance by commercial and industrial developers and owners, the central government and charities. In the final analysis, the central government would, in fact, be responsible for providing about 60 per cent of the capital required, including most of that for local authority and public utility investment, as well as that for the Development Corporation. It would make little difference if the capital was raised directly from the market, since the demand for fixed interest bearing stocks would be unaltered.

The surpluses on public authority housing would be very small and could easily be negative if costs have been slightly underestimated or rents overestimated. In practice this housing would be subsidised by the central government through housing subsidies, by local authorities through rates subsidies and by the Development Corporation, which would charge below the market price for the land. If the Corporation transferred land at the market price, the public housing account would be in deficit, but the Corporation's activities would show a much better and more realistic rate of return.[1]

A minimum net return of 8 per cent on capital invested in nationalised industries was set by a government White Paper and appears to have been applicable to Development Corporations in 1967.[2] Most of the Corporation's development work would have financial results substantially higher than this. Returns of 11 to 12 per cent would be obtained on most land sales, other than transfers to public housing. Equally satisfactory would be ground rents on central area sites and rack rents on central area buildings. However, both ground rents and rack rents on industrial sites and premises would be unsatisfactorily low, particularly the ground rents which would give only about half the target rate of return. Possibly the rents suggested were too low, although low rents might be needed initially to encourage firms to set up in new towns.

The returns on land sold for private housing would be substantially affected by marginal changes in density. The returns would also increase, other things being equal, with increases in the size of settlement which, except in remote areas, might cause increases in the basic cost of the site more than sufficient to absorb the addition to the surplus.

[1] This position has been changed by the Housing Finance Act, 1972.
[2] Treasury, *Nationalised Industries*.

The surpluses on land sales would be very sensitive to changes in the basic cost of the site, but not very sensitive to changes in main road costs.

Returns from rents seemed not much affected by the shape of settlement or the degree of centralisation. They were affected by size – increasing appreciably without necessarily any corresponding increase in development costs.

Town expansion rather than greenfield development increased costs more than revenue, so that the rates of return were depressed. Even central area returns might only just reach the minimum of 8 per cent with a five-fold expansion of the original town, and the smaller the expansion the lower the returns.

PHASING, ADAPTABILITY AND THE USE OF CAPITAL RESOURCES

It is likely to be most economic to develop settlement areas one by one in closely associated geographical groups. To avoid the temporary need for facilities on a scale greater than long-term requirements, there must be a balanced population intake. Many facilities which are needed in a settlement may be large and 'lumpy' investments, which can only be fully utilised over long periods. Often facilities in small units which can be fully utilised rapidly and are immediately viable are preferable to larger and more complex units, even though development of the latter is cheaper. Hence, other things being equal, smaller, simpler forms of settlement, which can be extended over time without either alterations to earlier development or development at an unnecessary scale in the early stages, are more economic in the long run. A cluster of small settlements which can be completed one at a time may in the end be considerably cheaper than a single large complex development.

Expansion of existing settlements has phasing advantages over greenfield development which may offset the additional costs of re-developing existing areas. Under-used facilities in the existing settlement may meet the needs of newcomers before additional facilities are provided.

For a variety of reasons it is unlikely that a completed settlement will be the size originally planned. While it is necessary to plan for an efficient size and form, it is also necessary to take into account the relative efficiencies should the plans need to be changed. This involves consideration of both the overall structure and the form of those settlement areas which serve the whole or large parts of the settlement. The central area is probably most affected and most difficult to plan for flexibility, especially if the settlement is centralised, and circular or square in shape. Road and rail systems also are difficult and expensive to expand to meet unplanned growth, and difficult to reduce in capacity if planned size is reduced. Public utility services and some buildings might also cause problems.

While the demographic structure of the population would change slowly and so would probably not cause difficulties of adaptation, increasing affluence might considerably affect the demand for better quality homes and other facilities. It might only be possible to meet this by extensive adaptation and some replacement of existing buildings. Growing affluence would also lead to a greater car ownership and much more traffic. Additional road capacity to meet this increased demand would be expensive and it might be necessary to change the modal split towards a greater use of buses.

Small, low-density, decentralised cluster settlements would generally be most easily adapted to meet changes in need. However, those forms of settlement which are least adaptable and contain the 'lumpiest' investments show the greatest economies from a rapid build-up of population. The faster the build-up the more important phasing becomes, and the greater the risks of difficulties and expensive adaptations as needs change.

Adequate phasing of settlement growth demands attention to many problems. Population growth and structure must be kept in step with the creation of jobs and with the supply of all types of services. Maintaining such a balance depends on attracting people and firms, and on the timing of facility provision – hence on phasing. Permissions for development, land acquisition, obtaining the necessary credit, all depend a great deal on the state of the national economy and government policy. Changes in these and in expectations about national population growth make forward phasing difficult.

A settlement built up rapidly is more likely to be designed to one set of standards and in one architectural idiom, so that it will date and need adaptation or possibly replacement in a comparatively short time. Again, a rapid build-up of population implies fast population growth in the settlement as the second generation is produced, which exacerbates the peaking of demand for age-related facilities and services. The second generation labour force is likely to have different skills from its parents, tending more towards skilled and office employment.

OPERATING COSTS AND VALUES AFFECTED BY URBAN FORM

Neither operating costs nor the values or benefits arising from the form of settlement have generally been examined in this book, except for transport and one or two types of building. However the factors which need to be taken into account in evaluating operating costs and values in particular settlements were considered. For convenience four types of people and corporate bodies were distinguished: existing land users, industrial and commercial firms, public and semi-public bodies, and persons – residents, visitors and commuters to the settlement.

Existing owners would be compensated through the price paid for the land and by grants for disturbance, but these might not fully cover the losses sustained and might be insufficient to secure equivalent properties elsewhere. Users not actually losing their properties might suffer losses for which they would not be compensated, or achieve windfall gains.[1]

The effect of urban form on businesses is relatively easy to measure, since it is entirely in terms of their revenue and expenditure. The major items affected are the costs of goods and services bought, of labour, of organisation, of dispatching and transporting products to their markets, and of premises and operations within them; also the size of the market.

While the charges for public utility services are generally uniform and other public services are supplied without direct charges, standards and the costs of services vary considerably with the size and form of settlement. Their capital costs are affected by density and topography, but size effects are soon exhausted. Services to dwellings vary in cost with density and the form of dwelling. The costs of education, social and recreational services, and their accessibility, are affected to some extent by the size and form of settlement, in particular the size, density and pattern of centres. The costs of the protection services are also affected by size and form of settlement, particularly density, and by the detailed layout of the built facilities.

Residents and those who use a settlement are affected in many ways by its size and form, partly through the standard of services, as described above, and partly through the environmental quality of each type of area and accessibility from the home of the various facilities within and outside the settlement. In the main centres there is likely to be some conflict between range and convenience of access, the former increasing and the latter declining with size. In evaluating alternatives it is necessary to consider perceived values of the users as well as costs-in-use.

Accessibility can be defined in two ways. First, it is the cost, time taken, comfort and convenience of making a journey, usually from the home to a particular facility, which depend on the mode of transport and its relationship with the origin and destination of a journey. Secondly, it can be defined in terms of the opportunity to use facilities after journeys of various lengths. It thus depends on the size and form of the settlement, and will usually increase the greater the density of

---

[1] Future legislation is, however, expected to meet these problems.

development and the more compact the settlement shape. Although the size and the relations between various settlement areas also affect accessibility, no simple generalisations are possible, since it varies too with the organisation of facilities within the areas. Accessibility will, however, be improved by a road system which minimises the distance-time of journeys, and by a convenient and regular system of public transport.

GROWING AND DECLINING SETTLEMENTS

Policies setting the scale of development of new and expanded settlements, and their national consequences for the growth, decline and viability of existing towns and cities must also be considered. At the rates of population growth currently expected, the scale now contemplated could lead to a substantial decline in the population of most existing metropolitan settlements, and possibly to a loss of economic activity, endangering their viability. Far too little is currently known about the costs and performance of settlements during their development, or as their population and economic activity is reduced. It is thus difficult to determine the full consequences of developing new and expanded settlements and city regions to house population from the larger cities and metropolitan areas, or to know whether current proposals are of the right order.

OPTIMUM SETTLEMENT FORMS AND URBAN POLICY

Very broadly, the settlement offering the lowest costs both for construction and the journey to work would be a small to medium-sized town, with a compact shape and with employment areas spread evenly over the town in relation to the residential areas. Densities should be low enough to be achieved with conventional two- and three-storey buildings and most of the car-parking should be at ground level. The main road system should probably be a grid with a central road box. There would be no particular advantage in attempting to induce workers to use buses for the journey to work rather than their private cars, and no advantage in providing a bus-only road system. If larger settlements were required, it might be cheaper to plan them as a cluster of smaller settlements, although how far this was worthwhile would depend on the extent to which workers were deterred by the length of the journey to work. The more this was so the more likely that clusters of small settlements would be cheaper than single large settlements. The way in which the settlements were arranged in clusters would probably be less important than their individual form and size. Expansion of existing towns, except where confined to infilling and rounding-off, is likely to add considerably to development costs. The costs *per capita* for town expansion would depend on the scale of growth, being generally lower for large-scale expansion than for small. The additional costs of expansion appear far more than those generally likely to arise from the more expensive forms of greenfield development, except perhaps at very high densities.

Financial returns to the Development Corporation would usually be highest when the development was cheapest. Differences in shape and centralisation would have little effect, but returns would be high for large rather than small settlements provided land costs were not too much influenced. Returns would also increase with density unless high buildings, multi-storey car-parking or decking had to be used. The additional costs of town expansion would generally seriously reduce the returns, often to unacceptable levels.

Not only the position at the maturity of the settlement, but costs and returns through the development period, need to be considered to determine the phasing which makes the best use of the capital employed. Since changes in needs during the development and after are inevitable, it is necessary to consider the flexibility and adaptability of various forms of development, taking into account operating costs and the values associated with different forms, as well as capital costs. Nor, if the best balance of national urban development is to be attained, is it sufficient to consider only the economies of new and expanded settlements and city regions; attention must equally be given to the way settlements decline, and the consequences for their costs and values and the viability of their economies. Unless the total consequences are considered it will not be possible to find the best balance of urban development for the country.

POPULATION AND GROWTH

DEMOGRAPHIC STRUCTURE

Frequency distributions of population by age are usually irregular or polymodal, which made comparison difficult. The conventional solution of changing the class limits was neither effective nor convenient, as it inevitably obscured essential detail. The distributions could be rearranged in a useful way, but the results could not be treated as a frequency distribution because they were not sequential. The groups used in this study were:

Children under school age
Primary schoolchildren
Secondary schoolchildren
Young adults

Men aged 20–64
Married women aged 20–59
Unmarried women aged 20–59
Persons of pensionable age

This was satisfactory for descriptive purposes, at least in the planning context, but a single derived statistic would be better for making comparisons. The annual rate of natural increase was suitable, being dependent not only upon age, sex and marital status, but also upon the demographic rates acting upon the population. It is also, in its own right, the most important feature of a population.

THE BASE POPULATION

Since one of the variables considered was the original size of the settlement to be expanded, it was necessary to discover whether the population structure varied with this size.

Proportions of the population in each age group, and of each sex and marital status, as well as rates of population increase, were used by Moser and Scott as measures of town characteristics.[1] The correlation coefficients between these measures and the population of the town did not indicate any relation between them (table A.1). However, only towns of population 50,000 or more were considered and the calculations were based on 1951 Census data. For 1951–61 the correlation coefficient between the annual rate of natural increase and town size, calculated from a one in ten sample of small towns (with a population

[1] C. A. Moser and W. Scott, *British Towns; a statistical study of their social and economic differences*, Edinburgh and London, Oliver and Boyd, 1961.

Table A.1. *Correlation coefficients between population characteristics and total population of a town*

Characteristic	Correlation coefficient with total population
Percentage of population aged 0–14	−0·011
Percentage of population aged 15–64	0·089
Percentage of population aged 65 and over	−0·044
Females per 1,000 males	−0·009
Females per 1,000 males, aged 25–44	−0·074
Percentage of females aged 20–24 ever married	−0·016
Total percentage population change 1931–51	−0·101
Total percentage population change 1931–51 due to births and deaths	−0·061
Total percentage population change 1931–51 excluding births and deaths	−0·107
Total percentage population change 1951–8	−0·135

SOURCE: Moser and Scott, *British Towns.*

Chart A.1. *Age structure of population in urban and rural areas, 1961*

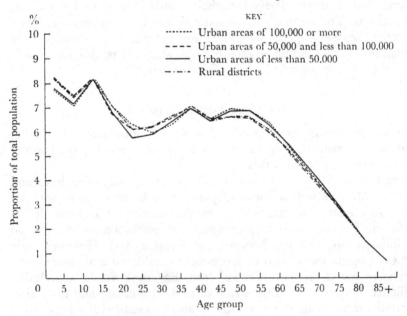

KEY
········ Urban areas of 100,000 or more
- - - - Urban areas of 50,000 and less than 100,000
——— Urban areas of less than 50,000
—·—·- Rural districts

SOURCE: *Census 1961. England and Wales, Age, Marital Condition and General Tables*, table 17, p. 54.

Chart A.2. *Rates of natural increase
in urban and rural areas, 1951–61*

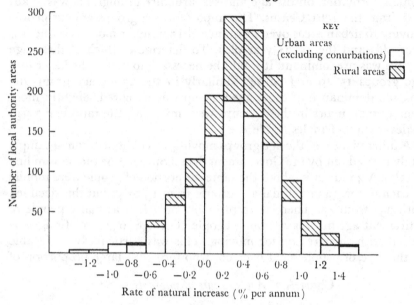

SOURCE: *Census 1961. England and Wales, Age, Marital Condition and General Tables.*

of less than 50,000) was 0·39. This was much higher than Moser and Scott's figure of 0·061 for larger towns, but still too small to indicate any marked relationship between size and growth rates.

In 1961, the age distributions in aggregates of urban local authority areas of various sizes and rural districts varied very little (chart A.1). It can be seen that the curves corresponded closely at all ages. Information from the 1961 Census on rates of natural increase, themselves a measure of population structure, indicated that towns were homogeneous from this point of view (chart A.2). The rates were distributed almost normally around the national average, the departure being too small to indicate any class of town with a particular population structure. Thus there was no evidence that demographic structure varied with town size, and the national structure could be used to estimate base populations. The evidence above also supported the use of national rates of natural increase.

CHARACTERISTICS OF MIGRANTS

Some information on the age and sex structure of migrants was available from the 1961 Census. The important age groups among people moving to urban areas over a distance of 15 miles or more were the 0–4 year olds and the 15–24 year olds. To determine which of these age groups was predominant, it would be necessary to divide the latter into age groups 15–19 and 20–24. Similarly in the 25–44 age group the possible dominance of those aged 25–29 was obscured. Slightly more females than males in these groups were migrants, the ratio being 946 males to 1,000 females (table A.2).

A fuller picture of the age groups moving was obtained from a sample study carried out by the Government Social Survey.[1] As the bottom line of table A.3 indicates, about the same proportion of people were mobile in each of the quinquennial age groups from 15 to 45 but this declined with age from 45. There were probably only half as many people of retirement age moving as young people. The age structure of migrants varied with their reason for moving. This was particularly noticeable in the case of people aged over 60, who formed a large proportion of

Chart A.3. *Age structure of migrants, 1961*

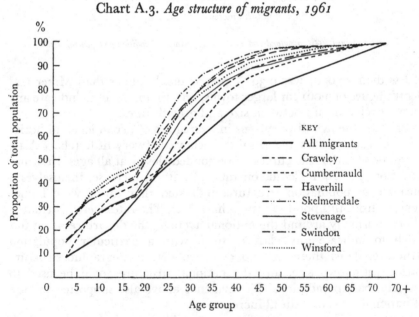

SOURCE: *Census 1961. England and Wales, Occupation, Industry and Socio-Economic Groups* (county volumes).

[1] Government Social Survey, *Labour Mobility in Great Britain, 1953–63*, by A. I. Harris and R. Clausen, London, HMSO, 1966.

Table A.2. *Age and sex structure of migrants*[a]

Percentages

Age group	Males	Females	Total
0–4	9·3	8·2	8·8
5–14	12·9	11·4	12·1
15–24	21·5	25·0	23·3
25–44	36·9	31·0	33·9
45–64	13·5	15·3	14·4
65+	5·9	9·0	7·5
All ages	100·0	100·0	100·0
Total nos.	330,620	349,570	680,190

SOURCE: *Census 1961. England and Wales, Migration Tables*, London, HMSO, 1966, table 9.

[a] People moving to urban areas over a distance of 15 miles or more.

Table A.3. *Persons moving 11 miles or more by age and reason for move*

Main reason for last move	Age groups							All ages[a]
	15–19	20–4	25–30	31–44	45–54	55–9	60+	
Had to – given notice – slum redevelopment	3	2	4	10	5	3	6	33
Wanted– better/modern accommodation – different-sized dwelling – house of own	37	33	61	157	60	19	41	408
Work reasons	115	80	134	376	199	72	94	1070
To be near relatives or friends	24	29	22	59	40	18	122	314
Better surroundings	23	16	27	86	60	27	82	321
Rents, rates etc. too high	7	8	6	18	12	6	27	84
Total	209	168	254	706	376	145	372	2230
Marriage (incl. prospect of)	28	79	28	15	2	1	—	153
Total	237	247	282	721	378	146	372	2383
Percentages	9·9	10·4	11·8	30·3	15·9	6·1	15·6	100

SOURCE: Based on figures given in *Labour Mobility in Great Britain, 1953–63*.

[a] Excluding children under 15.

those who moved to be near relatives, or because rents or rates were too high. On the other hand, few in this age group moved for reasons of work or to obtain a better dwelling or a home of their own. Two motives operated about equally on all age groups – eviction because of notice of redevelopment, and desire for better surroundings. Therefore the migrants resulting from overspill on redevelopment seemed likely to be more evenly spread over the age groups, and hence on average older, than migrants attracted by the jobs offered in the course of developing a new settlement.

Chart A.4. *Age structure of Crawley migrants, 1958 and 1964*

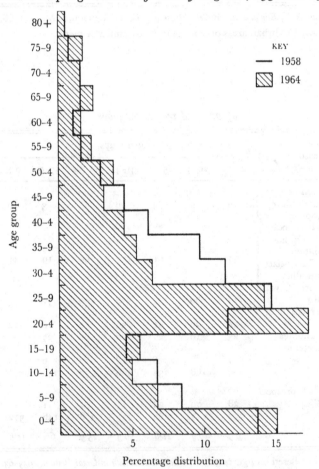

SOURCE: Ministry of Housing and Local Government, *Expansion of Ipswich, designation proposals* by Shankland, Cox and Associates, London, HMSO, 1966.

CHARACTERISTICS OF NEW TOWN MIGRANTS

While migrants to new and expanding towns were younger than migrants in general, migrants to expanding towns were younger than those to new towns (chart A.3). Town expansion under the Town Development Act, 1952, is usually related to official overspill schemes, whose migrants are mainly families on the housing lists of the exporting authorities, and hence fairly mature with a high proportion of children and young people. In contrast, migrants to new towns tend to be the more mobile young married couples with young children if any. The way that housing is allocated under the two types of development determines the nature of migration to new and expanding towns.

There was evidence that as new towns matured the proportion of older migrants rose. For example, of the migrants to Crawley, a higher proportion was over 65 in 1964 than in 1958, when the balance was younger and more concentrated in the 25–29 age group (chart A.4). This seemed a likely trend: as a settlement matures and acquires a better range of facilities, it will attract more general migrants and also the parents of those already living there.

Chart A.5. *Age structure of new town populations, 1961*

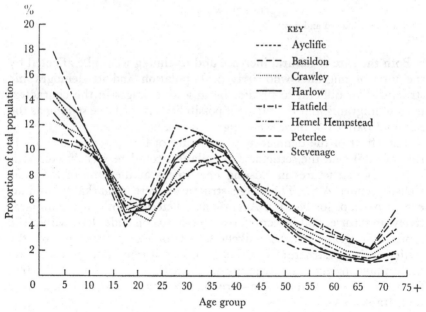

SOURCE: *Census 1961. England and Wales, Occupation, Industry and Socio-Economic Groups* (county volumes).

Table A.4. *Demographic structure of Crawley migrants, 1964*

Percentages

Age group	Single[a] Male	Single[a] Female	Married Male	Married Female	Total Male	Total Female
0–4	16·0	15·0	—	—	16·0	15·0
5–9	7·5	7·0	—	—	7·5	7·0
10–14	5·5	5·0	—	—	5·5	5·0
15–19	4·5	6·5	—	0·4	4·5	6·9
20–4	2·5	1·0	12·0	18·3	14·5	19·3
25–9	—	0·2	15·0	12·3	15·0	12·5
30–4	0·4	0·2	7·2	5·8	7·6	6·0
35–9	0·4	—	5·8	5·0	6·2	5·0
40–4	0·2	0·2	5·2	4·2	5·4	4·4
45–9	0·2	0·2	3·6	3·6	3·8	3·8
50–4	0·2	0·4	3·0	3·2	3·2	3·6
55–9	0·2	0·4	2·6	2·4	2·8	2·8
60–4	0·4	1·0	1·8	1·6	2·2	2·6
65–9	0·4	1·2	1·2	0·8	1·6	2·0
70–4	0·4	1·0	1·0	0·6	1·4	1·6
75–9	0·6	1·2	0·6	0·4	1·2	1·6
80–4	—	0·6	0·1	0·2	0·1	0·8
85+	—	—	0·1	0·1	0·1	0·1
Total	39·4	41·1	59·2	58·9	98·6	100·0

SOURCE: as chart A.4.

[a] Includes widowed and divorced.

Both the rate of natural increase and its timing would be affected by the type of migrants who arrived. Population and its demographic structure are difficult to predict because of changes in the characteristics of migrants, but the range of possibilities is not large so long as the national pattern of those who migrate remains the same.

The effect of the demographic structure of the migrants and of the rate of intake on the settlement population could be seen in comparisons of age structures in existing new towns at the time of the 1961 Census (chart A.5). These age structures were remarkably similar, except perhaps for Newton Aycliffe and Peterlee, both then comparatively immature, and it seemed reasonable to conclude that, within the limits of migrant structure likely to be found, its influence on the settlement's age structure was small, making it unnecessary to simulate more than one migrant structure in studying the economics of urban form. The best data available were for Crawley in 1964 and these were used (table A.4).

POPULATION ESTIMATES FOR A MODEL SETTLEMENT

To simulate the population structure of a model settlement three separate projections to 2001 were produced:[1] the first was from 1961 of 100,000 persons with the national structure for age, sex and marital status as shown in the 1961 Census; the second was of a migrant intake of 2,000 persons per annum for 5 years from 1961 to 1966 with the structure of 1964 Crawley immigrants; the third was the same as the second, but the period of intake was from 1991 to 1996. These were used as building blocks for the various population histories chosen for examination. For example, with a population of 25,000 expanded by means of 4,000 immigrants per annum over 15 years, the population structure at the end of migration was calculated as:

(Projection to 1976 of 100,000 persons in 1961 with national demographic structure) × 0·25 plus [(projection to 1976 + projection to 1971 + projection to 1966) of 2,000 migrants per annum 1961–6] × 2.[2]

The results are shown in table A.5.

[1] The basic work was done with a computer programme written by EMCON in Elliott Autocode, and run on an Elliott 803, using the cohort-component method of population projection. Legitimate age-specific fertility rates, with a constant proportional addition for illegitimate births and mortality rates differentiated according to marital status, were used, varying over time in the same way as the Government Actuary's rates in the official projection published in *Economic Trends*, no. 139, May 1965.

[2] This assumes that the effects in 1976 of migration in the quinquennia 1966–71 and 1971–6 are the same as the effects of migration in 1961–6 in 1971 and 1966 respectively. The third projection was made to check the general assumption that the effect at the end of quinquennium n of a batch of migrants in quinquennium $(n-r)$ is the same as that at the end of quinquennium $(r+1)$ of a batch of migrants in quinquennium 1, by providing the structure at the end of quinquennium 8 of a batch of migrants in quinquennium 7 for comparison with the second projection – the structure at the end of quinquennium 2 of a batch of migrants in quinquennium 1. The differences between these extreme cases, indicating the maximum error that the assumption could cause, are very small, as shown below:

	2nd projection	3rd projection
Under school age	1,807	1,777
Primary schoolchildren	2,074	2,065
Secondary schoolchildren	913	914
Young adults	452	451
Men aged 20–64	3,192	3,214
Married women aged 20–59	2,813	2,838
Unmarried women aged 20–59	302	290
Persons of pensionable age	767	805
Total	12,320	12,354

Table A.5. *Population projections to 2001*

	1961	1966	1971	1976	1981	1986	1991	1996	2001
National average									
Under school age	7,772	8,949	9,280	9,694	9,792	10,305	11,158	11,934	12,602
Primary schoolchildren	8,520	9,204	10,555	10,993	11,499	11,703	12,203	13,197	14,207
Secondary schoolchildren	8,044	7,080	7,544	8,753	9,105	9,552	9,732	10,104	10,923
Young adults	5,309	6,332	5,379	5,819	6,760	6,964	7,300	7,408	7,734
Men aged 20–64	28,534	28,862	29,482	29,497	29,994	31,287	32,568	34,285	36,168
Women aged 20–59									
Married	21,383	21,492	21,816	22,116	22,585	23,254	24,424	25,913	27,475
Unmarried	5,533	5,317	5,167	4,728	4,721	4,887	5,018	5,192	5,278
Persons of pensionable age	14,905	15,863	17,161	18,343	19,022	19,388	19,583	19,438	19,345
Total males	48,377	50,047	51,833	53,769	55,695	57,794	60,306	63,259	66,606
Total females	51,623	53,052	54,551	56,174	57,783	59,546	61,680	64,212	67,126
TOTAL	100,000	103,099	106,384	109,943	113,478	117,340	121,986	127,471	133,732
Migrants[a]									
Under school age	—	1,805	1,807	1,290	1,074	1,313	1,833	2,118	2,018
Primary schoolchildren	—	1,191	2,074	2,208	1,599	1,293	1,528	2,131	2,520
Secondary schoolchildren	—	574	913	1,674	1,892	1,371	1,075	1,228	1,732
Young adults	—	420	452	749	1,347	1,429	1,003	801	957
Men aged 20–64	—	3,108	3,192	3,326	3,666	4,337	4,950	5,241	5,246
Women aged 20–59									
Married	—	2,783	2,813	2,867	3,017	3,412	3,959	4,259	4,139
Unmarried	—	208	302	352	520	768	808	689	575
Persons of pensionable age	—	686	767	851	957	1,114	1,321	1,680	2,461
Total males	—	5,370	6,161	6,668	7,048	7,533	8,257	9,093	9,836
Total females	—	5,405	6,159	6,649	7,024	7,504	8,220	9,054	9,812
TOTAL	—	10,775	12,320	13,317	14,072	15,037	16,477	18,147	19,648

SOURCE: NIESR estimates.

a An input of 10,000 over a 5-year period.

MIGRATION AND GROWTH

The difference between a greenfield situation and town growth is one of degree not kind. Almost always a settlement will start with some development and hence some base population. As demonstrated, the demographic structure of the base population could be taken as that of the national population and that of the migrants as that of the 1964 Crawley intake. The demographic structure of the population at maturity depends also on the sizes of the base and mature populations, and on the period to maturity.

People emigrate from new settlements as well as migrating to them. The experience of new towns suggested that in the early years emigration was about 5 per cent a year and occurred mainly among the recent arrivals. The probability of emigration declined steeply with increasing length of residence, partly because of increasing connections and a sense of belonging, and partly because, with time, the inhabitants passed out of the age of maximum mobility. Since any emigration is likely to follow quite swiftly on arrival, it was reasonable to assume that the emigrants' age structure was similar to that of immigrants and to consider net migration.

The net rate of intake of migrants would vary with the overall policy and with the success with which that policy was implemented. National and local factors would affect the actual annual intake and its divergence

Table A.6. *Population growth hypotheses*

Reference number	Base size	Final size	Net annual migrant intake	Years to maturity
(1)		50,000	2,000	15
(2)	10,000		1,500	20
(3)		100,000	4,000	20
(4)			3,000	25
(5)		50,000	1,500	10
(6)			1,000	15
(7)		100,000	4,000	15
(8)	25,000		3,000	20
(9)			10,000	20
(10)		250,000	8,000	25
(11)			6,000	30
(12)		100,000	3,000	10
(13)			2,000	15
(14)	50,000		8,000	20
(15)		250,000	6,000	25
(16)			5,000	30
(17)			5,000	20
(18)	100,000	250,000	4,000	25

from the planned rate, which could be constant or could vary in a consistent manner to meet changes in phasing requirements as the settlement matured. To study the effect of the rate of intake on the population at maturity of the town, a range of base sizes, of constant net rates of intake and of maturity periods was needed and a set of 18 hypotheses was selected for study (table A.6).

POPULATION IN A MATURE SETTLEMENT

The demographic structures of the 18 populations were calculated both at maturity of the settlement, when migration was assumed to cease, and 40 years after the start of development. The variation at maturity in the demographic structure of the 18 populations was small in spite of the great range in base size, net annual intake and period to maturity

Table A.7. *Demographic structure of a mature settlement*

Percentages

Reference number (table A.6)	Under school age	Primary school-children	Secondary school-children	Young adults	Men aged 20–64	Women aged 20–59 Married women	Women aged 20–59 Unmarried women	Persons of pension-able age
(1)	12·4	13·9	8·5	4·6	26·5	22·5	2·8	8·7
(2)	11·1	13·1	9·5	5·9	26·4	22·1	3·1	8·8
(3)	11·6	13·6	9·8	5·9	26·3	22·5	2·9	7·5
(4)	10·9	12·5	9·6	6·6	26·9	22·4	3·4	7·7
(5)	10·7	12·0	8·2	5·0	26·7	21·3	3·5	12·6
(6)	11·4	11·6	6·8	4·6	27·5	22·0	3·8	12·3
(7)	12·2	13·7	8·5	4·7	26·5	22·4	2·9	9·1
(8)	11·0	12·9	9·5	5·9	26·4	22·0	3·1	9·3
(9)	10·9	12·5	9·6	6·6	26·9	22·4	3·4	7·7
(10)	11·5	13·6	9·8	5·9	26·3	22·5	2·9	7·5
(11)	10·9	11·8	9·0	6·5	27·4	22·7	3·7	8·0
(12)	11·4	11·6	6·8	4·6	27·5	22·0	3·8	12·3
(13)	10·7	12·0	8·2	4·9	26·7	21·4	3·5	12·6
(14)	11·1	13·2	9·6	5·9	26·4	22·1	3·0	8·7
(15)	10·6	12·1	9·4	6·5	26·9	22·1	3·5	8·9
(16)	10·7	11·6	8·9	6·4	27·3	22·3	3·7	9·0
(17)	10·3	12·2	9·1	5·9	26·4	21·4	3·4	11·3
(18)	10·0	11·4	9·0	6·3	26·8	21·4	3·7	11·3
Total	199·4	225·3	159·8	102·7	481·8	397·5	60·1	173·3
Mean	11·1	12·5	8·9	5·7	26·8	22·1	3·3	9·6
Range	2·4	2·5	3·0	2·0	1·2	1·3	1·0	5·3
Standard deviation	0·2	0·8	0·9	0·7	0·4	0·4	0·4	1·8
Coefficient of variation	1·8	6·4	10·1	12·3	1·5	1·8	12·1	18·8

SOURCE: NIESR estimates.

Table A.8. *Demographic structure of a settlement after 40 years*

Percentages

Reference number (table A.6)	Under school age	Primary school-children	Secondary school-children	Young adults	Men aged 20–64	Women aged 20–59 Married women	Unmarried women	Persons of pension-able age
(1)	10·7	11·2	7·6	5·2	28·2	22·3	3·8	10·9
(2)	10·3	10·7	7·9	6·0	28·2	22·3	4·1	10·5
(3)	10·4	10·8	7·8	6·0	28·4	22·6	4·1	9·9
(4)	9·9	10·9	8·7	6·6	28·0	22·3	4·0	9·6
(5)	10·1	11·0	7·8	5·5	27·7	21·5	3·9	12·5
(6)	10·1	11·4	8·0	5·3	27·4	21·3	3·7	12·9
(7)	10·6	11·2	7·6	5·3	28·1	22·2	3·8	11·1
(8)	10·2	10·7	7·9	6·0	28·2	22·2	4·1	10·7
(9)	10·0	10·9	8·7	6·6	28·0	22·3	4·0	9·5
(10)	10·4	10·8	7·8	6·0	28·4	22·6	4·1	9·9
(11)	9·9	11·6	9·2	6·4	27·6	22·2	3·8	9·3
(12)	10·1	11·4	8·0	5·3	27·4	21·3	3·7	12·8
(13)	10·1	11·0	7·8	5·5	27·7	21·5	3·9	12·5
(14)	10·3	10·8	7·9	6·0	28·2	22·3	4·1	10·4
(15)	9·9	10·8	8·6	6·5	27·9	22·1	4·0	10·2
(16)	9·9	11·4	9·0	6·3	27·5	22·0	3·9	9·9
(17)	10·0	10·7	8·0	5·9	27·9	21·8	4·0	11·7
(18)	9·8	10·8	8·5	6·3	27·6	21·6	4·0	11·4
Total	182·7	198·1	146·8	106·7	502·4	396·4	71·0	195·7
Mean	10·2	11·0	8·2	5·9	27·9	22·0	3·9	10·9
Range	0·9	0·9	1·6	1·4	1·0	1·3	0·4	3·6
Standard deviation	0·2	0·2	0·5	0·4	0·2	0·4	0·1	1·9
Coefficient of variation	1·6	1·9	5·5	7·4	0·8	1·8	2·1	17·8

SOURCE: NIESR estimates.

(table A.7). The greatest variation was in the smaller groups – secondary schoolchildren, young adults, unmarried women and persons of pensionable age. The variations after 40 years were markedly less than at maturity (table A.8).

An assessment of the facilities required in a mature settlement needed a complete breakdown of population by age and marital status. Since, as demonstrated, the structure was stable over the range of likely conditions, one typical structure was sufficient for this study. This was calculated for an average set of circumstances so that it was representative of various conditions of settlement growth (table A.9).

Table A.9. *Typical population of a mature settlement*[a]

Age group	Single		Married		Total		
	Male	Female	Male	Female	Male	Female	M+F
0–4	485	459	—	—	485	459	944
5–9	488	462	—	—	488	462	950
10–14	503	476	—	—	503	476	979
15–19	474	424	7	31	481	455	936
20–4	251	176	163	219	414	395	809
25–9	67	58	265	278	332	336	668
30–4	29	32	273	295	302	327	629
35–9	21	25	309	329	330	354	684
40–4	20	25	331	338	351	363	714
45–9	19	26	312	298	331	324	655
50–4	18	26	257	224	275	250	525
55–9	17	30	191	161	208	191	399
60–4	19	41	144	125	163	166	329
65–9	20	54	107	92	127	146	273
70–4	23	64	69	57	92	121	213
75–9	23	66	37	27	60	93	153
80–4	17	49	15	9	32	58	90
85+	10	31	5	4	15	35	50
Total	2,504	2,524	2,485	2,487	4,989	5,011	10,000

SOURCE: NIESR estimates.

[a] Per 10,000 population.

GROWTH IN A MATURE SETTLEMENT

After maturity of the settlement some migration in and out would continue as in ordinary towns. If the settlement was successful this movement would be very like the general national pattern. It was assumed in the population calculations that these movements would balance out and that the town's population would continue to grow by natural increase. The annual rates of growth of the population in the period after the end of immigration could vary considerably (table A.10).

As might be expected, these growth rates showed a strong correlation with the period over which migration occurred, the size of the annual intake and the scale of growth (table A.11). The policy for immigration is therefore very important and should be decided in broad outline at a very early stage, so that the physical planning can take into account the expected growth after the end of the planned population expansion. Clearly, the shorter the period of immigration, the smaller the annual intake and the smaller the proportionate expansion, the slower the future rate of growth and the more stable in size the settlement will be.

Table A.10. *Growth rates after the end of migration*

Reference number (table A.6)	Period of migration (years)	Population At maturity	After 40 years	Annual growth rates (%)
(1)	15	47,406	67,645	1·43
(2)	20	49,210	65,355	1·43
(3)	20	112,314	151,991	1·52
(4)	25	110,014	138,443	1·54
(5)	10	43,917	61,779	1·14
(6)	15	45,692	60,569	1·13
(7)	15	100,310	141,977	1·40
(8)	20	104,094	137,397	1·39
(9)	20	280,785	379,978	1·52
(10)	25	291,415	366,953	1·55
(11)	30	276,487	323,527	1·58
(12)	10	87,833	123,559	1·14
(13)	15	91,384	121,138	1·13
(14)	20	258,671	344,102	1·44
(15)	25	255,230	317,006	1·46
(16)	30	265,985	308,611	1·50
(17)	20	239,685	307,005	1·24
(18)	25	248,380	300,492	1·28

SOURCE: table A.5.

Table A.11. *Growth rates after the end of migration and migration policy*

Policy variables	Reference numbers (table A.6)	Average annual growth rates (%)
Immigration period		
10 years	(5) (12)	1·14
15 years	(1) (6) (7) (13)	1·27
20 years	(2) (3) (8) (9) (14) (17)	1·42
25 years	(4) (10) (15) (18)	1·46
30 years	(11) (16)	1·54
Migrant intake (annual)		
1,000–2,000	(1) (2) (5) (6) (13)	1·25
3,000–5,000	(3) (4) (7) (8) (12) (16) (17) (18)	1·38
6,000–10,000	(9) (10) (11) (14) (15)	1·51
Ratio of target to base population		
2:1 and 2·5:1	(5) (6) (12) (13) (17) (18)	1·18
4:1 and 5:1	(1) (2) (7) (8) (14) (15) (16)	1·44
10:1	(3) (4) (9) (10) (11)	1·54

SOURCE: table A.10.

Table A.12. *Quinquennial growth rates for one input
of 10,000 migrants over 5 years*

Years from start of migration	Total migrant population	Annual growth rates (%)
5	10,775	
		2·72
10	12,320	
		1·57
15	13,317	
		1·11
20	14,072	
		1·34
25	15,037	
		1·85
30	16,477	
		1·95
35	18,147	
		1·60
40	19,648	

SOURCE: table A.5.

Stability might be improved by varying the rate and structure of the intake, but any such policy would have to be reflected in policies for housing and industry. Whatever policy is followed, in the first year after the end of immigration a very high rate of increase is likely, decreasing irregularly as time goes by. An indication of this pattern was given by projecting the total of one quinquennial input over 40 years (table A.12).

APPENDIX B

LAND VALUES AND RENTS

Table B.1. *Prices per acre of freehold residential land*

£ thousands, 1967 prices

Density (dwellings per acre)	Size of settlement		
	50,000 persons	100,000 persons	250,000 persons
8	6·5	8·4	10·3
10	7·2	9·3	11·5
13	8·5	11·0	13·5
15	13·0	16·8	20·7
20	15·8	20·5	25·3
30	21·6	28·0	34·5

SOURCE: NIESR estimates.

Table B.2. *Prices per acre of freehold non-residential land*

£ thousands, 1967 prices

Charities: churches, social centres, etc.	2·5
Local authority	
Offices, libraries, schools	10·0
Open space	0·4
Public utilities	
Bus stations and garages, transformer stations	20·0
Sewerage and waterworks	0·5

SOURCE: NIESR estimates.

Table B.3. *Net annual rents^a for non-residential development*

	Ground rents for sites	Rack rents for buildings
	(£000s per acre)	(£s per sq. ft.)
Industry	0·85	0·42
Shopping		
Town centre	20·00	1·15
District centre	11·00	0·90
Offices	(0·10)^b	0·75

SOURCE: NIESR estimates.

^{a} In a settlement for 100,000 persons, at 1967 prices.
^{b} Expressed in £s per square foot of gross floor area to be developed.

Table B.4. *Net annual rents^a for public authority housing*

£s, 1967 prices

Dwelling size (persons)	Basic standard^b		Higher standard^c	
	House	Flat	House	Flat
1	..	85	..	..
2	117	130	..	180
3	130	156	..	225
4	163	182	..	270
5	176	195	260	..
6	194	..	300	..
7	208	..	350	..
8	215	..	..	..
Garage (extra)	23	23	—	30

SOURCE: NIESR estimates.

^{a} Net of maintenance and management charges.
^{b} Subsidised.
^{c} Unsubsidised.

LIST OF WORKS CITED

I. BOOKS, ARTICLES AND OTHER SOURCES

BECKERMAN, W. *The British Economy in 1975*, Cambridge University Press, 1965.

BEESLEY, M. E. 'The value of time spent in travelling: some new evidence', *Economica*, vol. 32, no. 126, May 1965, pp. 174–85.

BEST, R. H. *Land for New Towns*, London, Town and Country Planning Association, 1964.

Birmingham University (Department of Transportation and Environmental Planning). *Travel and Land Use Survey*, Birmingham, 1966.

BROWN, A. J. 'Regional problems and regional policy', *National Institute Economic Review*, no. 46, November 1968, pp. 42–51.

DOUBLEDAY, E. H. *The Future of Industry in Central Hertfordshire*, Hertford, Hertfordshire County Council Planning Department, 1956.

FAIRTHORNE, Q. 'The distances between pairs of points in forms of simple geometric shape', *Proceedings of the Second Symposium on the Theory of Traffic Flow* (ed. Joyce Almond), Paris, OECD, 1965.

FARBEY, B. A. and MURCHLAND, J. D. 'Towards an evaluation of road system designs', *Regional Studies*, vol. 1, no. 1, February 1967.

FOSTER, C. D. 'Public finance aspects of national settlement patterns', *Urban Studies*, vol. 9, no. 1, February 1972, pp. 79–99.

Freeman Fox, Wilbur Smith and Associates. *West Midlands Transport Study, Summary Report*, London, 1967.

GEORGE, R. D. *Productivity in Distribution*, Cambridge University Press, 1966.

GOLDSTEIN, A. *Motorway Route Location Studies*, Keele, Town and Country Planning Summer School, 1966.

Greater London Council. *London Traffic Survey*, vol. 2, London, 1966.

— *Report of Studies*, London, 1969.

Hamlyn Group. *'Commercial Motor' Tables of Operating Costs for Goods and Passenger Vehicles* (annual).

HOLMANS, A. E. 'Restriction of industrial expansion in South East England: a reappraisal', *Oxford Economic Papers*, vol. 16, no. 2, July 1964, pp. 235–61.

International Federation for Housing and Planning. *Growing Space Needs in Urbanized Regions*, Stockholm, 1965.

JAMIESON, G. B., MACKAY, W. K. and LATCHFORD, J. C. R. 'Transportation and land use structures', *Urban Studies*, vol. 4, no. 3, November 1967, pp. 201–17.

LOMAX, K. S. 'The relationship between expenditure per head and size of population of county boroughs in England and Wales', *Journal of the Royal Statistical Society*, vol. 106, part 1, 1943.

London County Council. *The Planning of a New Town*, London, 1961.

LUTTRELL, W. F. *Factory Location and Industrial Movement*, London, National Institute of Economic and Social Research, 1962.

McCLELLAND, W. G. *Studies in Retailing*, Oxford, Basil Blackwell, 1963.

Manchester City Transport. *Manchester Rapid Transit Study*, Manchester, De Leuw, Cather and Partners in association with Hennessey, Chadwick, Oh Eocha and Partners, 1967.

Middlesex County Council. *First Review of the Development Plan: report of a survey*, London, 1962,

MOSER, C. A. and SCOTT, W. *British Towns: a statistical study of their social and economic differences*, Edinburgh and London, Oliver and Boyd, 1961.

PARKER, T. W. 'Noise problems in buildings', *Royal Society of Health Journal*, no. 2, March 1961.

REYNOLDS, D. J. *Urban Layout and Transport Systems: a theoretical/practical study*, Ottawa, Roads and Transport Association of Canada, 1971.

SMEED, R. J. and HOLROYD, E. M. *Some Factors affecting Congestion in Towns*, Harmondsworth, Road Research Laboratory, 1963.

Spon Ltd. *Spon's Architects' and Builders' Price Book* (annual).

STEEL, R. 'Town development: roads and economics', *Journal of the Institution of Highway Engineers*, vol. 12, March 1965.

STONE, P. A. 'The impact of urban development on the use of land and other resources', *Journal of the Town Planning Institute*, vol. 47, no. 5, May 1961.

— *Housing, Town Development, Land and Costs*, London, Estates Gazette Ltd, 1963.

— 'The price of sites for residential building', *The Property Developer*, 1964, pp. 43–57.

— *Building Design Evaluation: costs-in-use*, London, Spon, 1967.

— *Urban Development in Britain: Standards, Costs and Resources, 1964–2004:*
    vol. I: *Population trends and housing*, Cambridge University Press, 1970
    vol. II: *Non-residential development* (forthcoming)

TANNER, J. C. 'Forecasts of vehicle ownership in Great Britain', *Roads and Road Construction*, November/December 1965.

TOWNSEND, C. B. 'The economics of waste water treatment', *Proceedings of the Institution of Civil Engineers*, vol. 15, no. 3, March 1960, p. 209.

WATTS, K. 'Functional control and town design', *Architects' Journal*, vol. 138, 23 October 1963.

II. OFFICIAL PUBLICATIONS

Central Statistical Office. *Annual Abstract of Statistics*.

Department of Economic Affairs. *A Strategy for the South East*, London, HMSO, 1967.

Department of Education and Science. *Playing Fields and Hard Surface Areas*, London, HMSO, 1966.

— *Statistics of Education, 1965*, part 2, London, HMSO, 1966.

General Register Office. *Census 1961. England and Wales*, London, HMSO:
    Age, Marital Condition and General Tables, 1964.
    Household Composition Tables, 1966.
    Industry Tables, part 1, 1966.
    Migration Tables, 1966.
    Occupation, Industry and Socio-Economic Groups (county volumes), 1966.

Government Social Survey. *Labour Mobility in Great Britain 1953–63* by A. I. Harris and R. Clausen, London, HMSO, 1966.

Ministry of Housing and Local Government. *Open Space*, Technical Memorandum no. 6, London, HMSO, 1956.

— *Ministry of Housing and Local Government Report, 1958*, Cmnd 737, London, HMSO, 1959.

— *Homes for Today and Tomorrow*, London, HMSO, 1961 [report of the Parker-Morris Committee].

— *Peterborough: an expansion study 1963* by Henry W. Wells, London, HMSO, 1963.

— *Worcester Expansion Study, June 1963* by J. H. D. Madin and Partners, London, HMSO, 1963.

— *Expansion of Ipswich: designation proposals* by Shankland, Cox and Associates, London, 1966.

— *New Towns Act 1965. Reports of the Development Corporations to March 31, 1970*, HC 64, London, HMSO, 1970.

Ministry of Labour. 'Forecasts of the working population, 1966–81', *Ministry of Labour Gazette*, November 1966.

Office of Population Censuses and Surveys. *Census 1971. Great Britain, Advance Analysis*, London, HMSO, 1972.

Department of Scientific and Industrial Research. *Structural Frameworks for Single-Storey Factory Buildings* by H. V. Apcar, London, HMSO, 1960.

— *Densities of Housing Areas* by P. H. H. Stevens, London, HMSO, 1960.

— *Factors affecting the amount of Travel* by J. C. Tanner, London, HMSO, 1961.

— *The Economics of Factory Buildings* by P. A. Stone, London, HMSO, 1962.

Board of Trade. *Report on the Census of Distribution and Other Services, 1961*, part 1 : *Establishment Tables*, London, HMSO, 1963.
— *Board of Trade Journal* (weekly).
Department of Trade and Industry. *Commission on the Third London Airport: papers and proceedings*, vol. 8, part 1 : *Stage III: Research and Investigation*, London, HMSO, 1970.
Ministry of Transport. *Traffic in Towns*, London, HMSO, 1963.
— *Research on Road Traffic*, London, HMSO, 1965.
— *Roads in Urban Areas*, London, HMSO, 1966.
— *National Travel Survey, 1964: preliminary report*, London, Ministry of Transport, 1967.
Treasury. *Nationalised Industries: a review of economic and financial objectives*, Cmnd 3437, London, HMSO, 1967.

United Nations Economic Commission for Europe. *Cost, Repetition and Maintenance: related aspects of building prices*, Geneva, United Nations, 1963.

INDEX

accessibility, 19, 21, 229–32, 252–3
affluence, 214–15, 236, 251; *see also* cars, private
amenities, 11, 26, 160–1, 227–9
Apcar, H. V., 107n

Beckerman, W., 58n
Beesley, M. E., 124n, 125n
Best, R. H., 26n, 28n, 30n, 31n, 34n, 37n, 38n
Birmingham University, 78n
Brown, A. J., 6n
Buchanan, Sir Colin, 78, 98
built environment, 1
bus-only roads, 24, 43, 138, 140–1, 247
bus routes, 41–3
buses, 74, 76, 138–43, 228, 247; and main road costs, 139–40; and road networks, 24, 138–9; costs-in-use, 176–8; economics, 141–3, 176–8; occupancy rates, 76, 77; operating costs, 125; *see also* public transport; travelling to work

capital resources, efficient use of, 208–11, 250–1
cars, private, 15, 24, 74–8, 137, 170, 247–8; operating costs, 124–5, 141–3, 171–2, 175–8, 230, 247; ownership, 65, 74, 76, 77, 78, 215, 247, 251; *see also* parking; travelling to work
Census 1951, 255
Census 1961, 45n, 57, 58, 256, 257, 258, 259
Census 1971, 233n
Census of Distribution 1961, 48, 52
central areas, 32, 34, 35–7, 38–40, 64, 65, 93, 170–2, 194, 195; adaptability, 212–13, 216; costs of construction, 116–18, 122
centralisation: and adaptability, 213, 215, 251; degree of, 22, 33, 34, 92–5, 131–3, 157–9, 175, 201, 244–5
centralised settlements, 38, 39, 41, 87, 92–4, 100, 126, 131–3, 135, 157–8, 228; costs-in-use, 172
civil engineering work, 121–2; *see also* sites
Clausen, R., 258n
climate, 9, 10
clusters of settlements, 1, 12, 22, 68–72, 144–6, 243–4; and capital costs of roads, 99–101; and travelling costs, 134–6, 178–9; cross, linear block, linear line, necklace, 33, 34, 100; *see also* sub-regional form

colleges of higher education, 35, 37, 38–9, 41, 54; costs of construction, 107, 115, 122, 156; expansion, 214; *see also* educational facilities
commercial centres, 15–16, 29, 35; costs-in-use, 30, 161; costs of construction, 29, 151, 152, 157, 194, 195, 245; density, 29, 152, 245; economies of scale, 156; space requirements, 28, 29, 62; *see also* service industry; shopping
communications: land for, 38; systems, 23–5, 40–3, 121, 185; *see also* transport
compensation for land, 221–2, 252
construction costs, 13, 102–10, 121–3, 163–6
costs-in-use, definition, 167
Crawley, 44, 57n, 258, 260–3, 265
cultural activities *see* minor building facilities; recreation
Cumbernauld, 28, 57n, 165, 213, 226, 258
cycling, 74–6, 77, 137

daylight, 25, 26, 160, 161
decentralisation, 6, 7
decentralised settlements, 38, 39, 41, 87, 92–5, 99–101, 126, 131–3; costs-in-use, 172
declining settlements, 234–8, 253
demographic structure, 27, 28, 44, 162–3, 208–9, 214, 219, 239, 255–62, 263–4, 266–8; *see also* population
density of development, 25–31, 32, 34, 151–2; and costs-in-use, 29, 167–70, 245; and development costs, 15, 29, 103–5, 111–15, 121–3; and road costs, 95–7; and travelling costs, 133–4; optimum, 29, 151; *see also* height of buildings; housing density
Department of Economic Affairs, 218n, 233n
Department of Scientific and Industrial Research, 25n, 29n, 30, 60, 62n, 67n, 68, 107n, 124n, 152n, 156n
developers, commercial and industrial, 191, 192, 198, 200, 202, 234; finance, 202, 206, 248–50
development, 191–206; adaptability, 3, 207; and existing development, 3, 10, 180–8, 205–6, 236–7, 248; costs, 1, 4, 151–66, 191–2, 204, 239–50, 254; dispersion, 6; duration, 4, 215–19; financial costs, 189–90; forms, 182; greenfield, 113, 151, 188, 190, 205–6, 248; phasing, 3, 207, 215–19, 250–1; scale, 233–4; *see also* town expansion
Development Areas, 218–19, 235

[276]

PUBLICATIONS OF THE
NATIONAL INSTITUTE OF ECONOMIC
AND SOCIAL RESEARCH

published by
THE CAMBRIDGE UNIVERSITY PRESS

Books published for the Institute by the Cambridge University Press are available through the ordinary booksellers. They appear in the five series below:

ECONOMIC & SOCIAL STUDIES

*I *Studies in the National Income, 1924–1938*
  Edited by A. L. BOWLEY. Reprinted with corrections, 1944. pp. 256.
*II *The Burden of British Taxation*
  By G. FINDLAY SHIRRAS and L. ROSTAS. 1942. pp. 140.
*III *Trade Regulations and Commercial Policy of the United Kingdom*
  By THE RESEARCH STAFF OF THE NATIONAL INSTITUTE OF ECONOMIC AND SOCIAL RESEARCH. 1943. pp. 275.
*IV *National Health Insurance: A Critical Study*
  By HERMAN LEVY. 1944. pp. 356.
*V *The Development of the Soviet Economic System: An Essay on the Experience of Planning in the U.S.S.R.*
  By ALEXANDER BAYKOV. 1946. pp. 530.
  (Out of print in this series, but reprinted 1970 in Cambridge University Press Library Edition, £7.50 net.)
*VI *Studies in Financial Organization.*
  By T. BALOGH. 1948. pp. 328.
*VII *Investment, Location, and Size of Plant: A Realistic Inquiry into the Structure of British and American Industries*
  By P. SARGANT FLORENCE, assisted by W. BALDAMUS. 1948. pp. 230.
*VIII *A Statistical Analysis of Advertising Expenditure and of the Revenue of the Press*
  By NICHOLAS KALDOR and RODNEY SILVERMAN. 1948. pp. 200.
*IX *The Distribution of Consumer Goods*
  By JAMES B. JEFFERYS, assisted by MARGARET MACCOLL and G. L. LEVETT. 1950. pp. 430.
*X *Lessons of the British War Economy*
  Edited by D. N. CHESTER. 1951. pp. 260.
*XI *Colonial Social Accounting*
  By PHYLLIS DEANE. 1953. pp. 360.
*XII *Migration and Economic Growth*
  By BRINLEY THOMAS. 1954. pp. 384.
*XIII *Retail Trading in Britain, 1850–1950*
  By JAMES B. JEFFERYS. 1954. pp. 490.
*XIV *British Economic Statistics*
  By CHARLES CARTER and A. D. ROY. 1954. pp. 192.
*XV *The Structure of British Industry: A Symposium*
  Edited by DUNCAN BURN. 1958. Vol. I. pp. 403. Vol. II. pp. 499.
*XVI *Concentration in British Industry*
  By RICHARD EVELY and I. M. D. LITTLE. 1960. pp. 357.
*XVII *Studies in Company Finance*
  Edited by BRIAN TEW and R. F. HENDERSON. 1959. pp. 301.

* At present out of print.

OCCASIONAL PAPERS

* At present out of print.

*XVII   *British Post-War Migration*
By JULIUS ISAAC. 1954. pp. 294.
*XVIII *The Cost of the National Health Service in England and Wales*
By BRIAN ABEL-SMITH and RICHARD M. TITMUSS. 1956. pp. 176.
*XIX   *Post-war Investment, Location and Size of Plant*
By P. SARGANT FLORENCE. 1962. pp. 51.
*XX   *Investment and Growth Policies in British Industrial Firms*
By TIBOR BARNA. 1962. pp. 71.
XXI   *Pricing and Employment in the Trade Cycle: A Study of British Manufacturing Industry, 1950–61*
By R. R. NEILD. 1963. pp. 73. 75p net.
*XXII   *Health and Welfare Services in Britain in 1975*
By DEBORAH PAIGE and KIT JONES. 1966. pp. 142.
XXIII   *Lancashire Textiles: A Case Study of Industrial Change*
By CAROLINE MILES. 1968. pp. 124. £1.05 net.
XXIV   *The Economic Impact of Commonwealth Immigration*
By K. JONES and A. D. SMITH. 1970. pp. 186. £1.75 net.
XXV   *The Analysis and Forecasting of the British Economy*
By M. J. C. SURREY. 1971. pp. 120. £1.20 net.
XXVI   *Mergers and Concentration in British Industry*
By P. E. HART, M. A. UTTON and G. WALSHE. 1973. p. 190. £1.80 net.

STUDIES IN THE NATIONAL INCOME AND EXPENDITURE OF THE UNITED KINGDOM

Published under the joint auspices of the National Institute and the Department of Applied Economics, Cambridge.

*1   *The Measurement of Consumers' Expenditure and Behaviour in the United Kingdom, 1920–1938* vol. I
By RICHARD STONE, assisted by D. A. ROWE and by W. J. CORLETT, RENEE HURSTFIELD, MURIEL POTTER. 1954. pp. 448.
2   *The Measurement of Consumers' Expenditure and Behaviour in the United Kingdom, 1920–1938* vol. II
By RICHARD STONE and D. A. ROWE. 1966. pp. 152. £6.00 net.
3   *Consumers' Expenditure in the United Kingdom, 1900–1919*
By A. R. PREST, assisted by A. A. ADAMS. 1954. pp. 196. £4.20 net.
4   *Domestic Capital Formation in the United Kingdom, 1920–1938*
By C. H. FEINSTEIN. 1965. pp. 284. £6.00 net.
5   *Wages and Salaries in the United Kingdom, 1920–1938*
By AGATHA CHAPMAN, assisted by ROSE KNIGHT. 1953. pp. 254. £6.00 net.
6   *National Income, Expenditure and Output of the United Kingdom, 1855–1965*
By C. H. FEINSTEIN. 1972. pp. 384. £10.40 net.

NIESR STUDENTS EDITION

1   *Growth and Trade* (abridged from *Industrial Growth and World Trade*)
By A. MAIZELS. 1970. pp. 312. £1.45 net.
2   *The Antitrust Laws of the U.S.A.* (2nd edition, unabridged)
By A. D. NEALE. 1970. pp. 544. £1.85 net.
3   *The Management of the British Economy, 1945–60* (unabridged)
By J. C. R. DOW. 1970. pp. 464. £1.10 net.

* At present out of print.

REGIONAL PAPERS

1 *The Anatomy of Regional Activity Rates* by JOHN BOWERS, and *Regional Social Accounts for the United Kingdom* by V. H. WOODWARD. 1970. pp. 192. £1.25 net.
2 *Regional Unemployment Differences in Great Britain* by P. C. CHESHIRE and *Interregional Migration Models and their Application to Great Britain* by R. WEEDEN. 1973. pp. 120. £2.00 net.

THE NATIONAL INSTITUTE OF ECONOMIC AND SOCIAL RESEARCH

publishes regularly

THE NATIONAL INSTITUTE ECONOMIC REVIEW

A quarterly analysis of the general economic stituation in the United Kingdom and the world overseas, with forecasts eighteen months ahead. The first issue each year is devoted entirely to the current situation and prospects both in the short and medium term. Other issues contain also special articles on subjects of interest to academic and business economists.

Annual subscriptions, £6.00, and single issues for the current year, £1.75 each, are available directly from NIESR, 2 Dean Trench Street, Smith Square, London, SW1P 3HE.

Subscriptions at the special reduced price of £2.50 p.a. are available to students in the United Kingdom and the Irish Republic on application to the Secretary of the Institute.

Back numbers, including reprints of those which have gone out of stock, are distributed by Wm. Dawson and Sons Ltd., Cannon House, Park Farm Road, Folkestone.

The Institute has also published

THE IVTH FRENCH PLAN

By FRANCOIS PERROUX, translated by Bruno Leblanc. 1965. pp. 72. 50p net.

This also is available directly from the Institute.

Published by Heinemann Educational Books

AN INCOMES POLICY FOR BRITAIN

Edited by FRANK BLACKABY. 1972. pp. 260. £4.00 net.

Available from booksellers.